GU01048564

MACROECONOMIC POLICY COORDINATION IN EUROPE

The ERM and Monetary Union

The National Institute of Economic and Social Research is an independent non-profit-making body whose object is to increase knowledge of the social and economic conditions of contemporary society. It conducts and publishes research by its own staff and in cooperation with the universities and other academic bodies.

MACROECONOMIC POLICY COORDINATION IN EUROPE
The ERM and Monetary Union

Edited by
Ray Barrell and John Whitley

SAGE Publications

National Institute of Economic and Social Research

© National Institute of Economic and Social Research 1992

First published 1992

All rights reserved. No part of this publication may be
reproduced, stored in a retrieval system, transmitted or
utilized in any form or by any means, electronic, mechanical,
photocopying, recording or otherwise, without permission in
writing from the Publishers.

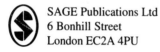 SAGE Publications Ltd
6 Bonhill Street
London EC2A 4PU

SAGE Publications Inc
2455 Teller Road
Newbury Park, California 91320

SAGE Publications India Pvt Ltd
32, M-Block Market
Greater Kailash - I
New Delhi 110 048

ISBN 0 8039 8764 1
ISBN 0 8039 8765 X pbk

Printed and bound in Great Britain by
Biddles Ltd, Guildford and King's Lynn

Contents

Contributors and Participants

Robert Anderton, National Institute of Economic and Social Research
Ray Barrell, National Institute of Economic and Social Research
Andrew Britton, National Institute of Economic and Social Research
Jean-Pierre Chauffour, Centre d'Etudes Prospectives et d'Informations, and Observatoire Français des Conjonctures Economiques
John Driffill, University of London
Hélène Harasty, Centre d'Etudes Prospectives et d'Informations, and Observatoire Français des Conjonctures Economiques
Gustav Adolf Horn, Deutsches Institut für Wirtschaftsforschung
Andrew Hughes Hallett, University of Strathclyde
Anthonie Knoester, Katholieke Universiteit Nijmegen
André Kolodziejak, Katholieke Universiteit Nijmegen
Jean Le Dem, Centre d'Etudes Prospectives et d'Informations, and Observatoire Français des Conjonctures Economiques
Paul R. Masson, International Monetary Fund
Marcus Miller, University of Warwick
Patrick Minford, University of Liverpool
Anupam Rastogi, University of Liverpool
Steven Symansky, International Monetary Fund
Hans R. Timmer, Netherlands Central Planning Bureau
Frank A.M. van Erp, Netherlands Central Planning Bureau
Nico I.M. van Leeuwen, Netherlands Central Planning Bureau
Jan Willem in't Veld, National Institute of Economic and Social Research
John Whitley, London Business School
Rudolf Zwiener, Deutsches Institut für Wirtschaftsforschunh

Other participants
Chris Allen, London Business School
Mike Artis, University of Manchester
Paul Atkinson, OECD
Tam Bayoumi, IMF and Bank of England
Op de Beke, European Commission
Alex Bowen, NEDO
John Bradley, Economic and Social Research Institute, Dublin

Andreas Brandsma, European Commission
Willem Boeschoten, Netherlands Bank
Fritz Breuss, WIFO
Ralph Bryant, Brookings Institution
Stephen Carse, Isle of Man Treasury
Guglielmo Caporale, National Institute of Economic and Social Research
Keith Church, University of Warwick
Roy Cromb, HM Treasury
David Currie, London Business School
Peter Curwen, HM Treasury
Keith Cuthbertson, University of Newcastle
Henri Delessy, CEPII
Michel Dombrecht, Bank of Belgium
Torbjorn Eika, Central Statistics Bureau, Oslo
Andrea Gubitz, Commerzbank, Frankfurt
Stephen Hall, London Business School
Jerome Henry, Bank of France
Sean Holly, University of Sheffield
Mary McCarthy, European Commission
Donal McGettigan, Bank of Ireland
Morris McGuire, Bank of Ireland
Dimitrios Malliaropulos, Deutsches Bundesbank
Marie-Calire Marchesi, Paris Chamber of Commerce
Geoff Meen, Oxford Economic Forecasting
Pete Mitchell, University of Warwick
Carlo Monticelli, Secretariat, Committee of European Central Bankers, BIS
Fergal O'Brolchain, Dept of Finance, Government of Ireland
Terry O'Shaugnessy, University of Oxford
Paolo Onofri, PROMETEIA
John Overend, Aston Business School
Nikitis Pittis, National Institute of Economic and Social Research
Pete Richardson, OECD
Chris Salmon, Bank of England
Berhard Seidel, Deutsches Institut für Wirtschaftsforschung
Edith Skriner, OPEC
John Grieve Smith, University of Cmabridge
Mike Stephenson, Bank of England
Henri Sterdyniak, OFCE
Christopher Taylor, Bank of England
Dave Turner, OECD
Marc Vanheukelen, EC Commission
Alpo Willman, Finlandsbank

Introduction

Ray Barrell and John Whitley

Despite the progression towards the formation of a European Monetary Union there still exists considerable disagreement between economists about the relative merits of the current European Monetary System (EMS), EMU and a return to independent policy under floating exchange rates. This volume results from a conference held at the University of Warwick in March 1992, under the auspices of the SPES programme of the European Commission. The conference was attended by multi-country modellers from different parts of Europe, by academic economists, and economists from European central banks, the OECD and the EC. Many of the contributions are highly empirical and are based on large-scale multi-country models which are regularly used for forecasting and policy analysis, thus increasing the practical relevance of many of the findings.

The empirical chapters illustrate some of the findings of studies which have attempted to evaluate EMS and EMU and highlight some of the critical features which influence the different findings. In particular the possible changes in wage bargaining under transition to EMU are analysed and their implications developed using empirical models. In addition some of the policy issues facing the European economies are discussed, such as the nature of the current balance constraint, the impact of German reunification and debt solvency requirements for convergence to EMU. The volume also includes some more theoretically based analyses which are also highly relevant in contemporary European discussions, such as the nature of credibility and the role of exchange-rate realignments in the process of adjustment to EMU.

The SPES programme has financed a network of multi-country modellers from Europe over the last two years and this volume represents an account of some of the comparative work that has been possible within the network. The core group of modellers comprise the National Institute of Economic and Social Research and the London Business School, using the model NiGEM developed by the Institute and jointly maintained with the LBS, the Observatoire Français des Conjunctures Economiques (OFCE) and the Centre d'Etudes Prospectives et d'Informations Internationales (CEPII) with their MIMOSA model; the Deutsches Institut für Wirtschaftforschung using the EC's QUEST model; Oxford Economic Forecasting; and the OECD with their INTERLINK model.

The evaluation of exchange-rate regimes

The opening chapters by Masson and Symansky and by Minford, Rastogi and Hughes Hallett are concerned with the evaluation of alternative policy regimes for the European economies, particularly EMS and EMU. They both use stochastic simulation methods to evaluate the variability of inflation and output under the various exchange-rate arrangements but come to quite different conclusions. Minford *et al.*, using the Liverpool annual global model, argue that EMS produces instability. This result is in sharp contrast to the results of the study by the EC Commission, *One market One money*, which concludes that EMS reduces average inflation variability (but at the cost of increased average output variability). Masson and Symansky in Chapter 1 provide a very useful comparative assessment of these studies and show that different findings result from differences in experimental design rather than differences between the models used in different exercises. They compare results from the IMF's MULTIMOD with those from the Liverpool model used by Minford and colleagues, and since MULTIMOD was used also by the EC Commission in its *One Market, One Money* study, they are able to illustrate the sensitivity of the results to certain key assumptions. One of these is the treatment of risk premia and the method by which these are estimated and therefore implicitly assumed to change under EMU. The problem of measuring the risk premia arises since in an uncovered interest parity (UIP) formulation of the exchange rate expectations are not actually observed and so ex-post deviations from UIP cannot be distinguished from expectations errors. Masson and Symansky show that the EC Commission's method of estimating risk premia produces gains from EMU that are far larger than obtained by other methods. In essence, quite large historical random shocks disappear completely under EMU so that a key source of instability disappears. On the other hand the Minford treatment of exchange-rate realignments under EMS is shown to cause most of the instability in their results. A further difference found by Masson and Symansky is the method of averaging output and inflation variability under the different exchange-rate regimes. They find that this explains some of the EC Commission's preference for EMU over floating. The overall conclusion of Masson and Symansky is that EMS is much less of a potential source of instability than implied by Minford and colleagues, but on the other hand they find no strong evidence to support EMU over the alternative regimes.

The study by Minford, Rastogi and Hughes Hallett, discussed by Masson and Symansky, argues that the best regime for the EC countries would be floating with monetary policies either coordinated worldwide or, if this is impossible, coordinated within an EC-wide coalition in a world of independent Nash behaviour. Otherwise the UK would gain from staying out of EMU, returning to a floating exchange-rate regime. Whilst accepting the importance of the treatment of risk premia on exchange rates (and rejecting the approach of the EC Commission) they argue that the exchange- rate errors used in the stochastic simulations should be derived from a fully model-consistent framework rather than by the random-walk model used by Masson and Symansky and they are probably correct to argue this case, especially since the practical difficulties are not insurmountable. Several of the models involved in the most recent Brooking comparison exercise (Bryant, *et al.,* 1992) did implement full model consistent stochastic simulations (see also Ireland and Westaway, 1991). The second theme of Chapter 2 concerns the choice of monetary policy under each regime. Three typical alternative forms of monetary policy are used in the various studies of EMS and EMU. The first is an interest-rate rule which targets inflation and real output. This is used in the EC Commission study and in the model-based simulation studies described elsewhere in this volume. The second form of monetary policy is money targeting and the third is nominal income targeting. Minford and colleagues reject the first option as potentially unstable for some shocks on the basis of some earlier results with other models. They argue that a proper comparison of the different exchange-rate regimes should involve the adoption of the most appropriate monetary policy for that regime, and hence monetary policy may, and should, vary across the alternative exchange-rate regimes. Their results suggest that nominal income targeting is more favourable for floating relative to EMU whereas the reverse may hold for fixed money supplies. Minford *et al.* also distinguish between purely automatic rules such as fixed money and non-automatic responses which include both non-cooperative Nash policies and EC cooperation. They argue that the optimum is a coalition of all EC countries for the management of their money supplies but under floating rates with EMU the next best, followed by worldwide cooperation under floating. There is not, however, full agreement between the EC countries on which option is best; Germany, France and Italy would benefit from EMU, the UK from floating. With respect to the rest of the world the US would prefer floating and Japan and Canada would be in favour of EMU.

Labour market convergence

The role of labour markets, and particularly the behaviour of wages, in relation to movement towards monetary union, is discussed in Chapters 3 and 4 by Anderton, Barrell and in't Veld and by Horn and Zweiner respectively.

Anderton, Barrell and in't Veld examine the structural stability of wage equations in the four main European economies with a view to judging whether the convergence of inflation in Europe can be ascribed to increased credibility of policy, changes in labour market structural characteristics or merely reflects the loss of monetary control under a fixed exchange-rate regime. They find no evidence of structural changes in the wage relationships for Germany and the UK (despite the 'Thatcher' reforms), nor of changes in France despite their labour market reforms. This latter case is suggestive therefore of a credibility effect. In the case of Italy they find strong evidence of a shift towards more forward-looking behaviour in recent years, which may or may not be related to the operation of EMS. They test the implications of forward-looking behaviour by subjecting the NiGEM model in response to both a fiscal and an oil price shock. This is done under the different assumptions of forward-looking expectations ('model-consistent') and backward-looking ('data-consistent') expectations for the expectations term in the wage equations under an EMU environment. Model-consistent expectations tend to produce a faster inflation response for a fiscal shock but the effects on a utility function containing both output and inflation depend on the degree of crowding out in the different European economies. In general, differences in the utility indices are not very marked across the different expectation-generating alternatives and the same is true of an external (oil price) shock. The results indicate, therefore, that the economies' response to the shocks does not depend critically on labour market participants believing policy commitments to reduce inflation. It is rather the successful operation of the monetary policy rule which relates interest rates to inflation and real output under EMU that ensures a successful outcome.

Horn and Zweiner consider in Chapter 4 how uniform behaviour in Europe might influence the competitiveness and shock absorption capabilities of the major European economies using the DIW version of the EC Commission's model QUEST. In particular they consider adjustment patterns that might arise if wage equations in the rest of Europe were identical to those in Germany. They find that wage behaviour in Germany is such that wages rise in line with productivity in the long run (a result consistent with that of Anderton *et al.* in the preceding chapter but who find that this is not a phenomenon peculiar to Germany). But in Germany also wages respond more sluggishly to inflationary pressures than elsewhere in Europe, at least in the short run (again consistent with the Anderton *et al.* findings). They find little difference in the response of real output and inflation in the European economies under a fiscal shock with German-style wage behaviour but more substantial effects for an oil price shock because the German wage adjustment to productivity now takes place in the other European economies and hence reduces the competitiveness gains to Germany itself. The implications for wage adjustment under EMU therefore depend upon the nature of the shocks occurring to the European economies but they also depend upon whether the style of wage bargaining can be said to be shifting towards that of Germany, and this is given little support by the stability analysis reported by Anderton *et al.* in the preceding chapter, except possibly for Italy. Furthermore German reunification may be changing wage adjustment in Germany itself.

The comparison and evaluation of large macro models

Macroeconomic models have a role to play in the analysis of economic policy, but before we use models for that purpose it is important that we understand their properties and the basic philosophies of their managers. Models may differ in their scope and in their data sources, and these factors may influence their properties. However, models cannot be constructed in a theoretical vacuum, and the imposition of statistically invalid constraints (or the avoidance of valid constraints) could distort model properties. One of the major aims of this SPES programme has been to undertake a set of model comparisons and evaluations. The first has been published in the *Journal of Forecasting* (Whitley, 1992). That paper involved the comparison of a set of standard simulations on our core set of models. The second comparison paper, in this volume, has been designed to bring out aspects of the models that are particularly relevant to policy analysis.

The comparison exercise was undertaken by Whitley, but the individual model groups undertook the programming and the simulations. In order to evaluate the policy conclusions that can be drawn from a set of models it is necessary to construct a set of standard rules of conduct for monetary and fiscal policy, and to agree a framework for the determination of exchange rates. This ensures that differences in outturns from different models will, in this exercise at least, be the result mainly of differences between models. We adopted the interest-rate targeting rule used by the Commission in *One market, One money*, and we also asked all modellers to implement a countercyclical fiscal policy rule. We were unable to implement model-consistent expectations in all the models in the programme, but we were able to ensure that exchange rates followed the open arbitrage path relating exchange rates to interest rates. Each modelling group was asked to implement a set of shocks to their models and to report them in a standard format. The results are reported in Chapter 5.

The Maastricht Treaty attempted to address the issues surrounding fiscal policy in a monetary union, and our first set of simulations was designed to throw light on this topic. Each model group increased government spending in each of the European economies in turn, and four different policy regimes were analysed:

— independent interest and exchange-rate targeting, with the intention of modelling floating exchange rates
— an EMS where internal exchange rates are fixed within bands, whilst interest rates and the exchange rate policy are determined by the Bundesbank, taking account of the deviation of German variables from their target values
— an EMU regime with a European central bank that targets aggregate European variables with ERM fiscal policies

— an EMU regime where fiscal policies have to be designed to fit inside a long-run fiscal policy constraint

Three of the models, NiGEM, Interlink, and OEF had fiscal policy multipliers that are generally below one, suggesting a substantial degree of crowding out, whilst the DIW-EC QUEST model generally displayed fiscal multipliers that are initially in excess of one.

The full results of the set of experiments are set out in Chapter 5, and we will only summarise the main features. Membership of the ERM gives the fiscal authorities in the UK, France, and Italy more leverage than is available to them under independent exchange-rate policies. The result may be unexpected, but it arises because the Bundesbank determines the interest-rate and exchange-rate reactions to all fiscal expansions, and we are assuming that it is targeting German variables and hence there is little additional pressure on interest rates within the expanding economy. The direct spillovers from fiscal expansions are small in all the models, and hence inflation and output do not rise very much in response to a fiscal impulse in another country. The Bundesbank interest-rate reaction is therefore muted, and hence the rise in the ecu exchange rate is small.

Under EMU we assume that the European central bank targets European-wide inflation and output, and as a result we observe a larger rise in interest rates in response to fiscal expansion in the UK, France and Italy than we observe in an EMS regime. The interest-rate response to a fiscal expansion in Germany is smaller under EMU than in the EMS. Fiscal multipliers are therefore lower in EMU for the former three countries, but larger for Germany. In no case do we observe the Walters phenomenon under EMS where fiscal expansions lead to higher inflation, lower real interest rates and hence a considerable increase in demand. The models considered in this volume all have real interest-rate effects that are sufficiently slow acting that they do not display unstable reactions to demand.

Fiscal expansion in Germany as a result of economic and political union in 1990 has been accompanied by an increase in interest rates. The IMF, in its *World Economic Outlook* in May 1992, has argued that the expansionary effect on the rest of Europe of this fiscal impulse has been more than offset by the effects of the associated rise in interest rates and exchange rates. Our simulations help throw light on this issue. The fiscal expansion that we have implemented in Germany under EMS rules generally leads to a slowdown in the rest of Europe. This message is clear from the simulations undertaken on NiGEM, OEF and Interlink. To the contrary, only the simulations on the DIW-EC QUEST model suggest that the trade effects outweigh the interest-rate and exchange-rate effects.

The importance of differences between models is further highlighted in the chapter on Strategic Model Choice by Andy Hughes-Hallett. He accepts that models will differ in their policy implications and hence policymakers' actions will depend upon the model that they choose to use. If policymakers in different countries choose to use different models then they may play inconsistent and suboptimal strategies. Disagreement over the true model increases expected losses, whether or not policymakers cooperate with each other, but cooperation over the choice of model will reduce expected losses. Hughes-Hallett finds that the gains from choosing the right model are much greater than the gains from policy cooperation between countries. This interesting result gives further weight to the need for effective model comparison exercises. Only one of the models involved in our comparison — an early version of the EC QUEST model — was included by Hughes Hallett, and it would be of interest to see his analysis extended to the set of models covered here.

The EMS and the path to EMU

Large-scale models are a useful test bed on which to evaluate policy regimes, but they are not the only one available to us. The chapters by Driffill and Miller and by Britton in this book address the evolution and future of the EMS. Driffill and Miller ask the question 'Is the Road to Monetary Union Paved with Recession', and their conditional answer to the question is yes. A successful monetary union requires that the members achieve a set of sustainable, or equilibrium, real exchange rates, and this requires that price levels adjust. It is not sufficient to achieve inflation convergence. Even if high inflation countries such as the UK join the proto-union at the correct real exchange rate, in the early years on the path to convergence inflation rates will be above those in Germany, and hence real exchange rates will become increasingly overvalued. Even when inflation converges the economies are out of equilibrium, and inflation has to fall below that in Germany for a number of years. Driffill and Miller demonstrate the importance of the credibility of the exchange-rate peg. If it is not credible, and wage contracts are forward looking, then the anticipation of devaluation will raise wage settlements and therefore inflation. The currency will become increasingly overvalued, and hence a recession will be induced. This recession will not be permanent, in that eventually wage bargainers will accept that the peg is credible, and will adjust their inflation expectations downwards, and the inflation rate will drop below that in Germany and then approach it from below, with unemployment falling back to equilibrium. The evidence from the set of models discussed in this volume is that this process could be rather extended.

The problem of learning about realignments is also addressed in the chapter by Britton. He argues that the EMS has been designed so that it is impossible for the markets to estimate the reaction function of the authorities, and hence it is not possible to forecast realignments with confidence. This lack of certainty has been induced by the continuous process of institutional change that the EMS has undergone. It has never been a fixed-rate or Bretton Woods-style adjustable peg system with agreed rules of the game, rather it has seen continually changing rules and the pegging system has evolved over time. Britton argues that if expectations do not depend on past realignments, then realignments are an attractive policy option because they give considerable real advantages in the short run. However, it is a weapon of last resort, in that it will often affect expectations, and this may well help to offset the real gains. If, though, a realignment can be undertaken without inducing a shock to expectations, then it is of value. That is why the Froot and Rogoff (1991) proposal of one last realignment just before irrevocably fixing exchange rates is so attractive. However, such an action may damage the credibility of the system as a whole. Britton argues that the survival of the ERM must be in question, because it has survived by relying on surprises, and eventually individuals will learn about the system. He suggests that the ERM can either emerge from its chrysalis into full-blown EMU, or it could collapse with Europe reverting to flexible exchange rates.

Using large models to analyse policy

In Chapter 9 Knoester and Kolodziejak discuss the role of supply-side policies and convergence to EMU. Their emphasis is on the effect of income taxes of wage bargaining (the so-called 'wedge' effect). They claim that there is convincing empirical evidence to support a supply-side effect of taxes through their impact on wages, despite the fact that these effects have never been very robust in empirical work and that Layard, Nickell and Jackman (1991) now argue that such influences should not appear in the long-run determination of wages (this issue is discussed in Chapter 3). Knoester and Kolodziejak use the tax effect to argue that policies which simultaneously reduces taxes and public spending can remove the negative consequences of otherwise more likely adjustment paths adopted by the European countries in an attempt to meet the convergence criteria set out at Maastricht. However their alternative policy scenarios assume also that there is an (exogenous) degree of wage moderation in the European countries without specifying how this is to be achieved, and how important this element is in the success of their proposed policies.

Van Erp, van Leeuwen and Timmer discuss the emerging pattern of the current account of the balance of payments in the European Community, the US and Japan in Chapter 10. Their study is based on simulations with the world model of the Dutch Central Planning Bureau. They find that flexible exchange rates alone cannot be relied upon to remedy current account imbalances and that fiscal policy is required, especially in a world of fixed nominal exchange rates. Current account imbalances are corrected more efficiently if there is a globally coordinated fiscal policy adjustment.

Chauffour, Harasty and Le Dem in Chapter 11 analyse the impact of German reunification and its effect upon Europe under alternative monetary arrangements. This is a good practical example of an asymmetrical shock and its potential effects are simulated using the MIMOSA model. The key questions raised are whether the effect of German reunification was beneficial to the rest of Europe and whether the shock might have been better managed under a different exchange-rate regime — either floating or EMU. The answer to the first question is a qualified yes since, although EMS transmitted higher German interest rates to the rest of the Community, this actually helped to promote faster convergence of interest rates and higher German inflation simultaneously reduced inflation differentials and enhanced credibility. Under the alternative of floating the D-Mark would have appreciated alone and activity would have been higher in the rest of the Community, although at the cost of higher inflation imported from Germany. Under EMU arrangements the outcome would have been between that of floating and EMS since the rise in interest rates would have been governed by average EC inflation. A particularly strong feature of the results is that the differences in the impact on EC output of German reunification under different exchange-rate arrangements would have persisted until well towards the end of the century.

Exchange-rate realignments and the EMS

The issue of realignments has often been discussed in the context of a single country adjusting its exchange rate against its partners within the ERM. As Driffill and Miller demonstrate, a devaluation may well induce forward-looking agents to anticipate further realignments and hence bargain with an anticipated rate of inflation that reflects this. Risk premiums could well emerge in interest rates as a result of the anticipation of further devaluations and higher inflation. There are a number of examples of this during the ERM period. In 1983 the Dutch government decided to realign against the D-Mark, and devalued by only 3 per cent. The previous commitment to the D-Mark parity had been seen as credible, and interest rates had essentially converged on German levels. The realignment caused a decline in the credibility of the exchange-rate peg, and an interest differential of almost ½ per cent emerged in short-term interest rates, and stayed there for several years (see in't Veld, 1992, for further discussion).

A realignment that is driven by the need to remove an undervaluation on the part of one currency may well have different effects on the credibility of the authorities. A concerted move to reduce the perceived undervaluation of the D-Mark in the post unification period could be seen as entirely beneficial.

No individual country is devaluing and breaking its commitment to the mechanism, and hence there is little reason for further devaluations to be anticipated. The realignment deals with a once-in-century shock (see Williamson, 1991) and does not signal a move back to a floating rate system. If expected inflation does not rise because of a devaluation premium, then the realignment will not be associated with the problems discussed in Chapter 7.

We would argue that such a costless realignment is possible at this stage of the evolution of the EMS towards monetary union. Britton and Minford *et al.* both argue (albeit from a different perspective) that the EMS cannot be seen as an enduring exchange-rate management arrangement. It must either progress to monetary union, or revert to a floating exchange-rate regime. The process of convergence is clearly under way, as is discussed in Chapter 9. There are some policy adjustments that are clearly required to meet the convergence criteria laid down at Maastricht. The single market programme is also of importance in the process of achieving convergence. In a more competitive Common Market the scope for significant differences in labour market behaviour are likely to be reduced. The convergence of labour market behaviour would greatly assist the convergence of economic performance, but the evidence in Anderton *et al.* suggests that this process has been taking place only slowly. (Anderton, Barrell and McHugh, 1992, discuss the relationship between product market competition and the wage bargaining process.) The achievement of convergence in economic performance without the convergence of labour market behaviour will be greatly aided by more coordinated monetary (and fiscal) policies, but as Hughes-Hallett argues, it is essential that the authorities in different countries agree on a model, or at least have some sort of agreed position on the likely responses of the world to their action.

The evaluation of EMU

The issue of coordinated policy is of particular importance when comparing the operation of the ERM to that of a potential EMU. Our results in Chapter 5 suggest that the response of the ERM to asymmetric shocks depends very much on the source and location of the shock. The response to German unification under ERM rules has been dominated by its inflationary effects on Germany. Interest rates have risen, and exchange rates have appreciated. There is some evidence that this has had a deleterious effect on the other European economies. Our common simulations and the chapter by Chauffour *et al.* both demonstrate that the shock may have been better accommodated under EMU as long as monetary policy is not dominated by German concerns. The inflationary consequences for the community as a whole are much less than for Germany, and hence the deflationary policy response would be much less severe if EMU was in place. The German inflation differential partly reflects the need for an appreciation of the real D-Mark exchange rate, and this would be better managed inside a monetary union. The ERM also has the possibility embedded in it of a destabilising response to shocks. If an inflationary shock hits a country other than Germany, then under ERM rules the interest rate cannot fully adjust, and hence the real interest rate in that economy will fall. A Walters effect of this sort could be destabilising in that it increases the expansionary effects of the initial shock. Although none of our simulations display this effect it must be seen as a serious possibility and it could lead to the collapse of the mechanism. Under an EMU operated by a European central bank with European objectives, interest rates throughout the Community would rise in response to an inflationary shock in any of its members. Some developments in the ERM are inevitable, and if it progressed to full EMU rather than collapsed, this would then solve many of the policy coordination problems that the current system faces.

Many of the issues addressed in this volume are not yet resolved, but it is encouraging that we find a relatively high degree of consensus between the models and the practitioners on many of the implications for policy. Comparative exercises of this sort can help the process of convergence towards an agreed model, and also hopefully towards a true model. Even without achieving this ideal aim this volume can be seen as an important contribution both to the policy process and to the coordination and dissemination of Pan-European macroeconomic research.

1

Evaluating the EMS and EMU Using Stochastic Simulations: Some Issues*

Paul R. Masson and Steven Symansky

Introduction

Since the Delors Report was published in April 1989, a lively debate has ensued about the costs and benefits of economic and monetary union in Europe (EMU). However, relatively little has been done using empirically-based macroeconomic models to evaluate the economic performance of monetary union relative to alternatives of floating exchange rates or the EMS as it currently operates, with occasional realignments. A notable exception was the EC Commission's study on monetary union: *One Market, One Money* (*European Economy*, no. 44, October 1990), which used stochastic simulations of the IMF's MULTIMOD model to compare variability of output and inflation under different exchange rate arrangements. This study was however criticised by Patrick Minford and Anupam Rastogi. In a series of papers, one of which is included in this volume, Minford and collaborators have presented their own simulations of the operation of the EMS and of monetary union, using a different model, the Liverpool World Model.

The EC Commission was sanguine about the favourable effects of monetary union: their simulations suggested that though the EMS of the mid-1980s produced more output variability (but less inflation variability) than freely floating rates, the evolving EMS and, even more so, EMU, would produce improvements in both output and inflation variability for the EMS countries taken together. The favourable overall result was only tempered by the fact that not all countries would necessarily improve both inflation and output variability when moving to a (symmetric) EMU; for instance where there are Europe-wide

*We are grateful to Alexander Italianer and Patrick Minford for giving us details of their simulations, and to them and to Leonardo Bartolini, Andrew Hughes Hallett, and Marcus Miller for helpful discussions. We also wish to thank Kote Nikoi and Susanna Mursula for research assistance. The views expressed here are personal to the authors and do not represent those of the International Monetary Fund.

targets for monetary policy, as opposed to an asymmetric EMU in which Germany sets monetary policy for Europe, both German and Italian GDP exhibited higher variability than under freely floating exchange rates (though inflation variability was lower for both countries).

In contrast, Minford and Rastogi (1990) conclude that EMU is unambiguously bad for the United Kingdom, and also bad for the other three major EC countries if the UK joins. Especially in the case where the EMS countries pursue monetary targets (either independent targets, as under floating, or a joint target, as would be the case in EMU), floating dominates monetary union. More recent work, included in this volume, concludes that preference for floating (over EMU) would be greatly strengthened if exchange-rate stability is not an objective. The EMS is criticised even more strongly according to Minford and associates; it is destabilising, and has only survived by becoming more rigid and undergoing institutional change.

The current chapter attempts to throw light on the difference between the conclusions reached by the two sets of studies. We focus on several aspects that seem to be crucial for the simulation exercise: first, how to model the EMS (in particular, realignments); second, how monetary policy would be determined in EMU; and third, what structural changes would result from EMU—in particular, how to estimate the effects of reductions in the risk premia in interest rates. Some of these methodological issues have already been raised by the EC Commission (1990), Minford and Rastogi (1990), and Emerson and Italianer (1990), but it may be useful for participants in the debate to get an outsider's view. Since we are able to redo the simulations on MULTIMOD, we may be able to discover how much of the difference in results is due to different assumptions or to different models.[1] We also raise the issue of what the criterion for evaluating EMU relative to alternatives should be: do national inflation rates matter, or just EC-wide inflation?

Since agreement was reached at Maastricht in December 1991 to proceed to full monetary union, it may be thought that the costs and benefits of monetary union are largely an academic question at this point. Even if this were true, the methodology would have wider application, and might have practical interest for evaluating other monetary unions—among the former Soviet republics, for instance—or other countries wanting to join EMU (including the United Kingdom). But more than this, the variability of output and inflation when monetary union is achieved in Europe might have implications for other macroeconomic policies, even if national exchange-rate policies were no longer at issue. In particular, how to run EC monetary policy still has to be determined—subject to the general objective of price stability—and national fiscal policies may have to be operated with more flexibility to compensate for constraints on monetary policies (see Masson and Melitz, 1991, and Hughes Hallett and Vines, 1991).

Method

Stochastic simulations

The method of stochastic simulations was used both by the EC Commission and by Minford and his associates; it is also used in the results presented below. This method, since it is familiar, can be described briefly. [2] A model, with estimated parameters, contains behavioural equations for private sector variables, including exchange rates, as well as variables for policy instruments, which may or may not be endogenous. The purpose of the exercise is to see to what extent different policy rules for the instruments affect the variability of macroeconomic variables such as output and inflation. Stochastic simulations assume that the error terms in behavioural equations are drawn from a given joint distribution—usually that estimated from historical data. In order to evaluate the policy rules, repeated drawings are made from that distribution, so that the policies are evaluated on the basis of the variance across drawings of the variables of interest.[3] This variability is calculated relative to a baseline path—in particular, the model's solution with errors set to zero.[4] Policies are judged more desirable, the more effective they are at stabilising target variables around baseline paths.[5]

While the general method is not contentious, apart from the possible objection that the model may not be 'structural', in the sense of not invariant to the policy rule, and hence open to the Lucas (1976) critique, there are at least two aspects as it applies to EMU that are: how to estimate the historical covariance matrix of the errors, and what measure of variability to use to evaluate the outcomes.

Risk premiums

Risk premium estimates are important because by moving to a single currency (and hence removing exchange-rate risk between the EMU countries) EMU does not remove all exchange-rate risk; there is still risk between the ecu and the currencies of the non-EMU countries. MULTIMOD expresses the exchange-rate risk relative to the dollar, so the equations for EMU countries were rewritten relative to either the D-Mark (for asymmetric EMU) or the ecu (for the symmetric system). EMU will change the error covariance matrix by eliminating risk premium shocks to interest parity, provided there are no differential credit risks. The covariance matrix emerges straightforwardly from the estimation of behavioural equations that do not have expectational variables. The real problem concerns the interest parity condition, which does not contain parameters to estimate, but in which shocks may be present that reflect 'risk premia'. Uncovered interest parity between Germany and another EMS country can be written as follows:

$$R = R_G + E^e - E + u \tag{1.1}$$

where R is the domestic interest rate (a G subscript indicates a German variable), E the log of the exchange rate (for example, FF/DM), an $'e'$ superscript the expectation of next period's value, and u is a risk premium shock.

The significance of risk premium shocks to the evaluation of EMU comes from the fact that when realignments are ruled out (and even more clearly, when there is just a single currency), the risk premium shocks between European currencies simply disappear. Therefore, monetary union reduces an element of uncertainty, which is larger or smaller depending on how large those shocks are judged to have been historically. The problem is, however, that expectations of the exchange rate are not observable, so that we cannot distinguish *ex post* deviations from uncovered interest parity from expectations errors—that is, making a wrong forecast of the exchange rate.

The EC Commission (1990) gives a cogent account of four possible strategies for estimating those shocks (here R^* is the US interest rate).

(i) Use the actual exchange rate next period (call it $E(+1)$) in place of its expected value, and calculate u as

$$u = R * -R - E(+1) + E$$

(ii) Assume that expectations are governed by the hypothesis of a random walk, so that the interest differential itself represents a risk premium (see Masson and Symansky in the stochastic simulations of MULTIMOD reported in Bryant *et al*, 1992).

$$u = R * -R$$

(iii) Use the model to solve for E^e, and calculate u accordingly.
(iv) Use a small, partial model to generate E^e such that it is consistent with gradual adjustment to an assumed value for the long-run real interest rate.

The EC Commission chooses option (iv), after pointing out some of the pitfalls associated with the other options. Minford and Rastogi (1990) also strongly reject options (i) and (ii), the first as wrong and the second because it is inconsistent with MULTIMOD, but they criticise the Commission for choosing (iv) on the grounds that it is also inconsistent with MULTIMOD. Furthermore it gives shocks which Minford and Rastogi consider 'strain credulity' because they are so large—standard deviations of 5 to 11 per cent. According to them, the closest to being correct is option (iii).

We disagree that option (iii) is the correct one in principle, and in practice implementing it involves formidable difficulties. To use the model to disentangle historical expectations errors from risk premium shocks requires that expectations of all the exogenous variables be specified over a sufficiently long horizon that terminal conditions on the jumping variables (that is, exchange rates, interest rates, inflation, human wealth, and the market value of the capital stock) have no significant effect. Since the model includes government spending, oil prices, monetary targets, and so on, as exogenous variables, all these variables would have to be modelled for each country—pushing the needed inputs to the exercise into higher dimensions of complexity. Obviously it is not enough simply to assume that expectations of exogenous variables are the same as their *ex post* outcomes; this simply shifts the mistake of option (i) on to another set of variables.

Instead of estimating models of the exogenous variables, our preferred approach is to use time-series models to proxy exchange-rate expectations, ensuring that expectations are consistent with the historical data in at least a rough sense. Such a method is analogous to an instrumental variable approach to estimation. The issue is not model consistency; it is rather to get reasonable empirical estimates of the size of the risk premiums. As Svensson (1991) argues, even with a large coefficient of relative risk aversion, risk premia would be only a small fraction of interest differentials. Since the latter are in the order of only a few percentage points within the EMS, the EC Commission's estimates seem much too large.

We therefore agree with Minford and Rastogi (1990) that these risk premium shocks are unreasonably large, but disagree that option (iii) is the correct method. Getting a reasonable empirical estimate was the rationale for the random walk assumption of (ii); in fact in Frenkel, Goldstein and Masson (1989) time series models were identified, and not surprisingly (given what we know, for example, from Meese and Rogoff, 1983), a unit autoregressive (that is, AR(1)) coefficient, or something near it, describes the exchange-rate data well. For the other variables for which expectations need to be generated, for example, short-term interest rates, we estimated more complicated AR models. For exchange rates, it would therefore be unrealistic to assume that market forecasts are very different from the current rate, if one is considering a short-term horizon (one year in MULTIMOD). The fact that these forecasts are very different in the Commission study—the result of using option (iv)—explains the very large risk premium errors that they find. What is needed are estimates of the shocks that are consistent with the historical data, and a generalised option (ii) seems to us the best way of achieving this. We will consider below, in the fourth section, how the size of the estimates of risk premium shocks affects estimated gains from EMU.

Measuring variability

The second important issue in evaluating EMU is what measure of variability to use. Essentially, this amounts to asking what is the appropriate objective function (though in this chapter we do not assume anything about the relative importance of output versus inflation variability). The issue is whether we care about the variance of European *aggregates* (whatever their variability across countries) or rather about the variability of *each country's* variable.

This issue does not seem to have received any attention in the literature. However, Hughes Hallett and Vines (1991), in their evaluation of EMU, assume that national objective functions change. Welfare evaluations usually assume that the European objective function is a simple average of each country's objective function, which is typically quadratic in deviations from target (see, for example, Minford *et al.* in this volume). For instance, if each country's objective function is

$$L_i = E\{(q_i)^2 + \alpha(\pi_i)^2\} \qquad (1.2)$$

(where E is the mathematical expectation) and the global welfare function is

$$G = L_1 + L_2 \qquad (1.3)$$

then the global objective function is a simple weighted average of the variability of national output and inflation in the two countries

$$G = E[(q_1)^2 + (q_2)^2] + \alpha\ E[(\pi_1)^2 + (\pi_2)^2] \qquad (1.4)$$

This is the procedure followed by Minford and associates, and also implicitly by the EC Commission, since they calculate European variability by weighting together mean square deviations from baseline of each country's variable, and taking the square root of the result.

While this seems plausible for output, it does not make as much sense for inflation. In a single currency area, changes in relative prices should not matter in themselves, if they do not have harmful real effects. On the contrary, relative price changes are necessary for real adjustment. In the long run, all regions will share the same rate of inflation, which will be the result of the currency area's common monetary policy. The distribution of money balances across regions will be endogenous, as will movements in relative prices. It is the overall inflation rate and its variance in the face of shocks that are the source of important welfare costs. Just as there would only be a single money target in a currency union, there would likely only be a single objective for inflation— although the Maastricht agreement does not specify how 'price stability' should be defined. Flexibility of prices across regions in response to asymmetric shocks would be a desirable feature because it would facilitate adjustment— provided the overall inflation rate was not affected.

This reasoning suggests that the proper variability measure is $E[(\pi_1 + \pi_2)/2]^2$, the variability of European inflation, which depends on the covariances between inflation rates in the following way:

$$E[(\pi_1 + \pi_2)/2]^2 = [E(\pi_1)^2 + E(\pi_2)^2 + 2\operatorname{cov}(\pi_1, \pi_2)]/4$$

Exchange-rate changes between EMS currencies due to risk premium shocks tend to induce a negative covariance, lowering the variability of *aggregate* EC inflation. EMU, by eliminating those exchange-rate changes, may not therefore reduce this measure of inflation variability as much as the average of national inflation variances.

In the simulations presented below in the third and fourth sections, we therefore use a hybrid set of measures for European variability: for output, we calculate an average of each country's root mean square errors, since it matters whether some countries are adversely hit even if others benefit. For inflation, in contrast, we report the variability of European inflation, calculated as the variability of a GDP-weighted average of the constituent countries' inflation rates (or equivalently, the variability of the change in the European price level). In the fourth section, we consider the effect of using other criteria.

Furthermore, the choice of what variables to use in evaluating different regimes is obviously important. Minford *et al.* (in this volume), who calculate welfare functions that depend on various combinations of output, the price level, real interest rates, the real exchange rate, and money supply growth, argue that the inclusion of the exchange rate is essential to the spirit and substance of the exercise. An alternative approach, followed by the EC Commission (1990) is to cite root mean squared error values for a large set of variables, and allow the reader to impose his preferences. In what follows, for conciseness we present graphs of output and inflation variability (calculated as described above), but details on other variables are available from the authors.

Modelling monetary policy
Important issues are the choice of the baseline rule for monetary policy and how to model it in the EMS and EMU. These choices are critical from a number of aspects. First, the benchmark of floating exchange rates requires an anchor for monetary policy: is this a money target or a target for nominal income, for instance, or rather the optimal uncoordinated setting of a monetary instrument, leading to a Nash equilibrium as each country optimises independently? Second, since there are margins of fluctuations for exchange rates within the EMS, monetary policy is only constrained when obliged to defend the band: what does it do within the band? Finally, EMU requires a rule for European monetary policy, which can range over a number of alternatives, just as it can for an individual country operating a floating exchange rate. It is conceivable that

EMU might be better than floating for one intermediate target, but worse for another.

The various studies differ in the choice of monetary policy assumptions. MULTIMOD has, in its standard version, the default assumption that countries target base money, but in such a way that they smooth interest rate fluctuations (otherwise, an attempt to hit money exactly each period might provoke large fluctuations in rates).[6] Such a rule for monetary policy is assumed to apply to each of the industrial countries, except for those in the EMS; the latter are assumed to change interest rates in order to resist movements away from their central parities against the D-Mark, while Germany targets base money.

The EC Commission chose a different intermediate target, namely a modified form of nominal income targeting in which the target depends on the rate of inflation (not the price level) and the log of output relative to its baseline level. Moreover, a greater weight was put on inflation (2.0) than on output (0.4). The use of inflation was justified by the argument that central banks do not care about the price level *per se* and hence do not try to roll back past price increases.

In Minford *et al.* (this volume), two alternatives are given with respect to monetary policies. In the first, there is a fixed target for the money supply, which is hit exactly (the fixed money case), while in the second, governments are assumed to set their money supplies in an optimal way in response to shocks (the strategic response case). Thus, in the latter case monetary policy is actively adjusted, at least in the case of floating rates. Under EMU, the European money supply is again alternatively forced to follow a fixed target or set optimally to respond to shocks, while exchange rates among EC countries remain fixed.

In the simulations reported below, we alternatively assume a nominal income target or a money supply target. These targets apply under floating rates, under an EMS regime, and (for an EC-wide aggregate) under EMU. Using alternative targets helps in assessing the sensitivity of the results to the choice of intermediate target. We do not consider strategic responses by policymakers.

Modelling the EMS

How to model the existing EMS is important for judging whether the status quo is better or worse than EMU. There is a consensus for assuming that Germany sets monetary policy for the EMS; that is, either its money supply, value of nominal income, or optimal policy setting is taken as given by other countries, who must devote their monetary policy instruments to defending their parities vis-à-vis the D-Mark (at least when the band is threatened). However, there are two major areas of disagreement: (a) treatment of the way countries defend their parities, including the operation of monetary policy within the band; and (b) how realignments are modelled.

Intervention to defend the band

In the standard MULTIMOD (see Masson, Symansky, and Meredith, 1990), other EMS countries vary their interest rate or their money supply as a function of the deviation of the exchange rate from its central parity. The function chosen is a cubic, following Edison, Miller, and Williamson (1987), but rewritten in terms of the money supply (with the interest rate determined by the equality with money demand). The equation was rewritten in terms of deviations of the money supply from an exogenous target since this formulation permitted various alternative specifications to be nested in a common specification. In the model used in the simulations reported below, the monetary policy function (for example, for France) is written

$$M - MT = a(E - E_p)^3 \qquad (1.5)$$

where M is the log of the French money supply, MT the log of its money target, and E is the log of the exchange rate (in FF per DM), and the 'p' subscript refers to its central parity.[7] In this formulation, there is no explicit band; however, choice of the value of 'a' will determine how close the exchange rate stays to its parity, in the face of shocks. As it is currently parameterised in MULTIMOD, we have found that even in the face of sizeable shocks, EMS exchange rates stay within about ±1 per cent of parity (which is consistent with the practice of some EMS countries, in particular Belgium and the Netherlands, to aim for smaller bands than the statutory ±2.25 per cent that is mandated by commitment to the narrow band of the ERM). Equation (1.5) implies that the closer E is to its parity, the closer M will be to MT, that is, the more importance will be given to the domestic money target.

In EC Commission (1990), bands are also not explicitly defended, but a different function is used, in order to impose very strong non-linearity beyond ±1 per cent. This is also combined with a weight on the hybrid nominal income target described above, so that when the exchange rate is close to the centre of the band, the monetary authorities set policy to aim at the domestic target. The resulting function is

$$R - R^b = 200[(E - E_p) + 2.1 \times 10^{18}(E - E_p)^{11}] + \\ 100[2(\pi - \pi^b) + 0.4(q - q^b)] \qquad (1.6)$$

where here, the interest rate is varied relative to its baseline value R^b, π is the rate of inflation and q is the log of output. Both rules (1.5) and (1.6) allow for intramarginal intervention.

Finally, Minford and others assume that, within the band, money is exogenous (when money is not adjusted strategically). They assume an explicit band, however, which has to be defended, and at the edge of the band, money becomes endogenous. It changes by whatever amount is necessary to prevent the exchange rate from going outside the band, and intervention only occurs at the edges of the band.

Realignments

The EC Commission and Minford and others differ fundamentally on how to model realignments—what triggers them and how the amount of realignment is determined. The EC Commission bases its model on historical experience of realignments in the 1985-7 period, during which the average size of realignments was 3.5 per cent, and realignments offset about 50 per cent of price differentials. Consequently, they assume that a realignment is triggered by an 8 per cent overvaluation (or undervaluation) of price levels relative to Germany, but the size of the realignment against the D-Mark is limited to 4 per cent, and it occurs in the following period.

In contrast, Minford and others assume that realignments are triggered by the knowledge (assuming perfect foresight) that, in the absence of new shocks, the exchange rate, if it were flexible, would be outside of the band next period. However, parities have to be defended this period; there is a one-period lag in making the parity adjustment that has been decided. The amount of the realignment is the multiple of ±5 per cent necessary to put the exchange rate back in the band next period, in the absence of future shocks (of course, new shocks next period may force the authorities to defend the new band by varying the money supply).

Simulating the existing EMS

As discussed above, there is disagreement concerning how to model the current operation of the EMS, or at least, the EMS as it operated from 1985-7; it could be argued that realignments have been ruled out since the last substantial realignment in February 1987; there have been subsequent public commitments of some countries not to realign again, and the Maastricht agreement also makes realignments less likely. However, understanding how the EMS operated in the past is still important.

Minford *et al.* (this volume) consider that the EMS induces instability, because realignments occur at discrete intervals, after potentially destabilising attempts of monetary policy to prevent the exchange rate from going outside the band:

'The EMS is a system prone to acute instability in the face of shocks. Particularly vulnerable are the dependent-EMS countries. The reason for this instability seems to lie in the non-linearity of the fixed-but-adjustable system's response to shocks, with large shocks creating a sharp response, and in deflationary circumstances the perverse trade-off in dependent-

EMS countries inducing monetary over-reaction.'

In contrast, the simulation results of the EC Commission show that the EMS reduces average inflation variability but increases average output variability of the EMS countries taken together. The reasons for the tradeoff in effects is described as follows in EC Commission (1990)—henceforth, ECC (1990):

'The reduction in inflation variability is the consequence of the reduction in asymmetric intra-Community exchange rate shocks and wage and price discipline effects... The increase in output variability is due to the constraint on monetary policy from the peg to the DM for the countries other than Germany. The wage and price discipline effects .... [are] apparently not large enough to compensate for the reduced room for manoeuvre in monetary policy, except in Germany...'(p. 154)

All in all, however, the impact of the EMS relative to floating is not dramatic. In the stochastic simulations reported in Chapter 2, welfare losses from the EMS under fixed money are many multiples of the welfare costs that shocks produce in a floating rate regime (see, for instance, table 2.2 in the next chapter). Not only are EMS countries, except Germany (which has a small gain), worse off, but the same is true of non-EMS countries (see Chapter 2, table 2.2). This is the case we will discuss; the welfare losses under strategic policymaking are even larger.

In order to understand the source of the difference in results, we simulated both sets of realignment rules with MULTIMOD, and compared the results, which are plotted in chart 1.1. This chart gives the two alternatives described above: (1) A 4 per cent realignment is triggered by prices being out of line by 8 per cent relative to Germany but is delayed until the next period (the EC Commission's rule). (2) A realignment in multiples of 5 per cent is triggered by a forward-looking assessment of whether, given monetary policy, the exchange rate would be outside the band next period, but the realignment is also delayed until next period (the rule of Minford and associates). The chart also looks at the effect of not realigning at all—that is, of having fixed central parities with bands around them—and the effects of the band width[8] on the variability of output and inflation. Obviously, the narrower the band width, the closer the regime with fixed parities resembles EMU, while the wider the bands, the closer it resembles freely floating rates.

It can be seen from chart 1.1 that stochastic simulations of MULTIMOD strongly suggest that the instability found by Minford *et al* is a result of their choice of realignment rule. For all EMS countries except Germany, output and inflation variability are dramatically higher when this rule is in place. It should be noted that we did not modify wage setting behaviour to reflect anticipated devaluations, as did Minford *et al*, but our inflation equation embodies a combination of forward- and backward-looking elements (see Chadha, Masson and Meredith, 1991), so that when downward realignments are triggered, inflation

Chart 1.1 Realignment rules, when money is exogenous within the band

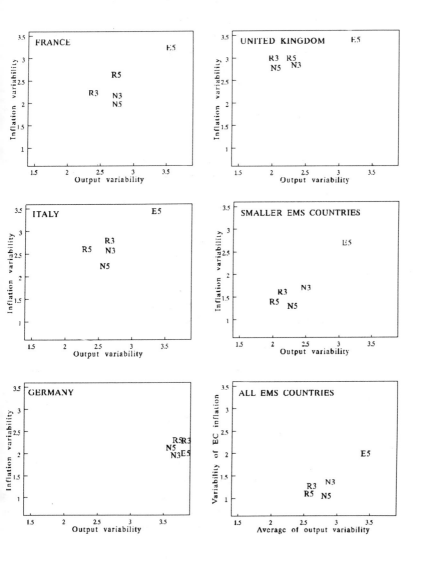

N3 = no realignment, 3% bands
N5 = no realignment, 5% bands
E5 = equilibrium realignment next period, 5% bands
R3 = real exchange rate trigger, 3% bands
R5 = real exchange rate trigger, 5% bands

is increased immediately, before the realignment occurs. It seems that even for the EC Commission's realignment rule, that effect produces the result that absence of realignments lowers inflation variability in all countries.

As to the effect of changes of the band width, differences are not dramatic, although the wider band width dominates for all countries if there are no realignments. In principle, two effects are involved (the same as when considering the stabilisation effects of a currency union): a narrower band enhances inflation discipline, while a wider band allows monetary policy greater flexibility to respond to shocks. In these simulations, however, we keep the money supply exogenous within the band (that is, unless the exchange rate threatens to go outside it), so that the latter effect only operates through the mechanism that a change in real income and prices (for instance, due to a negative demand shock) will lower the demand for money, and hence allow lower interest rates. For all countries, a wider band when there are no realignments leads to somewhat lower output variability, but differences are small. When realignments are allowed the superiority of a wider band no longer holds. Only the smaller EMS countries[9] and Italy are clearly better off with the wider bands.

As for the effect on non-EMS countries, not reported in the chart, we found no evidence that the operating rules of the EMS (nor the choice of EMS countries between floating and EMU) had anything more than a trivial effect on their output and inflation variability (or on other variables). For instance, under floating rates and the various alternatives plotted in chart 1.1, US output variability was between 2.12 and 2.14, and US inflation variability was between 1.38 and 1.39, while comparable ranges for Canada were 2.75-2.80 and 1.99-2.00, respectively. As one would expect, a monetary arrangement among European countries, which have the largest amount of trade among themselves, does not in itself seem to have major impacts on foreign countries.

Simulating EMU

In this section, we present our simulations of monetary union, and compare the resulting variability of output and inflation to their values under floating or the EMS. We consider two key aspects of the comparison, namely the assumption concerning the stance of monetary policy, and the method chosen to calculate the risk premium errors, discussed in the second section above. The studies by Minford and associates and by the EC Commission differ in these two aspects, and it is important to understand how they contribute to the difference in conclusions.

As is the case for the EMS, it is important to specify what is the default stance for monetary policy. Minford *et al.* present two alternatives: money targets and 'strategic money', that is, the choice of the optimal money supply setting in a Nash, non-cooperative setting. The EC Commission uses nominal income,

Chart 1.2 Money versus nominal income targeting, with floating rates or EMU

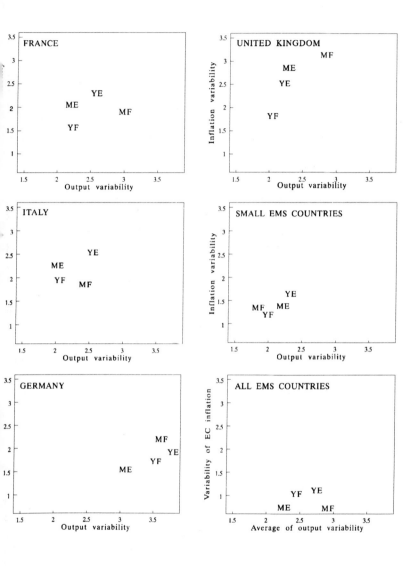

MF = money target, floating rates
ME = money target, symmetric EMU
YF = nominal income target, floating rate
YE = nominal income target, symmetric EMU

or, more precisely, a combination of inflation and output, with greater weight on the former (see our second section above). The simulations we have done with MULTIMOD assume either a money target (hit exactly period by period, rather than with smoothing of interest rates as in the published version of MULTIMOD, in order to be as close as possible to other studies), or a nominal income target. In choosing the latter, instead of the EC's weighted average of output and inflation, we verified that simulations using either gave similar root mean square errors—so we are not deviating substantially from what the EC Commission did. Nominal income has the advantage of simplicity and, for our model, gave much easier convergence to a solution—perhaps because a nominal anchor in the form of the level of prices or the money supply is necessary to prevent nominal variables from wandering off—that is, being indeterminate in long-run equilibrium—as we have argued elsewhere, for example, Frenkel, Goldstein and Masson (1989).

Chart 1.2 gives a comparison of EMU with floating rates for European countries, under the alternative assumptions of money targets and nominal income targets (further details are available from the authors).[10] EMU is modelled as completely fixed rates among all EC countries, which we assume to be equivalent to a single currency. It is assumed to be a symmetric regime, in the sense that Germany no longer has a preponderant role in setting monetary policy. Instead, the European central bank targets a European aggregate, defined as either the aggregate monetary base of the member countries (whose demand is assumed to be consistent with aggregating existing money demand functions), or European nominal income calculated as the sum of national variables. The non-European countries are in each case assumed to target the monetary base, and to float their currencies.

Some care must be taken in interpreting the chart. While the comparison of EMU and floating is straightforward (for the same targeted variable, money or nominal income), comparison of money with nominal income targeting is sensitive to the choice of feedback parameter on the latter. The money supply in the simulations is equal to its target, but instrument instability prevents hitting a nominal income target exactly. Larger feedback parameters can achieve lower variability for output and inflation, but at the expense of much higher interest rate variability. However, we have verified that the ranking of EMU and floating under a nominal income target seems unaffected by the choice of feedback parameter.

The chart suggests that the ranking of the regimes differs across countries: there is no obvious dominance of either EMU or floating over the other. Though the variability of European output and inflation is lowest under EMU with money targeting, the difference for Europe between floating and EMU with nominal income targeting is very small. This reflects our choice of measures for European variability, which imply a concern for individual countries' output fluctuations but only for aggregate European inflation variability. Floating rates give lower inflation variability than EMU under nominal income targets for every country (using national criteria), but for aggregate EMS inflation, the dominance of floating disappears. For one country, the United Kingdom, floating with nominal income targeting seems to give the best outcome in terms of both output and inflation variability—but floating with fixed money the worst.

To some extent (though not as concerns money, which they assume is the target), our results echo those of Minford and associates, who found that in some circumstances France, Germany and Italy would benefit from EMU, while the United Kingdom would not. Our results with money targeting show that the United Kingdom benefits from EMU. However, we do not find, for the aggregate EC, that floating dominates under fixed money, contrary to Minford *et al.*, where, under fixed money, floating gives a lower welfare cost than EMU for an EC constituted of Germany, France, Italy and the UK. On the contrary, we find that, for money targeting, EMU would be preferred to floating. Since we do not calculate welfare function values, we present the variability of EC inflation, and we include smaller EC countries in our calculations, our results cannot be compared directly; however, it would seem that differences derive mainly from the models used (and their associated historical error distributions) rather than in the way monetary policy is specified.

If EMU does not seem to be clearly preferable to floating, how do we explain the strong EC Commission conclusions in favor of EMU? To elucidate this question, we present a range of simulations that includes the alternatives that are given prominence in their report. Their results indicate that for the EC as a whole, a move from floating to the mid-1980s version of the EMS led to lower inflation variability but somewhat higher output variability, but further moves to a tighter EMS and to EMU lead to improvements in both dimensions, and results that dominate floating (Graph 6.10 of ECC, 1990, p.154, reproduced below as chart 1.3).

In chart 1.4, which presents our simulation results, there is no clear progression in terms of reduction in variability when moving from the EMS to monetary union. As in ECC (1990), for illustrative purposes, two forms of monetary union are considered (both use money as target, since it dominated nominal income for EMU in chart 1.2): one in which Germany continues to set EC monetary policy (asymmetric EMU), and one in which a joint European target prevails (symmetric EMU). The latter does better than the former for all countries individually, and also for the aggregate—a result consistent with what the EC Commission found. However, contrary to their findings, for the aggregate of EMS countries floating dominates the EMS of the mid-1980s and both of these regimes dominate an asymmetric EMU. For the EC as a whole, however, floating does about as well as symmetric EMU in reducing the variability of aggregate EC inflation.

Chart 1.3 Macroeconomic stability of EMU

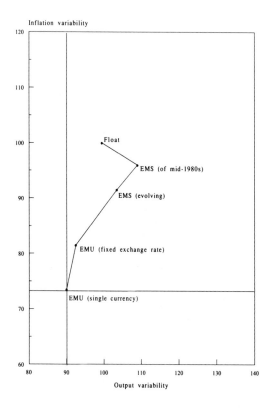

Inflation variability

EMS (of mid-1980s)

Float

EMS (evolving)

EMU (fixed exchange rate)

EMU (single currency)

Output variability

Indices EC average, free float = 100
Source: EC Commission (1990), graph 6.10, p.154.

It is clear that for some shocks the differences in outcomes must be considerable, but on average there does not seem to be too great a difference among the four regimes in our simulations, using the historical distribution of shocks. This result seems somewhat surprising on the face of it, especially concerning inflation. But it must be recalled that there is nothing in the model that captures the 'monetary discipline' argument in favour of either the EMS or EMU, because under all regimes, monetary targets are assumed to be consistent with the same long-run rate of inflation. As discussed above, the levels of variables (including

Chart 1.4 Floating exchange rates versus the EMS and symmetric or asymmetric EMU, with money exogenous

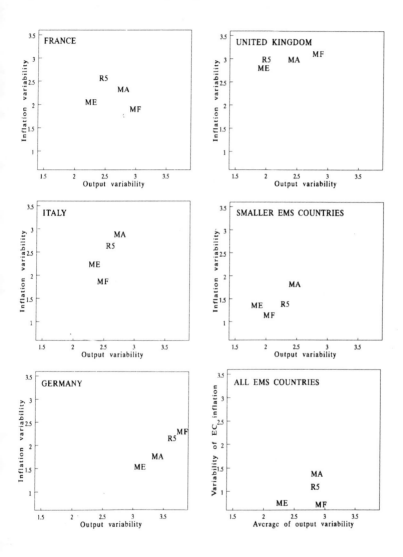

MF = floating rates
R5 = EMS with realignment triggered by real exchange rate
ME = symmetric EMU, European money target
MA = asymmetric EMU, German money target

inflation) are not assumed to be affected by the stochastic shocks, and the stance of monetary policy is not tighter on average in one regime than in another. We suggest that this possibility is no doubt an important feature of EMU, but more in the realm of political economy, and one that depends importantly on the incentives facing those who will run the new European Central Bank (see, for instance, Alesina and Grilli, 1992). It is not, to our knowledge, captured in simulations reported by either the EC Commission or Minford and associates.

How then to square our results with the large gains from EMU found by the EC Commission? To understand the role of the risk premium shocks and the measurement of variability, we present some alternative calculations in table 1.1 that are closer conceptually to those of the EC Commission. For the risk premium, we compare our estimates (which use the predictions of a random walk model for the exchange rate, and which are labelled 'method b' in the table), with the estimates of the EC Commission for those shocks, labelled 'method d' (see table E.7 of ECC, 1990, p. 321). It can be seen that the standard deviations of the latter are several times those used in our simulations.

In order to see the effect of the larger shocks, we simulate floating and EMU, assuming money supply targets, with errors drawn from these two sets of estimates.[11] In order to parallel their results more closely, we aggregate over only the four largest EC countries. Table 1.1 shows that the EC Commission's method implies much more dramatic improvement from EMU compared to floating. This is not surprising, since under their assumptions about risk premiums, exchange markets under floating are subject to major speculative shifts that would be eliminated by EMU. In this view of the world, major instability in exchange markets can be eliminated by a move to a single currency (or irrevocably fixed rates). Our estimates of the risk premium, in contrast, attribute a relatively small role to these shocks in causing macroeconomic instability.

A second comparison that can be made from the table is between the variability of European variables (for example, the sum of EC output or average European inflation) and the weighted average of the four countries' variability. Recall that our EMS results in charts 1.1, 1.2, and 1.4 use the first measure for inflation, and the second measure for output, while the studies by Minford and associates and the EC Commission use the second measure (weighted variability) for both output and inflation. The second measure indicates a much larger improvement of inflation variability when comparing floating with EMU, when the larger risk premium shocks are imposed (those estimated by the EC Commission). In contrast, if the criterion is EMS inflation (not national inflation rates), risk premium shocks have little importance for inflation variability, since they increase one country's prices but reduce another's, leaving the average roughly unchanged. So this dimension also helps explain the larger gains from EMU in reducing inflation variability in the EC Commission results compared to ours.

Table 1.1 Four EC countries: standard deviations of risk premium shocks and simulated output and inflation variability (per cent)

	Germany	France	Italy	UK	EC4 ave. variability (d)	Variability of EC4 aggregate (e)
Standard deviation of risk premium shocks relative to D-Mark						
Method b (b)	-	1.3	1.5	1.7		
Method d (c)	-	4.2	2.9	6.5		
Output variability (a)						
(i) Float						
Method b (b)	3.8	2.8	2.3	2.6	3.1	1.8
Method d (c)	5.2	2.9	2.6	2.7	3.8	2.0
(ii) EMU						
Method b (b)	3.2	2.4	2.2	2.1	2.6	1.6
Method d (c)	3.3	2.4	2.2	2.1	2.7	1.6
Inflation variability (a)						
(i) Float						
Method b (b)	2.2	1.9	1.9	3.1	2.3	1.1
Method d (c)	4.0	2.1	2.9	3.3	3.2	1.2
(ii) EMU						
Method b (b)	1.6	2.1	2.3	2.8	2.2	0.9
Method d (c)	1.7	2.1	2.4	2.8	2.2	0.9

Notes:
(a) Root mean square percentage deviations from baseline. Money is assumed to be exogenous in each case.
(b) Method b assumes random walk hypothesis to generate exchange-rate expectations. It was used in the simulations in the rest of this chapter. The figure given is the standard error of a regression over the period 1979-90 of the interest differential on its lagged value and a time trend.
(c) Method d uses a small model to generate risk premiums; it was used by the EC Commission. Figures taken from table E.7, EC (1990), p.321.
(d) The result of averaging the four countries mean square errors using GDP weights, and taking the square root.
(e) EC4 aggregate is calculated by summing the four countries' percentage deviations from baseline using GDP weights. Its variability is then calculated.

Conclusions

Our aim has been to understand the sharply contrasting conclusions of two significant model simulation studies of monetary union—those done by the EC Commission and by Minford and associates. In so doing, we have raised some methodological issues and also perhaps helped to identify areas which are particularly important for an evaluation of exchange-rate regimes. Our major conclusion is that the EMS seems to be much less of an engine of instability than is implied by the studies of Minford and associates, but we also do not, on the basis of stochastic simulations that admittedly account for only a limited set of factors, find a strong case for EMU.

The differences relate seemingly to fairly arbitrary choices in modelling realignments and in estimating the size of risk premiums in foreign exchange markets. On the one hand, the treatment of realignments by Minford and associates seems to be the cause of instability in their results, and their choice of the rule as a description of how the EMS actually operates (or did, when there were realignments) does not seem to us particularly convincing. Moreover, the fact that the rest of the world seems to be severely affected by the EMS throws doubt on their results.

On the other hand, the EC Commission's method of estimating risk premia produces gains from EMU that are much larger than obtained when other methods are used. It may well be that our models are not well suited to capture the advantages of a common currency, because they do not capture the saving of transactions costs and the anti-inflationary discipline resulting from a more disciplined, multilateral central bank. In the absence of these model features, and if the uncertainty related to separate currencies is assumed to take the form of shocks to interest parity conditions, then these shocks have to be very large for the gains from EMU to offset the loss of flexibility to respond to other shocks. It is also important in the evaluation to decide whether in a monetary union individual countries' inflation rates are important in themselves, or only the union's inflation rate. The justification for the latter is that, in a common currency area, there is only one underlying long-run inflation rate. However, this complicates the comparison with floating, because in the absence of a single currency, different national inflation rates are possible, and they are plausibly included separately in welfare functions. In our simulations, unlike those of the EC Commission, we do not find a clear improvement in average inflation variability (under either measure) when comparing EMU to floating exchange rates, though output variability does decline substantially.

It should also be recognised that in several respects our models are not completely adequate representations of either the EMS or EMU. They do not incorporate the 'bias in the band' and 'smooth pasting': in a perfectly credible target zone, there is a tendency for the exchange rate to revert towards the centre of the band.[12] At the edges, this implies that the exchange rate is certain to move in one direction rather than in another and this gives rise to 'smooth pasting.' However, empirical evidence in favour of this non-linearity has been weak (see, for instance, Flood, Rose and Mathieson, 1990). The difficulty in incorporating the results of this literature is that analytical solutions found there assume relatively simple processes for the 'fundamentals' in continuous time, while our macro-models are in discrete time and have very complicated dynamic processes for the variables determining interest rates. Using a linear approximation, like Svensson's (1991), for the expected exchange rate within the band would be possible, but this would not incorporate 'smooth pasting.' However, its weak empirical support makes us agree with Minford *et al.* that 'smooth pasting' would only produce a minor difference in the results.

A more serious limitation in our view is the treatment of credibility—both the credibility of the exchange-rate commitment within the EMS and the commitment to price stability in EMU. In our (and other) stochastic simulations, expectations are formed on the basis of certainty equivalence, and this implies for instance that a realignment is either expected to occur with certainty, or else the peg is expected to be successfully defended. In practice, the shocks that occur next period may invalidate those expectations. A more satisfactory framework would allow for a non-zero probability to be given to the two outcomes, and would make that probability endogenous. A preliminary attempt along these lines, applied to disinflation policies, was made in Masson and Symansky (1992); we hope to extend this analysis to exchange rates in subsequent work. A conceptual framework for considering the effects of the formation of a European Central Bank on anti-inflationary credibility is presented in Currie (1992).

Notes

1 We are not able to simulate the Liverpool World Model, however, so we cannot replicate the EC Commission's methodology on that model. A further caveat is that MULTIMOD has evolved somewhat since the version used by the Commission.
2 A more complete description is given in the Appendix to Frenkel, Goldstein, and Masson (1989) and in Masson and Symansky (1992).
3 The model contains expectations variables that are consistent with the model's solution in the absence of shocks, but these expectations may be falsified by errors in subsequent periods. A drawing for the errors in period t is made, the model is solved forward to calculate model-consistent expectations, then a drawing for the errors in period $t+1$ is made, and so on.

4   More properly, the mean path of the endogenous variables when a large number of drawings is made for the errors. In practice, this path is likely to be well approximated by the deterministic simulation with errors equal to zero.

5   In principle, the level of variables would also be of interest; for instance, lower inflation might permanently raise output above its baseline value. However, most models do not incorporate such linkages; instead, inclusion of the inflation rate in the objective function is intended to capture them in an *ad hoc* way.

6   However, this is much less true in the current version of the model, in which money demand contains no lagged interest rate.

7   It is assumed for convenience here that in the baseline, the exchange rate is always equal to its parity. Note that the notation here also differs somewhat from that used in MULTIMOD.

8   The band widths—3 and 5 per cent on either side of the central parity—are meant to be illustrative. They were chosen to be the same as in Minford *et al.*, rather than to conform to the existing narrow or wide bands of the ERM, respectively ± 2.25 and ± 6 per cent.

9   What we term 'smaller EMS countries' are in fact the countries of the smaller industrial country block of MULTIMOD, so that some non-EMS countries are also included in this group.

10 The parameters for the nominal income rule used in this chapter were made as close to the EC Commission values as possible. However, with real income and inflation targets their parameterisation did not always converge and we therefore used somewhat smaller reaction coefficients. The same feedback coefficient was then used in the nominal income rule. It turned out that a substantially larger coefficient (by a factor of ten) could have been used for targeting nominal income. It should be noted that the EC Commission reduced the size of their shocks by a factor of ten in order to do the simulations—perhaps an indication of convergence problems when the larger shocks were used.

11 Correlation coefficients among the errors were assumed to be unaffected, so both the relevant diagonal and the off-diagonal elements of the error covariance matrix were rescaled to reflect the estimated variability of risk premium shocks.

12 See Krugman and Miller (1991) for a compilation of some of the recent literature on target zone models.

2

ERM and EMU – Survival, Costs and Prospects[1]

Patrick Minford, Anupam Rastogi and Andrew Hughes Hallett

The Exchange Rate Mechanism (ERM) of the European Monetary System (EMS) has survived its twelfth birthday, and acquired an important new member, the UK. The process seems inexorable towards monetary union (EMU). But what are the costs and benefits in macroeconomic stability of these arrangements, actual and potential?

The existing literature is econometric in approach, that is, it attempts to estimate relationships in which the regime shift to ERM is captured by shifts in parameters, as well as in the means and variances of macro variables. These econometric attempts to disentangle the effects of ERM are useful but cannot satisfactorily answer the question we have posed, which requires careful setting up of the 'counterfactual' world — what would have been without ERM. As for EMU, econometrics can barely begin: the attempts to examine it in the literature are mainly either historical or use frankly theoretical structures without empirical backing. One exception — but as we shall argue a deeply flawed one — stands out, that by the EC Commission to use simulation analysis.

Our own approach is of this latter sort: we wish to set up a counterfactual world in which the ERM and EMU do not exist and compare it with a world in which they do — in possibly a wide variety of alternative forms. We have been working along these lines for a number of years and some provisional results of this work have already been published. In this chapter we draw together the main features of our latest results, to be found in full in Hughes-Hallett and Minford (1990) and Minford and Rastogi (1990a). This chapter is in effect a much-shortened version of both these two papers.

The European Monetary System — the issues

The EMS has been justified in one of at least four ways. First as a device for reducing uncertainty: exchange-rate variability (especially within the EMS but also overall) is to be reduced, preferably without any increase in the uncertainty surrounding other variables, such as interest rates or output. Second, as a device to achieve price discipline, an alternative to its achievement via domestic monetary targets. Third, as a route to the ultimate objective of European Monetary Union, the gains from which would take the form of lower monetary transactions costs. The objective would be advanced by progressive reduction in exchange-rate variability. Fourth, as a surrogate for explicit cooperation: cooperation would avoid 'beggar-my-neighbour' exchange-rate policies, whether of depreciation (for trade balance—output reasons) or of appreciation (for inflation reasons). The EMS prevents such policies by its rules.

In this chapter we try to shed some empirical light on these four arguments, using the method of model simulation and optimisation. The alternative empirical method is to go directly to the facts and estimate the observable effects of the EMS. Neither method is free of difficulties. In direct estimation it is hard to disentangle the EMS effect from the rest. Furthermore, actual policies may not have been optimal so that the EMS's relative performance is not gauged by estimation. Historical data can only show what did happen, not what could have happened. Our optimisation approach compares the EMS regime's performance with that of floating (which we take as a benchmark), both at their best. Our approach is reliant on the parameters of a model, and these are vulnerable to estimation difficulties as well as instability under regime change. We can, however, minimise this vulnerability by sensitivity analysis across parameter values and we have done this here to a substantial degree.

The main advantage in our approach lies in our ability to explore, with the powerful techniques of stochastic simulation and optimal control, a wide variety of alternative EMS regimes and concomitant policy behaviour. During the EMS period from 1979, the actual regime followed has been in more or less continuous flux, starting with largely independent monetary policy, wide bands and frequent parity changes, supported by stringent capital controls, and ending today with narrow bands, rare realignments, substantial monetary cooperation and no capital controls. In this chapter we ask how various EMS regimes would have stood up, in terms of stability, to the shocks experienced during the estimation sample period 1955-85.

Our concern is that the problems of market management induced by fixed-but-adjustable peg systems cause serious instability in the face of shocks above a certain threshold, akin to the failure of a bridge in the face of large traffic volumes. We explore the features of an EMS regime that could be expected to avoid such instability. From that exploration, we try to explain why the EMS has survived for more than a decade without the breakdown many predicted, and also to examine the claims for the EMS listed above. Throughout the chapter the Liverpool world model (a linked system of nine country models, all similar in design to the Liverpool model of the UK) is used as the empirical framework (see Minford *et al.*, 1986, for a full account). Key features of this model, which has been estimated largely on annual data, are rational expectations, perfect capital mobility, and wealth effects on consumption; markets clear continuously in an annual framework subject to a range of nominal contracts (especially bonds and wages, though the latter have a maximum maturity of one year).[2]

Previous work

Earlier work has been exclusively, as far as we know, along the lines of direct estimation, formal or informal, from the observed facts. A number of early studies computed comparative descriptive statistics for variables of interest, pre- and post-EMS, for EMS and non-EMS countries, the latter being a control. These include Collins (1987), de Grauwe (1987), Giavazzi and Giovannini (1989) and Ungerer *et al.* (1986). Vaubel (1989) offers a useful summary of these and of a number of other German studies (in German, for details see Vaubel) in the following negative terms:

'To sum up: the exchange rate mechanism of the EMS does not seem to have contributed to reducing nominal effective exchange rate variations, inflation and inflation differences of the member currencies, or to increasing intra-ERM trade, investment and growth in the member countries.'

Recently two studies, Artis and Taylor (1988) and Fratianni and von Hagen (1990), have used ARCH autoregression to examine whether there have been shifts in the (conditional) variances of the exchange rate and other series. Both find that the bilateral intra-EMS exchange-rate variances, real and nominal, have fallen post-EMS. But the record on trade-weighted exchange rates, real and nominal, is ambiguous, as the bilateral variances against non-EMS currencies have risen. Given that events other than the EMS have been at work since 1979 (shifts in monetary policies, swings in fiscal policy, oil developments) and that policies may have been sub-optimal, this evidence sheds little light on whether the EMS has succeeded in its principal appointed task of lowering overall (as opposed to intra-EMS) exchange-rate uncertainty.

As for inflation, Fratianni and von Hagen find that its conditional variance (as well as its trend) has fallen post-EMS in the EMS countries but that this is matched in the non-EMS countries. There is also evidence of greater covariance within (but not between) both EMS and non-EMS countries suggesting some degree of policy coordination within, but again not between, each group.

Modelling the EMS

The European Monetary System is a supplement to domestic monetary systems. Quite how it works depends on the countries involved. For example,

Holland treats the D-Mark—Guilder link as effectively fixed. Italy and France by contrast allow devaluations periodically, after discussions with EMS partners, principally Germany.

As argued in Minford (1989a), fixed and floating rate systems differ little in their transmission of real shocks. As for monetary shocks, though the direction of impact of foreign monetary shocks is altered, floating does not insulate against these shocks because the exchange rate tends to move sharply in response. While fixed rates eliminate any domestic monetary variance, and foreign monetary variance dominates, floating provides a mixture of domestic and foreign monetary variance. This combined variance may be greater or less for prices or output than under fixed rates depending on model structure and the variance—covariance structure of the shocks.

This suggests that abstracting from transitional costs a country will be attracted to a fully fixed system if the dominant foreign money in it exhibits low variance: in this case it is unlikely that the floating variance combination will be as low. This seems to be the position of Holland.

What then of EMS in less than fully fixed systems? Here we face a problem of evaluating the system behaviour. It turns out (Hughes Hallett and Minford, 1989, 1990) that behaviour depends crucially on the parameters of flexibility; that is, on the size of the permitted parity changes, on the margins around those parities, and on how long the parities must be held.

At the one extreme where the margins are wide, the parity may be adjusted in small steps, and may be adjusted frequently, the system is indistinguishable from free floating. Clearly, in the early days of, for example, the Italian association with EMS, this was the regime it followed. But nowadays such a regime is not fashionable; even Spain, having entered on a wide band, has been unwilling to allow its parity to be devalued, in spite of reported urgings from the Bundesbank.

What can happen when the limits are set more tightly? In effect there is a clash between two monetary systems. Monetary growth may be set independently over the medium term and yet exchange rates are not allowed to respond to this monetary divergence except discretely. Hence the length of time between realignments (and perhaps the size of the realignments) is likely to be crucial. Unfortunately there are no rules governing how realignments should be undertaken. Indeed the arguments between the French and the Germans in late 1989 suggest that realignments are now being put off as long as possible.

How do people expect this clash to be resolved? We may distinguish two cases: perfect capital mobility with only limited exchange controls (so that uncovered interest parity prevails, except at moments of speculative crisis when it is assumed for a time at least controls must bind) and fully and permanently effective exchange controls where the central bank can use sterilised intervention to fix the exchange rate while setting interest rates via monetary policy. Under perfect capital mobility, by contrast, during the period when the exchange rate is being pegged temporarily, the central bank cannot fix the money supply as well: it has to let money supply adjust to whatever the exchange-rate peg dictates. We will call the limited exchange control set-up 'no controls' in what follows, to indicate that UIP holds in this case.

In setting up our model of the EMS, we assume that German money supply growth is fixed by the Bundesbank, with no constraints from the monetary policies of other EMS countries. These others, however, are constrained by German money supply growth in so far as their parity (assumed to be set against the D-Mark) is held. These assumptions apply to the automatic workings of the EMS. But they do not rule out German strategic reactions to other EMS monetary policies in the short run when these can have spillover effects on Germany. Nor of course do they rule out short and long-run independence of Germany by these other countries, both within the parity limits and via parity changes.

This may seem an over-strong 'German dominance' view. Fratianni and von Hagen (1990) argue that Germany has not been dominant within the EMS. By dominance they mean that other EMS money supplies have had no independence of German money supply and that the German money supply has been independent of these others. They find from vector autoregression that other EMS money supplies are not exclusively affected by the German one in either short or long run, responding to both world and other EMS money supplies (de Grauwe, 1988, also finds that this is true of their interest rates related to German and other interest rates). They also find no effect of other EMS money supplies on Germany's in the long run though some marginally significant effect in the short.

It is clear that these results are entirely in line with our assumptions. It is the element of exchange-rate flexibility in the EMS that permits both some monetary independence by other EMS countries and some German strategic response to this independence.

The basic EMS version of the model

We assume to begin with, as our 'default' model, that, under the EMS, regime parities (initially set along an equilibrium trajectory, given anticipated events) must be held for at least one year after a shock has occurred. During this time, the exchange rate cannot move beyond the margins, set at ± 3 per cent around parity. A new parity trajectory may then be set to achieve expected exchange-rate equilibrium, given that shock and its anticipated consequences: the parity can only be moved in multiples of ± 5 per cent but the expected exchange rate can move flexibly because parity change plus the margins spans the whole exchange-rate space. It has been suggested that the rules restrict not only the frequency of parity changes but also their size (say to less than 10 per cent); furthermore that the frequency permitted may be diminishing (say to two years between changes). Such restrictions are, we have found in previous work (Hughes Hallett and Minford, 1989), potentially crucial to the system's stability. There we investigated a lower frequency of parity change: a two-year gap creates enormous instability because parity changes which are fully anticipated but stored up by the two-year rule actually exaggerate the current disequilibrium and trigger a future backlash. In this chapter we look at this issue again within a stochastic framework, as well as at the consequences of imposing restrictions on the size of parity changes.

A regime change such as the EMS may provoke change in supposedly structural equations (Lucas, 1976). In particular, under the EMS we have to modify our usual wage equation, which is not set up for policy conflict and sudden switches of regime. It seems likely that faced with the prospect of a sudden devaluation/price jump of uncertain timing, unions would take precautionary action to raise contracted wages in advance of the expected price jump. Another reason for preemptive action would be overlaps in contract periods. The model assumes that, in normal times of smooth price behaviour, this is of no importance, because such devices as bonus variation could iron out temporary anomalies in the contract as other workers get ahead or behind. But for extreme jumps these devices would be inadequate and we could expect the contract to reflect the likely overlap; as Taylor (1979) has showed this creates a serially correlated pattern of wage movements in response to a shock in expected prices, starting from the quarter of the shock.

Together these factors argue for a special adjustment of current wages in response to the prospect of future devaluation. The adjustment we make for illustrative purposes is equal to approximately one third of the parity change expected in the following year.

The effect of this anticipatory movement in wages is to push up prices rather faster than the exchange-rate peg would normally permit: consequently the real exchange rate tends to be pushed up, very much a feature of the EMS experience of those other countries, notably France and Italy, whose underlying inflation has exceeded Germany's.

It must be stressed that this adjustment is illustrative. As noted above, the EMS has been not one but a series of regimes, differing both across countries and across time periods. What we are doing here is taking Lucas's critique seriously and making a correction to an estimated structure for a hypothetical regime change. In order to allow for potential error in setting the parameter's size, we have checked for sensitivity to it: it turns out that our results do not vary much qualitatively even if the parameter is not included at all — see below.

Empirically, we can find some support for our correction in Italian and

French experience since the EMS began in 1979. Italy has pursued monetary policy that has generated systematically and substantially more inflation than in Germany. Real wages have turned out higher than predicted, indicating an effect from anticipated devaluation not allowed for in the model.

The case of France is an interesting contrast. First in the early 1980s Mitterrand had his 'dash for growth' which involved frequent devaluation. Then from '1983' he changed tack, pursuing a tough monetary policy using the EMS as an excuse (Minford, 1989c). To bring about convergence of inflation with Germany, money was tightened more than there, so that by 1990 the two countries' inflation rates were the same. One finds that in the early period French real wages lie above the prediction based on pre-1979 data, whereas in the later period they lie below. Both results are consistent with our proposed correction.

In other respects, the model's set-up is easily described under the two EMS regimes. Without exchange controls, the model is solved as if on fixed rates (money supply temporarily endogenous) when the exchange rate hits the EMS limit; otherwise it solves in the standard floating mode with money supply exogenous. With exchange controls, the model is solved with money supply exogenous throughout; but when the exchange rate hits the limit, it is fixed and the uncovered interest parity condition suspended. Interest rates are then set by the interaction of money demand (prices being set by the exchange rate and wages) and money supply.

This describes how the EMS model adjusts in the year of the shock. For the year after — when the parity can change — the exchange rate moves to find an equilibrium within the limits, with the money supply exogenous; if it cannot find one then the parity changes (by one or more multiples of a predetermined step size) until it does. Thereafter, the parity moves again whenever needed to find an equilibrium, with the money supply exogenous. This sequence is repeated every time a shock occurs: in year 1 adjustment without parity change, thereafter parity change until an exchange rate equilibrium is found.

The key difference between the two regimes is in the behaviour of interest rates (which then has impacts elsewhere in the model). Under no controls interest rates must rise sharply in response to the prospect of devaluation as dictated by uncovered interest parity. This is obviously deflationary. It is this that creates pressure for exchange controls in this partially flexible EMS system. The authorities may be compelled, in Tobin's phrase, to throw sand in the machinery of international arbitrage. As the time of a parity change approaches, the system becomes unmanageable without controls: we assume in the 'no-control' case that the authorities deliberately create uncertainty over the exact timing within the year for this reason, as well as using temporary controls *ad hoc* to boost manageability near the time of parity changes.

If they do resort to total controls, then interest rates will be kept low by the monetary expansion, permitting a more reflationary impact; the resulting speculation against the currency is simply frustrated by the controls. The catch is that real interest rates are held below going world rates, causing a micro distortion of the domestic capital market, subsidising capital investment and taxing saving. If the policy becomes systematic, this could cause a serious cost to be incurred.

Simulations of monetary independence under the EMS
We have undertaken a number of simulations with our model, and they are reported in detail elsewhere (see Minford *et al.*, 1990). We have analysed four regimes; floating exchange rates, the EMS with exchange controls and the EMS without controls. In all cases, the country is assumed to pursue a policy of temporary reflation, two years of 4 per cent money growth and 8 per cent in total by year 2 regardless of intervention in year 1 in the no controls case.

Under floating this reflation has the familiar effects. Prices rise, with inflation in the first year rising by 3 to 4 per cent in the UK and Italy and by rather more in France. The exchange rate falls rather sharply, and the real exchange rate initially falls as real wages are depressed by the unexpected inflation. Output rises, with net exports stimulated by higher competitiveness and domestic demand stimulated by lower real interest rates, with lower real financial wealth restraining this effect (in some cases offsetting it). In the longer term the nominal exchange rate stabilises and the real exchange rate returns to its base level.

The EMS without controls upsets this familiar scene. Wages and prices rise, though not so much as in floating because they are restrained by the exchange-rate limits. In the first year the real exchange rate actually rises because prices are pushed up relative to the exchange-rate depreciation by the anticipatory wage pressure. Interest rates, real and nominal, rise because of the need to maintain uncovered arbitrage, with nominal and real exchange rates expected to fall next year. Output falls as net exports are hit by the lower competiveness and domestic demand is hit both by the higher real interest rate and by the drop in real financial wealth. The picture is of a reflation frustrated, even reversed, on real variables, yet having much of the inflationary effects on nominal variables: the mechanism of frustration is the exchange rate and its sympathetic link with interest rates.

The EMS with exchange controls (with their micro costs, of course, not considered here), can at least cut this link. Interest rates now move in line with domestic monetary conditions only, so with this reflation they rise less and may fall, which reduces the immediate deflationary effect on output compared with the no-control case. However, output contracts in year 2 as the delayed inflation

in that year causes a negative wealth effect and a fall in expenditure. The delay
to inflation thus lessens the Phillips curve stimulus, while leaving unchanged
the overall expenditure contraction across years 1 and 2 as inflation reduces
wealth.

In our EMS simulations we hve assumed that wage behaviour will change.
If it does not, then in the EMS the real exchange rate falls as under floating.
But, as in the exchange control case, the delayed inflation causes output to fall
in year 2 after a stimulus in year 1; the output reaction (both up and down) is
smaller because real interest rates fall much less than when exchange controls
uncouple them from the real exchange rate (through UIP). We show below
the results we report are not in fact at all sensitive to the assumptions about
either wages or exchange controls. The essence of the ERM difference appears
to lie in the way it delays the inflation shock.

Evaluating the EMS

The simulations described above demonstrate the own-country responses to a
standardised variation in the macroeconomic instrument under floating and
under the EMS. These responses are now used as a set of multipliers to evaluate
how the world will respond to a variety of situations under the two different
regimes of floating and EMS. We will use these to judge whether the EMS
achieves its four possible aims in terms of its operating properties.

Stabilisation properties of EMS

There are at least two ways one could define a world regime under EMS or
floating. There could be a general decision to follow fixed policies, with no
reaction to shocks: or there could be strategic policymaking, with each country
reacting to changes in the environment, including changes in other countries'
policies (generating a non-cooperative, Nash equilibrium). Call these the
fixed-rule and the Nash cases respectively. We will try to analyse both cases.
In the Nash case, we do not permit time-inconsistency; a country is allowed
to select one reaction to events (under perfect foresight and after iterating with
the reactions of other countries) and it is then forced to stick to it by some penalty
function (for example, the fear of losing credibility). There are good reasons
to suppose such penalty functions do hold, in view of the disastrous results were
they not to. An empirical assessment of just how disastrous the alternative
consequence could be is provided by Minford (1989b) using the Liverpool
model of the UK.

Our benchmark is a floating regime without cooperation. It may be
regarded as the status quo, since countries are currently free to react as they
please to domestic and foreign shocks with no agreed constraints. It is

true that the Louvre Accord existed and some have argued that it represented a move towards exchange-rate limits. However, since the Accord was not formally binding, it is hard to see what effect it had. We have four possible systems, floating fixed-rule or non-cooperative, Nash, and EMS fixed-rule. We will consider later a last theoretical system of full cooperation. This is the ultimate in strategic policymaking, but it is obviously more relevant under the EMS than under floating. We find that the cooperative bargains which are feasible (that is, make all parties better off) involve different welfare weights and, of course, policies, for each shock. The practical difficulties of identifying the shock and then of resetting the welfare weights are in our view likely to be insuperable, when all the G7 are involved. Brandsma and Hughes-Hallett (1989) look at this issue and find that cooperative policies are hard to sustain as the distribution of gains keeps altering. However, the same argument may not apply to a smaller coalition within the EMS, which can be regarded as a cohesive group of countries committed to pegging their bilateral exchange rates.

We undertake two parallel simulation exercises. First, we consider a set of deterministic shocks in some detail. Second, we carry out a set of stochastic simulations, using the distributions of all the model's equation errors over the sample period, 1955-85.

We evaluate the effects of stability by the standard method of a quadratic welfare function, which in effect attaches penalty weights to the variances (around the desired trajectory) of output, the price level, real interest rates, the real exchange rate and the monetary instrument. This function is also the maximand of each government. The weights are set to penalise equally the following deviations from the desired trajectory in each period: 1 per cent on the level of output and prices, 1 per cent per annum (1 percentage point) on the short-run real interest rate and the real exchange rate, and 3 per cent per annum (3 percentage points) on the rate of growth of the money supply. For France and Italy, we multiplied the weights on all targets other than prices by 2 and 10 respectively to dampen rather extreme instability in use of the monetary instrument.

The exchange-rate target in particular is of key importance in assessing the EMS, whose objective after all is the stabilisation of exchange rates. If this objective is removed, then, while of course floating still appears highly desirable relative to EMS, the ranking of different EMS regimes alters materially. While therefore the size of weighting given to possible targets has generally been found to matter little (Hughes-Hallett, 1987), nevertheless in this particular case it appears essential to the spirit and substance of the exercise to include the exchange rate prominently among the targets. We set the desired or ideal trajectories, for this exercise, equal to the baseline solution of the model: we do this in order to abstract entirely from the initial conditions, which might otherwise dominate the effects of the shocks and so bias the exercise.

Deterministic shock

In the deterministic exercise we look at a basket of seven shocks: six of them are to individual EMS countries (France, Italy and the UK) — a monetary shock each (a 4 per cent reduction in real money demand for two years) and a real shock each (a 5 per cent rise in the real exchange rate for one year) — and one shock is global (a 50 per cent rise in the dollar prices of oil and other commodities permanently).

The results for this limited set of shocks, taken as a group, are shown in table 2.1. There are two sources of the instability found here with this EMS regime. First, there is model instability, holding money supplies constant: the EMS default regime produces larger reactions of the target variables to these shocks than floating for France and Italy. This instability arises for a dependent-currency EMS country (one of the 'EMS3') whenever a shock produces a parity change: this occurs for France and Italy under their money demand shocks, hence their poor results under EMS. The other countries benefit because the spillovers on them from these two countries for these shocks are smaller under EMS.

Table 2.1 Welfare costs of shocks under EMS and floating

	EMS	Floating	Ratio	EMS	Floating	Ratio
	(Money fixed)		E/F	(Nash reaction)		E/F
US	552	522	1.06	540,446	2,325	232.00
Canada	1,587	1,375	1.15	476,487	411,305	1.16
Japan	194	165	1.18	66,316	21,103	3.14
Germany	11	9	1.22	394,834	3,862	102
France	4,833	1,296	3.73	613,191	5,059	121
Italy	7,346	2,636	2.79	126,447	440,646	0.29
UK	38	43	0.88	433,702	695	624

Second, there is instrument instability: EMS countries (and as a result some non-EMS countries too) are induced into large money supply changes by the peculiar responses of their economies to the monetary instrument under the

EMS. These changes in turn provoke sharp responses from other countries, notably the US. The resulting large variability in relative money supplies causes massive real exchange-rate variability. Welfare costs consequently soar under EMS compared with floating, as table 2.1 shows. The one exception here is Italy which experiences more instability under floating than EMS for the oil and Italian money demand shocks. Its money supply reacts sharply under floating.

The greater model instability under EMS arises from the one-year delay after a shock in the reaction of the exchange rate and so of prices. Under floating the impact effects of the shocks are concentrated (with offsetting effects) in year 1, whilst the EMS delays them. The adjustment lags then damp down the economy one year later than under floating. The adjustment to those shocks, at least as implied by our model, are of interest. Under EMS reactions they can be perverse in a non-cooperative world, and they can also be more deflationary.

The key to these two features lies in the perversity of response to monetary policy under EMS. Under EMS, monetary expansion by the three main EMS countries raises home prices, but it lowers home output (and raises the real exchange rate and interest rates) perversely. Abroad (even in other EMS countries), it similarly lowers output instead of the normal effect under floating of raising it; the effect on prices abroad under EMS is mixed but on average there is a slight lowering as against the more substantial lowering under floating.

This perversity under EMS of both the direct effect of EC reflation on home output and the spillover effect on foreign output means that the EC responds to more rest of the world reflation by more home reflation (offsetting the foreign expansionary spillover on output). As for the rest of the world, it reacts to the negative spillover from more EC reflation by reflating more itself. The sharper insular deflation by the EC under EMS arises from the need to offset the effects of the oil shock, which are negative on output and positive on prices.

The case of Italy under floating is of interest. Italy has a near-vertical Phillips curve under floating — very weak response of output to money — because of its high degree of wage indexation: hence when it reacts (with normal slope) to rest of the world reflation it takes much sharper deflationary action to obtain the necessary offset. It is this that causes its instability under floating. Under EMS, the negative spillovers of fellow EMS members' Nash reflation largely offset the positive spillovers from the rest of the world. As a result its own money supply is left to react little in the Nash equilibrium. However, though Italy avoids domestic monetary instability under EMS, it suffers from the instability induced among others. This will be apparent when we consider the wider range of stochastic simulations below.

The fundamental problem with the EMS regime is clear. The inelasticity of the current parity, combined with the anticipation of parity changes when there are no capital controls, destabilises both the economy and policy responses.

Stochastic simulations

Thirty-eight sets of sequential shocks for six years each were applied to the two regimes, EMS-Nash and floating-Nash; 192 shocks in all for each regime. The shocks were drawings from the single equation residuals estimated for the model over the sample period (1957-81 for the most part). The average welfare cost for the 38 sets is shown in table 2.2. Model instability is apparent in the EMS results, holding money supply constant. The third column of the table shows the ratio of welfare costs under EMS and floating, with no policy responses. There is clearly a serious problem with the EMS regime.

Table 2.2 Average welfare costs across all shocks: by country

	EMS	Floating	Ratio	Floating	EMS	Ratio
	(Money fixed)		E/F	(Nash reaction)		E/F
US	1,779	315	5.6	1,028	316,674	308.0
Canada	40,525	4,816	8.4	47,423	507,385	10.7
Japan	1,294	743	1.7	6,818	64,180	9.4
Germany	3,530	2,024	1.7	1,828	204,083	112.0
France	3,530	737	4.8	896	299,724	334.0
Italy	3,191	187	17.1	41,550	68,439	1.6
UK	2,048	79	25.9	201	211,743	1,053.0

Nash instrument responses add materially to the model instability, as money supplies react in the way discussed in the deterministic case. The last column highlights the extremely high ratio of EMS to floating costs, when money supplies do react.

As our earlier discussion should have made clear, the extraordinarily high welfare cost under the Nash default-EMS compared with Nash floating arises from interactive overuse of the monetary instrument (and the associated real exchange-rate instability). The relatively high fixed money cost of EMS versus floating arises from greater variance of both output and inflation, as well as of real exchange rates and real interest rates: in other words there is a widely spread increase in variance across all countries and target variables.

The essential point of these results seems to be unavoidable. The EMS is a system prone to acute instability in the face of shocks. Particularly vulnerable are the dependent-EMS countries. The reason for this instability seems to lie in the non-linearity of the fixed-but-adjustable system's response to shocks, with large shocks creating a sharp response, and in deflationary circumstances the perverse trade-off in dependent-EMS countries inducing monetary over-reaction.

Alternative EMS regimes

It may well be said, in response to our analysis, that the fault must lie in our modelling of the EMS or choice of EMS regime. Clearly, the EMS has survived for ten years, most recently without capital controls. One could argue that the shocks in the 1980s have been small, but this seems improbable; though there has been only a mild recession (1982), there was a large oil price shock, an international debt crisis, domestic crises in the core EMS countries (for example, Mitterand's difficulties in 1982-3), and a gyrating dollar.

We therefore examined the model's sensitivity to different assumptions. We looked at our anticipation parameter for wages and at the choice of regime. We examined variations in the rules of the regime: in the period of delay before the parity can be changed and in the size of the parity change permitted. We also considered capital controls. Finally, we considered variations in policy reactions that might have helped. Clearly, having no money supply reaction is no help against model instability, but it would prevent instrument instability of course, and cooperation — or a coalition among EMS members — could help to offset model instability.

Slightly lengthening the period of delay badly worsens instability: we tried raising it to two years from the default one year, with severe problems of convergence. This result also emerged from our earlier non-stochastic study (Hughes-Hallett and Minford, 1989). The reason is that putting adjustment off does not diminish the size of the adjustment necessary and may even increase it (if the EMS-induced price change goes in the opposite direction to the floating solution, it may go further before having to be reversed); the expectation of this is deferred one year but that year's event still impinges on the current year's outcome through expectations.

The core of our result is shown in the summary table 2.3. The table is organised to show the welfare costs for different EMS regimes. It begins with the default EMS model, assuming Nash non-cooperative reactions; then in turn one assumption is relaxed at a time. Not all permutations can be shown in this summary table, but in the following discussion we mention some that are of interest.

Table 2.3 Average welfare costs* of the EMS under alternative assumptions (average for countries)

	ROW**	EMS4**	All
Default EMS (Nash)	296	196	239
Model Sensitivity:			
No wage reaction	208	209	209
Parity rules:			
Parity change limited (Max.5%)	300	86	178
No parity change	13	1.7	6.5
Capital controls:	228	170	195
Monetary policy rules:			
High penalty on money (Fr./It./UK only) - Nash	41	37	39
Fixed money	16	3	8
Worldwide cooperation (default EMS)	10	2	5.4
EMS coalition (default EMS)	25	1	11
EMU	8.5	0.5	3.9

*Thousands of welfare cost units.
**ROW: rest of world; EMS4: Germany, France, Italy, UK.

Capital controls are in existence to some degree through all these model-regime combinations: as explained above, some controls are needed in periods preceding well-anticipated parity changes to avoid massive interest rate movements. Indeed, the 'abolition' of exchange controls that was effected within the EMS in 1990 specifically provides for their temporary use in such circumstances. The fears of such as Giavazzi and Spaventa (1990) are that this temporary use may not be effective: once deregulation has occurred in normal times, evasion may be much easier in times of crisis. We could not deal with this problem in our modelling efforts here because our model is annual (too time-aggregated), to capture it. We have modelled permanently tough exchange controls as opposed to temporarily invoked controls, our default assumption. Permanent controls in fact make little difference to model instability across all countries but under the non-cooperative Nash assumption they do slightly reduce instrument instability, presumably because the model has a less perverse Phillips curve trade-off. This shows that provided capital controls can be used effectively in crisis, they are not mandatory or desirable at other times within the EMS. The qualification must remain that their effectiveness in crisis may be impaired if they are only used then.

If the model is varied to eliminate the wage reaction, instability is somewhat reduced but is still serious. This shows that the parity delay itself alters the system's adjustment in a similar direction (towards a perverse Phillips curve trade-off) and this destabilises the Nash equilibrium. Limits on the size of parity change are also not much help. They do markedly reduce instability for the EMS4. But they increase it for ROW; and in any case they leave marked instability, because there is still substantial scope for conflicting policy even with these limits.

Preventing parity change altogether transforms the situation. The reason is that it effectively prevents any independent use of monetary policy and hence the destabilising Nash reactions. The margins are insignificant in this context. This reveals that big gains appear when Nash independence is effectively abandoned. Like no parity change, fixed money supplies, unresponsive to shocks, reduce costs sharply. Worldwide cooperation reduces costs further, but as argued earlier such cooperation is probably infeasible. A coalition of the EMS countries (playing Nash with other countries, the US, Canada and Japan) is far more realistic. For the EMS4, either such a coalition or worldwide cooperation or fixed money are very similar. The EMS4 in fact fully maximise their collective welfare under EMU, the ultimately rigid system (modelled here as no parity change and zero margins). The rest of the world also prefers EMU because it reduces the EMS propensity to instability the most effectively.

What this analysis appears to indicate is that the EMS has survived by becoming more rigid (permitting less and less parity adjustment) and by the resulting monetary cooperation between member countries. It could not afford for long the luxury of frequent parity changes and of independent monetary policies by member countries, because these would have seriously destabilised it. In short, to survive the EMS had to become more than its overt rules, it had to develop into a monetary coalition. There is no viable halfway house between full monetary integration and floating, essentially as argued by Walters (1990). This conclusion validates the fears of many sceptics at the EMS' founding that the EMS could not survive without institutional change. The EMS has been forced into greater integration by the need to avoid the great potential instability of the original specification.

As for exchange controls, temporary ones are recognised to be necessary to prevent EMS breakdown when parity changes are allowed; but temporary or permanent, our work shows they do not avoid the instability of the basic regime design. Their weakening in 1990 has obviously been another factor hastening institutional change, but in a way we have not modelled here.

Finally, we may note (as shown in table 2.4) the comparison — regime by regime — between floating and its EMS equivalent. Throughout, the floating regime dominates its equivalent, exhibiting the point that floating provides a useful extra degree of freedom in economic adjustment.

Table 2.4 Floating and EMS regimes compared (ratio of floating/EMS welfare cost)

	ROW	EMS4	All
Fixed money: (Floating/EMS)	2/16	0.7/3	0.8/8
Nash (independence)	18/296	11/196	14/239
Nash (EMS coalition)	3.3/25	0.3/1	0.5/11
Worldwide cooperation	1.4/10	0.7/2	2/5.4

Notes: see table 2.3.

The EMS as creator of price discipline, a route to EMU and a surrogate for explicit cooperation

Sufficient should have been said to establish our key finding. This is that the EMS creates greater instability for dependent EMS countries than they would experience under floating. This property arises from the peculiar responses of the economy to their monetary instruments under the EMS. This instrument is hobbled effectively by the EMS; a monetary stimulus fails to stimulate output, perversely strengthens the real exchange rate, and yet fails to prevent inflation.

There can be little doubt that this is precisely the intention of the EMS. This is the mechanism by which the EMS creates price discipline; deviations from monetary consistency with the inflation rate of the reserve currency are penalised by these unpleasant consequences. There is a parallel with the aversion therapy sometimes used for cigarette smokers where a drug is taken which causes smoking to be accompanied by nausea.

Whether one undertakes such a style of cure depends on the alternatives open to one. It has been argued both in the case of France and Italy (for example, Giavazzi and Pagano, 1988, and Sachs and Wyplosz, 1986) that the EMS made it politically possible to pursue tough monetary policies in a way that purely domestic mechanisms could not. Essentially the EMS had the appeal of pan-Europeanism: people would endure the hardships of tight money for the sake of preserving Europe.

This is a highly persuasive account of why the EMS has been accepted as a counter-inflation framework in continental Europe. The facts are also clear that the framework has produced convergence of French and (to some degree) Italian inflation on the German rate. Episodes of independent monetary expansion in these two countries have become rarer as their counter-productiveness has come to be appreciated. At the same time there is some evidence that macroeconomic performance other than for inflation has been poor: growth has been slower and unemployment higher as compared both with these two countries' past and with performance elsewhere. De Grauwe (1989) has also argued plausibly that in practice the EMS exchange-rate discipline has acted in a more gradualist way than the domestic monetary shock treatment used in the US and the UK in the early 1980s.

It is well known that, faced with these choices, the UK has (until recently) preferred to use domestic monetary discipline. But this is not to deny that, compared with nothing at all, the EMS creates price discipline: the simulation analysis here clearly shows that it does and by what means.

But most importantly of all, the joint challenges to EMS members posed by the system's potential instability seem to have forced their central banks to abandon independence and cooperate to a degree never originally laid down. In this respect, therefore, the EMS has been indeed both a step to EMU and a producer of cooperation; while not a surrogate for it, its existence has certainly acted as a source of it. EMU must be closer once such cooperation is established.

Overall evaluation

We have attempted to evaluate the EMS with the use of a full macroeconometric model fitted to postwar data, and adjusted in a few key coefficients to deal with the post-1979 EMS phenomenon. We have used optimisation methods to ask what overall effects would occur under the EMS as compared with floating on the assumption that all governments react to events and strategically to each other; while there are inevitably arbitrary assumptions in the work here our overall conclusion is not enormously surprising. It is that the EMS acts as a hobbling-device on the monetary policy of EMS countries which do not control the key currency (that is, the D-Mark). They find that monetary policy creates unpleasant and destabilising results. This fact discourages them from using it — hence the encouragement of convergence and price discipline. However, by the same token the behaviour of their economies in response to shocks when they do use their monetary instrument under EMS is significantly worse than under floating.

We found that an EMS with no parity change and fixed money supplies exhibited reasonable stability, though still less than a floating regime where money supplies could be varied independently and non-cooperatively. This is not an entirely surprising conclusion. The stability problems of the EMS arise because parities can move and monetary independence is therefore exercised. To remove these problems requires the removal of both parity change and monetary independence. Yet such removal also takes away the ability of monetary policy to respond flexibly to shocks, and therefore floating, which preserves that ability without concomitant instability, appears from the general world viewpoint a superior regime.

The achievement of the EMS is to have survived by discovering how to alleviate these problems and by that discovery to have launched participating countries onto a fast tract to monetary unification. Nevertheless, it has done so at the cost of sacrificing the greater stability both inside and outside the EMS offered by the floating environment.

The price of EMU

Every schoolboy knows the advantages in principle of a common currency, even if he has never travelled abroad and recently the EC Commission (1990) has made a heroic attempt to measure them. Their efforts run to 351 pages and they suggest that the efficiency gain from removing currency uncertainty and exchange costs may be worth as much as 10 per cent of EC GNP. Virtually all of this comes from the effect of a supposed reduction in the risk premium on the cost of capital. Various other gains are adduced from the common currency, including those of increased price stability (including through enhanced credibility), more disciplined public finance and greater macroeconomic stability.

However, price stability is attainable with or without EMU, as is credibility. Whether EMU makes them more easily attainable is a matter of political economy, which is not tackled by the EC's report: what will the Euro-Fed's powers and incentives be, as opposed to those of existing monetary authorities? These questions raise wide considerations and are not easily settled. We will not pursue them in this chapter, but merely note that there are strong arguments to suggest that agreement between twelve democratic governments on a Euro-Bank devoted solely to tight money and unaccountable to the participating democracies is unattainable. These arguments are not addressed in the EC report but merely assumed away.

By 'discipline on public finance' seems to be meant the inability of a regional government to raise taxation through seigniorage. Here a virtue is made of what in the literature is regarded as a problem, making optimal taxation more difficult. Again we will not pursue this matter in this chapter.

Merely consider for example in passing the parlous financial state of the Italian government since the withdrawal of its powers to levy a sizeable inflation tax on the otherwise tax-free zone of the shadow economy, especially in the South. Whatever else the new tight ERM has done for Italy it has made the prospect of reaching budget balance much more distant, if it has not disappeared altogether: Ponzi-like, the Italian government goes on borrowing at an overvalued exchange rate sustained by exchange-rate support which guarantees returns for large capital inflows. The EC report offers no mechanisms, only pious hopes, for achieving movement to fiscal balance under EMU. No seigniorage and no alternative fiscal mechanism: it hardly seems to constitute a fiscal improvement.

Analytically, the efficiency gain claimed by the EC report comes from removing the transaction costs of currency exchange and the hedging costs of guarding against currency uncertainty. Whether the estimate is reasonable or not, we do not know. There are three qualitative arguments which suggest it may be on the high side:

(1) Currency risk is diversifiable in a world of many currencies and investment vehicles whose risks are correlated with currency risk. Hence the cost of hedging should tend to the premium on specific risk, namely zero.

(2) A transaction involving currency exchange should not, on the face of it (given the negligible cost of keying in electronic orders), cost any extra in credit transactions than an ordinary transaction in home currency, other than the cost of hedging net balances in one currency any one currency between clearings.

(1) and (2) suggest that the only saving comes in the exchange of notes and coin. But this is extremely limited: notes and coin are generally used in a small percentage of all transactions (with one or two exceptions such as Italy) and that part of it which is exchanged for foreign notes and coin is a small percentage of that again.

The EC commission's estimate of the transactions cost saving on its own is 0.4 per cent of GDP; this is based on a survey of financial firms' commission charges, and these are applied to estimates of the volume of business attracting these charges. While this is a more believable estimate than the huge aggregate figure it may still be on the high side; indeed, the report suggests that it is heavily concentrated among the smaller countries with less sophisticated banking systems.

(3) If the gain were as large as the EC estimate, then other pairs of nations enjoying a similar degree of inter-trade would have surely actively considered a common currency. Yet the countries of EFTA, of North America, of Eastern Europe, to name but a few candidates, have never seemed to put this idea seriously on the treaty agenda.

This last point suggests that whatever the truth in the EC Commission's estimate the key point in inducing nations to have a common currency must lie elsewhere, in the balance of other gains and losses. Indeed, it is that assumption that lies behind the extensive literature on the 'optimal' common currency area; that literature invokes a variety of criteria — for example, the degree of labour and capital mobility and the extent of fiscal transfers — but the extent of foreign exchange transactions does not figure importantly, if at all, among them.

Our purpose here is to examine this balance of other gains and losses and specifically those coming from the loss of a flexible exchange rate and so individual monetary policy in reacting to stochastic shocks — which we shall loosely call the stabilisation aspect.

Stabilisation gains and losses

In evaluating the stabilisation aspect for any given common currency proposal, one must make assumptions about the institutional framework. It makes a lot of difference whether there is a high degree of labour mobility and what the fiscal transfer arrangements are.

In the case of the EC it has been noted by Eichengreen (1990) that the fiscal offset to any national or regional decline in GDP is less than 1 per cent (as against 30 per cent in the US for instance); nor are there any plans to raise this offset coefficient to any number remotely comparable with the US one. The Delors Committee (Delors, 1989) called for a doubling but even that may well not be agreed by the nations that have to double their fiscal contribution to Brussels.

For the vast bulk of nationals in the richer countries of the EC, labour mobility is also limited. The key reason appears to be language and cultural differences, which make for instance a Frenchman pause before resettling in Frankfurt. What significant migration there is is from the poorer countries to the richer, since immigration controls that normally stop this are invalidated. But even this is not great because capital mobility within the free EC market enables workers in poor countries such as Spain, parts of the UK and of Italy, on the periphery of the EC, to attract investment and enjoy improved wages without the cost of moving; capital mobility and free trade act therefore as a substitute for labour mobility, as stressed in the Heckscher-Ohlin theory.

It is obvious as the optimum currency area literature stresses that whatever stabilisation task is performed by flexible exchange rates and divergent monetary policy, it can be partially substituted for by either labour mobility or fiscal transfers. To that extent, the EC is handicapped in its bid to be an optimum currency area. Our calculations below reflect this handicap. (If EMU goes ahead regardless, that might well lead to demands for further progress on fiscal policy and labour mobility, but that is another matter.)

Stochastic simulations

In the previous section we 'predicted' that ERM would evolve either into a 'tight ERM' (coalition) or back towards *de facto* floating; or finally towards a combination of both, a two-tier system with some countries adopting a 'tight ERM' and others opting for floating. Such a prediction is of course gratifyingly close to what has actually evolved in the past decade since the EMS started in 1979. We wish to evaluate the relative stability of EMU. For the countries deciding whether to go ahead with it (viz here Germany, France, Italy and the UK) we ask two sets of questions.

(1)   How does EMU compare with floating?
(2)   Given that EMU goes ahead, (a) will any country wish not to participate? (b) What will the rest of the world do in reaction to it?

EMU for all EC: how does it compare with floating?

How either floating or EMU behaves in the face of shocks depends on how monetary policy behaves. We distinguish two main possibilities: money supply targets pursued without response to shocks ('fixed money'), and continuous money supply optimisation in response to events (including those produced by other countries' responses, the non-cooperative Nash strategy assumption) 'strategic money'. Under EMU clearly the latter monetary response is the result of some sort of cooperation between EC countries; to model this we assume that each country's preferences are given an equal weight in this cooperative decision making. In practice, as we only model four

Table 2.5 Costs of EMU and floating (Nash)

	EMU	Floating	Prefers
EC			
Germany	0.2	1.8	EMU
France	0.4	0.9	EMU
Italy	0.5	41.6	EMU
UK	0.6	0.2	Floating
Row			
US	1.6	1.0	Floating
Canada	20.3	47.4	EMU
Japan	3.6	6.8	EMU

Table 2.6 Joint EC costs of feasible EC regimes

| | Fixed money | Nash independent | All | Nash coalitions in EC | | | World cooperation |
				ex-UK	ex-France	ex-Italy	
Floating	3.0	44.5	1.1	13.2	209.2	5.6	2.2
EMU	4.8	-	1.8	2.2	4.4	3.2	5.0

of the EC countries explicitly – Germany, France, Italy and the UK – this equality is limited to them. Table 2.5 shows the costs of these two regimes under the assumption that countries not within the ERM or EMU choose independent money supply growth rates to minimise their welfare costs subject to the choices of others. Under floating the EC countries each also behave in this way. Under EMU, Germany is assumed to set its money supply, minimising EC joint welfare costs – a coalition differing from ERM through the absence of any margins of intra-EC currency fluctuation at all.

It can be seen that, if this is the relevant choice set, then there is not full agreement between EC countries on which is best; Germany, France and Italy prefer EMU, the UK floating. In case other countries' preferences have any influence, they too can be seen to differ, with the US urging floating on the EC and Japan and Canada urging EMU.

Beside this money supply regime, it would be possible to imagine completely fixed money supplies (following a Friedman rule) or money supplies coordinated worldwide to minimise joint world welfare costs. Of course the first is not generally practised while the second would require a level of international agreement that is currently absent.

However unlikely, all these regimes are shown in table 2.6 with the joint welfare costs of EC countries that result from them. A rational way for the EC to choose a regime would be to settle on that exchange-rate-monetary regime combination which minimised their joint welfare costs; then side-payments (or equivalent compensation) could be made to those who lose out.

Table 2.6 reveals that the optimum is a coalition of all EC countries for the management of their money supplies but under floating rates. The next best is EMU, followed by worldwide cooperation under floating; this last would also be the first choice of the world community, which could presumably make it worth the EC's while. It would seem therefore that the global optimum for the EC is to float but to coordinate monetary policies. Furthermore, the rest of the world has an interest in coordinating with them too, offering the EC countries the necessary inducements.

If EMU goes ahead, who will participate?
We assume that EMU goes ahead for independent (perhaps political) reasons. Let us assume that Germany is committed to being part of EMU, since it has the central bank around which the ERM has been organised. Our work establishes that both France and Italy prefer to stay in whereas the UK prefers to stay out. The remaining three also still find EMU preferable to a return to floating, given that the UK stays out. They are not tempted back to floating without a coalition, though it remains preferable to float with a coalition including the UK.

How would the rest of the world react to an EMU (excluding the UK)?
In table 2.7 we show the gains achievable by world cooperation in monetary policy, given that the EC pursued an EMU excluding the UK. It pays the rest of the world to adopt a coordinated strategy in line with that of the EMU members.

Table 2.7 Costs of EMU (excluding UK) versus worldwide monetary cooperation with EMU bloc

	EMU ex-UK	Worldwide cooperation with EMU ex-UK
US	1.7	1.6
Canada	24.3	20.7
Japan	4.0	2.2
ROW	30.0	24.5
Germany	0.4	0.8
France	0.9	2.3
Italy	0.7	1.9
UK	0.2	0.2
EC	2.2	5.2
World	32.2	29.7

Conclusions

We have found that the best regime for the EC would be floating with monetary policies either coordinated worldwide or, if this is impossible, coordinated within an EC-wide coalition in a world of independent Nash behaviour. However, if for other reasons EMU goes ahead then it would pay the UK (alone) to stay out and float. The rest of the world, UK included, would still profit from coordinating with the EC's EMU as would they, but it may not be practicable.

This analysis has used a welfare cost measure with five components: output, price, real interest rate and real exchange-rate variances. However, decomposition of this measure shows that when only the first two components are included in conventional manner, then the EC preference for floating would be greatly strengthened, as one might reasonably expect when exchange-rate stability is not an objective. There would be a strong opposition on all sides to EMU, making further analysis of its precise form of little interest. Hence our central conclusion is substantially strengthened, implying that our actual choice of welfare weights is necessary to give the analysis any point at all. If exchange-rate stability is not an objective, then EMU will not be a starter.

Notes

1 This work was financed by the ESRC consortium for Modelling and Forecasting the economy. Hughes-Hallett is at the University of Strathclyde, Minford and Rastogi at the University of Liverpool. We are grateful for research assistance to Gary Hutson and Eric Nowell. We thank for their comments at various stages Charles Adams, Matthew Canzoneri, Nicos Christodoulakis, Neil Ericsson, Michele Fratianni, Paul De Grauwe, Jurgen von Hagen, Catherine Mann, Manfred Neumann, Michael Farkin, Jean Pisani-Ferry, Roland Vaubel, Walter Wasserfallen and Charles Wyplosz as well as other participants in the 1989 Konstanz Seminar and the 1990 Brookings workshop on policy rules.

2 The latter feature distinguishes it from 'disequilibrium' rational expectations models with a high degree of nominal rigidity such as Taylor (1988), McKibbin-Sach's model MSG2 (Ishii *et al.*, 1985), Minimod and more recently Multimod of Haas and Masson (1986) and Masson *et al.*(1988). For a more detailed comparison of these models see Bryant *et al.*, (1988).

3

Forward-Looking Wages and the Analysis of Monetary Union

Bob Anderton, Ray Barrell and Jan Willem in't Veld*

Introduction

This chapter discusses the role of forward-looking behaviour in labour markets in Europe and analyses the implications of such behaviour in the context of a monetary union. The first section discusses the literature on labour markets and the ERM. The second discusses empirical work undertaken at the National Institute on European labour markets. Our analysis is set up in a bargaining framework, and our empirical work finds a significant role for price inflation expectations in the process of wage determination. The final section embeds these forward-looking wage equations into the National Institute Global Econometric Model (NiGEM) and we undertake a number of policy analyses in the context of Monetary Union. We conclude that a successful anti-inflationary policy depends more on the reactions of the authorities than on the credibility of a monetary union.

Labour markets and the ERM

Membership of the ERM and a reduction in inflation appear to have been statistically associated over the last twelve years. Inflation has tended to converge on German standards amongst ERM members, and this convergence has been most marked since around 1985. However, there are a number of possible explanations. Membership of the ERM could have increased the credibility of the authorities and hence changed the nature of wage bargaining, increasing the effects of deflationary policies. Other forces may

*We would like to thank our colleagues at NIESR for advice and input into this chapter. Andrew Gurney, Andrew Britton, Jimmy McHugh, Nigel Pain, Soterios Soteri, Peter Westaway and Garry Young in particular all contributed in some way. This chapter has been greatly improved by useful comments provided by John Whitley. The model used is a version of that developed by the National Institute and jointly maintained with the LBS.

also have been causing changes in labour market structures. Alternatively, all we may be observing is that a commitment to a fixed exchange rate mechanism must be associated with loss of direct control over the money supply and hence ultimately over the price level.

If one country in a fixed exchange rate mechanism is the dominant player then it will tend to dictate the inflation rate in the long run. At minimum this will operate through a process of disequilibrium in other countries. If, for instance, Germany is dominant and France inflates faster than Germany then it will become increasingly uncompetitive, exports will fall increasingly below their constant competitiveness path, and imports will rise correspondingly. Current account deficits will cause wealth to decumulate, and aggregate demand will become increasingly depressed. Inflation will, as a result, have to fall until the price level reaches some equilibrium relationship with that in Germany. Evidence to support recession-generated convergence is given by Artis and Ormerod (1991), and the bivariate causality tests reported by Artis and Nachane (1990) also suggest that German inflation has affected inflation elsewhere in the ERM.

Inflation reduction could be produced in other ways. It is argued that German leadership allows other countries to adopt the Bundesbank anti-inflationary mantle.[1] Increased credibility supposedly changes both the degree of forward lookingness and the speed of response in the labour market, and this in turn improves the sacrifice ratio by causing the structure of bargaining to change. The evidence on this hypothesis is mixed. Dornbusch (1991) provides a cautious assessment, and Artis and Ormerod (1991) suggest that, after a period of deflationary turbulence, labour market behaviour outside Germany has returned to its previous pattern. The work by Barrell, Darby and Donaldson (1990)[2] is slightly more optimistic about the possibility of change, but locates the change in the positive transformation of institutions rather than as a 'manna from heaven' break in behaviour.

Wage behaviour

In order to assess the process of structural change in labour markets we have to understand the process of wage determination, both in long-run equilibrium and also in terms of its dynamic evolution. As up to three quarters of all workers in Europe are covered directly or indirectly by collective bargaining, we feel that it is productive to work in the bargaining framework discussed in Layard, Nickell and Jackman (1991). This is the latest in a series of papers[3] that have developed this approach. The bargaining framework produces a reduced-form wage equation that encapsulates the demand for labour and the supply of labour as well as the role of trade unions. The most common approach assumes that firms have the 'right to manage'. The wage rate is determined by the bargain

between employers, unions and workers, and then the employers have the right
to choose the number of employees. Hence, given the wage, they are able to
stay on their demand curve for labour.

The outcome of any bargaining process will depend upon the objectives of
the bargainers, their relative strengths and the environment within which they
find themselves. The obvious objective for the firm to consider is to maximise
its profits, and the profit function will also depend upon the price of other inputs,
on the production technology and on demand conditions. We will assume
that the union is interested in the welfare of its members, both those who remain
in the firm and those who are outside it. The Nash approach to bargaining
derives the equilibrium as

$$\max_{w}(U(W) - \overline{U})^{\beta}(\pi(W) - \overline{\pi})$$

where β is an indicator of union power, U is the utility of the union, W is the
wage, $\overline{U}$ is the fall-back utility level that the union will not go below, π is the
firm's profits, and $\overline{\pi}$ is the fall-back level of profits (which should over the
longer term be non-negative).

The bargain should result in a wage above the competitive level, and as a
result employment in the industries covered will be below that of a perfectly
competitive market. Not all workers remain 'insiders', some are outsiders, and
receive either the non-unionised wage or the level of unemployment benefit.
(The 'outsiders' may also be of no importance to the union when striking its
bargain.)

The bargain determines the mark-up of unionised wages over non-unionised
wages. This mark-up will depend upon the production technology, the degree
of product market competition, and the strength of trade unions. Unionised
workers face direct and indirect taxes whether or not they are in employment,
and hence these taxes only affect the mark-up if there are either inhomogeneities
in the tax system or non-homotheticity in the utility functions of individuals.
We would also expect the bargain to be independent of the level of productivity,
and hence real wages in the unionised sector may rise in line with productivity
in the long run. It is not clear that the bargain will be influenced by short-run
dynamics, and we discuss these below.

The determination of the wage (or benefit) received by those not employed
by the firm is clearly of considerable importance in the determination of the
economy-wide real wage. First of all it determines the wage of some proportion
of the work force, and given the constancy of the mark-up of the unionised over
the non-unionised wage it will influence the aggregate wage in the economy.
We would expect the reservation wage in the non-unionised sector, and hence
the overall wage, to be positively related to the level of benefits available to the
unemployed. Unemployment may also affect the reservation wage and it may

affect the relative power of unions and employers. A large pool of unemployed may make union members more fearful for their jobs, and it may also make it easier for firms to find alternative sources of labour.

Taxation and the real exchange rate may also have a role in the determination of equilibrium wages in the economy as a whole, even if they do not affect the union mark up. The real consumption wage R may be written as

$$R = W(1 - t^d) / PC$$

where $$PC = (sP + (1-s)PM)(1+t^i)$$

where W is the nominal wage, t^d is the rate of direct taxation, and PC is the price of consumer goods. Consumers buy both home produced goods and imported goods, and $(1-s)$ is the proportion of consumption devoted to imported goods priced at PM and the rest of expenditure is on home produced goods priced at P. We assume that indirect taxes t^i are paid on all goods. Consumers receive the real consumption wage, whilst employers pay the real producer wage, $w(1+t^e)/P$, where t^e is the employers' tax. The bargain can be defined in terms of either of these. We can write the multiplicative identity linking consumption and production wage, WP, as

$$R = WP(1 - t^d) / [(s + (1-s)PM / P)(1+t^e)(1+t^i)]$$

The factor multiplying WP is the tax and real exchange-rate wedge. This wedge affects both the union wage and the fall back wage, and hence should not affect the mark-up of the union over the non-unionised wage in the long run. Layard, Nickell and Jackman (1991) argue that this wedge should therefore not permanently affect the level of real wages. However, this would only be the case if either all workers were covered by the bargain or if the elasticity of supply of labour to the non-unionised sector were zero. If the wedge affects the quantity of labour supplied, and hence the wage, in the secondary sector it should affect the overall level of wages. Of course the smaller the secondary sector and the less elastic the supply of labour the less important is the wedge in determining wages.

The equilibrium real wage will therefore potentially depend upon unemployment U, the power of unions β, the degree of product market competition K, the production technology α, and the wedge. We may write this schematically as

$$W / P = f(U, \beta, (Y / L), K, \alpha, wedge)$$

where *Y/L* is the level of productivity implied by the production function. If union power, unemployment, the degree of product market power and the essential production technology all remain unchanged and the elasticity of supply of labour to the non-unionised sector is zero then we would expect real wages to grow in line with productivity.

We have spelled out the factors affecting the bargain in order to demonstrate that we would not expect them to be affected by the policy credibility of the authorities or by the exchange-rate regime it chooses. If the exchange-rate regime is to have an effect on the structure of the wage-price system we must look for it elsewhere. However, our analysis does allow us to bring out some institutional differences between the countries of the community. These affect both the structure of the bargain and the dynamics of the wage-price system, and it is in the dynamics of the wage-price system that we should see credibility effects from exchange-rate systems.

The dynamic responses we observe in wage equations are not the result of accidents but follow from the conscious construction of labour market institutions. Bargainers construct the institutions partly in the light of the policy credibility of the authorities. If the authorities have a poor anti-inflationary record then bargainers will not wish to have too long a period between renegotiating contracts. They will expect inflationary shocks to be validated and not reversed, and hence they will want short contracting periods. The shorter the contracting period the less nominal wage rigidity we would expect to observe. Shocks to prices will be quickly absorbed into wages, and as a result real wages are likely to be less flexible.

There are other ways in which the credibility of the authorities will affect the dynamics of the wage-price system. In countries such as Italy the low anti-inflationary credibility of the authorities led to widespread contract indexation in the 1970s. Indeed in Italy up until 1983 money wages were uprated in line with inflation once a quarter. Indexation mechanisms of this sort produce considerable rigidities in real wages and rapid propagation of shocks. They imply that the effects of a series of leap frogging wage demands, or the effects of an oil price shock, could easily lead to a rapid acceleration in inflation. [4]

Contracting periods and indexation mechanisms are not the only factors affecting the process of dynamic adjustment of wages. For instance, Taylor (1979) argues that we should expect to observe both backward and forward indexation in wage negotiations. For a given contracting period we would expect that less wage inertia would be observed when wages were more forward looking. There would still be some inertia because wage contracts are in general staggered, and not all wages can react immediately to current information. The shorter the contract period, the less wage inertia we would expect to observe because current information will be fed more rapidly both into backward indexed contracts and into contracts based on expected inflation.

Individuals have to form expectations about the future and they bargain over the expected real wage. If they form expectations then their expectations generating mechanisms may depend on the credibility of the authorities. If expectations are based in part on current and past data then history will affect the evolution of the wage bargain. The more credible the authorities' anti-inflation stance the less may bargainers change these expectations in response to current news. If the authorities' stance becomes more credible, or the optimal information set changes, then we would expect the expectations generating mechanism to change. Anderton, Barrell and McHugh (1992) and Artis and Nachane (1990) both demonstrate that the optimal (in the sense of minimising least squares errors) information set changed in the 1980s, with German inflation becoming an important predictor of inflation elsewhere. These changes are already well documented, and we wish to investigate whether or not a change in perceived credibility changes the structure of the wage bargaining process rather than just affecting one of the inputs into the bargain. We also wish to look at its implications for policy analysis in Europe.

Estimating wage equations

Our general approach has been to estimate wage equations that include both the long-run factors affecting the wage and the bargain, and also the factors affecting the dynamic process of wage adjustment. We analyse producer wage equations specified as:

$$\Delta \log W = a + b_1 \log W(-1)$$
$$+ b_2 \log(Y/L) + b_3 \log P(-1)$$
$$+ b_4 \log (WED) + b_5 U(-1) + b_6 PE$$
$$+ \text{Dynamics}$$

where W is the nominal wage per person hour, P is the price level of domestically produced output, Y/L is the long-run level of labour productivity per person hour. The tax and exchange-rate wedge is defined above. We use the level of the rate of unemployment and PE is the rate of inflation expected over the next quarter.[5]

Our hypotheses on this relationship are then

(1) Real wages rise in line with productivity to $b_1 = -b_3 = -b_2$.
(2) The tax and real exchange-rate wedge should have a non-negative effect in a producer wage equation.
(3) Unemployment should have a non-positive effect on wages.
(4) The coefficient on expectations will depend upon the proportion of the workforce covered by forward-looking wage bargains.

There is of course a great deal of debate over the variables that we might use in studying wage relationships. The current level of unemployment may not be a good indicator of the effect of unemployment on the wage bargain. If there is a large proportion of long-term unemployed who may have become deskilled and demotivated then their presence in our unemployment count may change its effect on the wage bargain. Union power often cycles with the state of the economy, and we presume that it changes in line with the business cycle indicators that we include. If the wage bargaining system includes some automatic backward indexation then there are groups whose wage bargain will not be affected by expectations. This situation was clearly the case with quarterly backward indexation in Italy under the *Scala Mobile*, and it also holds for groups whose contracts are governed by law, such as civil servants and those on minimum wages. As a result we would expect to see a mixture of backward and forward inflation indicators to enter our wage equation.

If the ERM changes wage behaviour then we should expect to see systematic change in the pattern of dynamics in our equations. Institutional change may also change the level of real wages and the dynamics of wage setting. Such institutional changes seem to be endemic in Europe in the early 1980s, and there is some evidence in Anderton, Barrell and McHugh (1992) that these changes were reflected in wage bargaining. If backward indexation is removed then we should expect to see the role of expectations enhanced. If the ERM alters the effective contracting period then we would expect the mean lag in our equations to change. Our empirical work is based on that reported in Anderton and Barrell (1992) where we have undertaken extensive tests for structural change. We have looked at the stability of our estimated equations in two ways. We have taken as our null hypothesis that there is no structural change and we have then tested for systematic change in the whole relationship starting in the period 1979Q1.[6] Although this test is statistically correct, it is weak, and we have also investigated the stability of individual parameters in our relationship.

Testing wage equations
The diverse inflationary experience of the four large European economies is widely documented. Both the UK and Italy have experienced two major inflationary episodes in the last twenty years, whilst consumer inflation in Germany has never risen above 7 per cent at an annual rate over this period. These differences in experience should, we believe, be reflected in wage bargaining and hence in our estimated equations. We would expect the countries with more variable inflation would have some role for expected inflation in the bargain, and indeed our equations for Italy, UK and France all have a role for expectations whilst that for Germany does not. We could find no role for a long-run tax and real exchange-rate wedge in the UK, France and Germany,

but the use of the consumer price (CED) in the dynamics (in contrast to the producer price in the long-run relationship) does leave a short-run impact from changes in the wedge. Table 3.1 contains our equations.

Table 3.1 Forward-looking wage equations (Δlog (W/E))

	Germany	France	UK	Italy
Constant	1.355	0.2326	0.741	1.61
	(5.89)	(1.22)	(3.7)	(2.29)
Error correction	-0.279	-0.051	-0.171	-0.135
	(6.06)	(1.39)	(3.79)	(2.33)
Δ Compensation (-1)	-0.349			
	(3.77)			
Δ Compensation (-2)	-0.211		0.338	
	(2.02)		(4.3)	
Δ Compensation (-3)	-0.304			
	(3.14)			
Δ CED(-1)		0.608	0.197	
		(4.03)	(2.5)	
Δ CED(-2)				0.707[a]
				(4.35)
Δ CED(-4)			0.281	
			(3.94)	
Unemployment (-1)	-0.007	-0.0025	-0.00074	-0.0013[b]
	(7.68)	(4.32)	(1.84)	(2.33)
Expected inflation		0.419	0.309	0.586[b]
		(1.65)	(2.51)	(2.31)
Standard error	0.011	0.0057	0.008	0.0148
Serial correlation (LM(4))	7.77	1.66	2.49	2.25
Sargan test of instruments		12.86	2.40	13.26
		(χ^2(8))	(χ^2(4))	(χ^2(10))
Data Period	*70Q2-91Q1*	*71Q2-90Q1*	*69Q4-90Q2*	*72Q3-90Q1:*

(a) Before 1982Q1

(b) Current period after 1982Q1. t ratios in brackets

Note: The dependent variable is the change in the log of compensation per person hour, and the error correction term is the divergence between the log of real producer wages per person hour and average productivity. Further details can be found in Anderton and Barrell (1992). All variables (except unemployment and expected inflation) are in logarithms. Δ denotes a change from the previous period.

Germany

All of our work on Germany suggests that there has been no systematic change in the structure of wage determination over the last twenty years. Inflation has been low, and collective bargaining has been relatively centralised. Contractual indexation of wages has been illegal in Germany over the period of our study. Our results suggest that unemployment has played a significant role in wage determination. In the short run neither price inflation expectations nor backward changes in prices appear to enter the German wage bargain, whilst in the long run wages rise in line with prices. This in part reflects the long and stable contracting round in the German economy.

Our German wage equation is given in table 3.1. It shows no sign of structural instability. We first estimated it using IV on a forward-looking price expectations term, but there was no evidence for its effect. The absence of significant inflation effects in our German wage equation may reflect the low level and low variability of German inflation over our data period. This makes it more difficult to pick up significant effects and also less necessary for bargainers to expend resources updating their expectations. There is also no role for wedge effects, and in the long run real wages rise in line with productivity.

UK

The UK economy saw a particularly severe period of deflation in the early 1980s. This was associated with a change in government, and the Thatcher administration clearly wanted to introduce a new regime into wage bargaining. The new administration's programme was essentially monetarist and anti-inflation policy was based upon targets for the growth rate of the money supply, and micro policies aimed at improving the supply-side of the economy were adopted. During the Conservative's first term in office, trade union reforms were introduced, credit markets were liberalised, government expenditure cutbacks were introduced and unemployment rose above three million. It was widely believed that these policies had transformed the behaviour of the labour market. In particular it is generally agreed that wage bargaining became more decentralised during the 1980s.

We estimated a general wage equation for the UK and sequentially eliminated terms. We found no long-run role for wedge effects, and the imposition of a unit coefficient on productivity was valid. Our results suggest that there is a role for forward-looking prices in the UK. We have instrumented price expectations with current and lagged changes in prices and with capacity utilisation and lagged unemployment. Our final equation is given in table 3.1. Our instruments are exogenous (the Sargan test) and the equation properties are acceptable. The Thatcher revolution may well have changed behaviour, and hence we tested the equation for stability in 1980Q1. The equation passed the stability test. (Further details can be found in Anderton and Barrell (1992). Our equation has a role for both backward and forward inflation terms, and there is a significant role for unemployment in this relationship.

Italy

After the rise in inflation during the early 1970s many countries adopted either formal or informal wage indexation procedures. The construction and subsequent reform of the wage indexation mechanism in Italy has been particularly instructive. In that country the process of wage indexation became formalised in a set of agreements characterised as the '*Scala Mobile*'. Formal indexation agreements can be very informationally efficient if the authorities have a reputation for validating shocks and this was indeed the case in Italy during the 1970s. The Italian authorities' commitment to the ERM in 1979 was accompanied by a clear change in their anti-inflationary stance. However this shift and its sustainability were not obvious even in the early 1980s, and the process of removing the *Scala Mobile* was long and painful.

Reforms to the *Scala Mobile* were introduced in 1977 and 1983, but the most significant changes were enacted in 1985. Automatic indexation had existed in Italy since the early 1950s, but price indexation was not particularly important in a period when real wages were growing rapidly. However, during the 1970s real wage growth slowed considerably. In 1975 and 1977 the coverage of the *Scala Mobile* increased, and Bank of Italy estimates suggest that the proportion of wage changes 'caused' by the *Scala Mobile* rose from 60 per cent in 1975 to around 80 per cent by 1978. In 1983 the mechanism was modified, and the degree of indexation was reduced from 1.0 to 0.85. However the most important reform took place in 1985. Firstly the frequency of adjustments was reduced from quarterly to half-yearly, slowing down the speed of pass through of prices to wages. Secondly the indexation rules were modified so that only those on low wages were compensated fully. Wages above a rather low minimum were either partially indexed or not indexed at all. These changes in the *Scala Mobile* do appear to have had a significant effect on the wage–price spiral in Italy, and have contributed to observed changes in behaviour. However it is fair to say that these changes were rather slow to come after the formation of the ERM, and they were painful to introduce. The authorities tried to remove the last vestiges of the *Scala Mobile* in the summer of 1990, but they were prevented from doing so by trade union pressure. Negotiations have continued after the 1992 General Election.

We estimated an equation for Italy using Instrumental Variables techniques over the whole period, and it exhibited instability around 1982. The reform of the wage bargaining system in Italy and the removal of the *Scala Mobile* indexation system are associated with large changes in the structure of our equation for Italy. We respecified the equation with all variables included both for the whole sample period and also for the period after 1982. We then tested down, eliminating insignificant variables. Our final equation contains a backward-looking inflation indicator for the period before 1982 and no effect from unemployment. After 1982 there is a significant role for forward-looking expectations and for unemployment, but no role for backward-looking inflation. The reform of the Italian wage bargaining system appears to have changed real and nominal wage flexibility by a significant amount. Further details can be found in Anderton and Barrell (1992).

France

There have been a large number of labour market reforms in France over the last decade. The two that have been most discussed have been the gradual decentralisation of collective bargaining and the removal of stringent redundancy regulations. In the 1970s and early 1980s much of French bargaining was both national and industrial, a pattern similar to that seen in Germany. Many agreements had automatic backward-looking indexation included in them, reducing the degree of real wage flexibility. Over the 1980s bargaining moved increasingly to the firm and plant level, and has become much more like that in the UK. In 1986 there were major changes in redundancy regulations, making severance much easier. This deregulation has raised the degree of labour market flexibility. All redundancies previously had to be notified and approved. These regulations appear to have reduced hirings for a given macro-environment and hence raised the equilibrium level of unemployment by extending the period of search between jobs (OECD, 1989). However, there is little evidence that the change in regulations on either redundancy or indexation has changed the speed of pass through of shocks to prices and wages or of prices to wages and *vice versa*.

French inflation has come down over the last ten years. The early years of the 1980s saw the failure of the Mitterand dash for growth. Wages and prices were frozen in 1982 and price controls were strengthened in 1983. These measures were accompanied by fiscal and monetary tightening which, along with increased exchange controls, reduced demand through the effects of higher interest rates and less government spending. These measures were a success, but they do not necessarily imply a change in the structure of wage and price behaviour. They could be associated with a change in the credibility of the authorities that would change the inflation expectations generating mechanism. Without observed expectations measures it is difficult to test this hypothesis, and anyway it is possible that their relevance may be low as French wage bargaining is still dominated by backward-looking compensation for past inflation.

Structural changes in the French labour market have come in three forms. The most significant for our purposes has probably been changes in minimum wage legislation. The most important element of the French wage structure for the analysis of inflation has been the minimum wage. The legal minimum was formally disindexed in 1983. However the annual resetting of the minimum wage during the second half of the 1980s has meant that it has kept up with average manual wages, and its coverage has actually increased. The minimum wage might be less significant if its coverage were not so extensive. As the French economy has moved to more decentralised bargaining in the last few years the minimum wage system, which covers 40 per cent of the workforce, has been increasingly used as the basis for wage settlements that have been designed to maintain an existing pattern of differentials. This is clearly informationally efficient because decentralised bargaining reduces common information.

We estimated an equation for wage setting in France, and we instrumented price expectations. The resulting equation is given in table 3.1. We tested for overall stability after the formation of the ERM, and the equation was stable over the break. The inflation measures in this equation split between backward and forward in the ratio 3:2, in part reflecting the nature of the French labour market. There is also a significant effect from unemployment.

Conclusions on labour markets
There have been some changes in the structure of European labour markets in the last decade, but it is not clear that these changes have been the result of increased credibility on the part of the monetary authorities. The process of dismantling the *Scala Mobile* in Italy has been long and painful. It may not have been possible without ERM membership but it cannot be seen as manna from heaven. It is possible to produce indices of real and nominal wage flexibility. These so called sacrifice ratios will depend upon the interaction of wage and price determination processes and are difficult to calculate from single reduced form equations. It is, however, possible to produce some indices of wage flexibility. Table 3.2 sets out our overall results. The first row gives an indication of wage flexibility in response to a rise in unemployment. The second gives the long-run coefficient on unemployment. The sacrifice ratio indicates the percentage point rise in unemployment that is required to reduce inflation by 1 per cent in the first year. The long-run coefficient on unemployment indicates the effect on the real wage of a permanent 1 per cent rise in unemployment. The third row gives an indicator of the degree of forward-looking behaviour in prices. The fourth and fifth rows give various indicators of the speed of response to increases in prices (given consistent expectations). Germany has systematically a slower impact and long-run response to increases in prices. This reflects a great deal about the success of the Bundesbank policy over the last decade.

Table 3.2 Wage flexibility

	Germany	France	UK	Italy[b]
Sacrifice ratio[a]	0.591	0.396	0.625	1.93
				(∞)
Long-run unemployment coefficient	-0.026	-0.052	-0.0043	-0.0096
Ratio of backward to forward expectations	no forward	6:4	5:3	switches in 1982
Mean lag in prices (in quarters)	6.26	7.73	1.08	7.41 (2.17)
Median lag in prices (range between 2 quarters)	[4-5]	[0-1]	[2-3]	[4-5] ([1-2])

(a) Sacrifice ratio: Mean lag in prices divided by long-run unemployment coefficient, and rescaled by .0025 for comparability with Layard, Nickell and Jackman (1991).
(b) Italian figures are for the post-1982 period, those in brackets beneath these figures are for the pre-1982 period.

NiGEM with forward-looking wages[7]

The four bargaining equations for wages that are described above have been embedded into the most recent version of NiGEM. The model is described fully in the May 1992 Manual (NIESR, 1992). It contains detailed models of the major seven economies with full stock and flow equilibrium embedded in them. It can be operated under various policy rules for interest rates, exchange rates and fiscal policy. Interest rates can be set to target either money supply, or a combination of real GDP and inflation or forward-looking real short interest rates. Long rates can be either forward-looking or backward-looking, as can the exchange rate. If the exchange rate is endogenous it always follows the open arbitrage path, and it will sometimes 'jump' if a shock changes the path for the expected interest-rate differential. The stock of government debt enters personal sector wealth, and hence the government financing rule is significant. The model can be run without a government financing constraint, or with a fiscal solvency constraint imposed in the form of a deficit target.

We have undertaken a set of fixed exchange-rate runs with forward-looking long-term interest rates. We have implemented inflation and GDP targeting along the lines described in 'European Economy no 44 (*One market, one money*)'. It targets both real GDP and inflation, with inflation having five times the weight of GDP. This rule will accommodate step changes in the price level, but will not accommodate permanent inflation.

We have added to this model the set of wage equations described above. Some of these equations have forward-looking price terms. The latter have been programmed up in two alternative ways. First they have been implemented with model consistent expectations. This requires the use of a terminal condition for each forward-looking variable and we have implemented a standard constant rate of growth condition on the price level.[8] Our solution method is a variant of forward shooting, and is described in Barrell and Gurney (1991). However, model consistent expectations is a strong set of assumptions for policy analysis purposes. We estimated our equations by Instrumental Variables, and the auxiliary instrumenting regression can be seen as a description of a data consistent expectations generating mechanism that is on average accurate. As an alternative to model consistent expectations, a fixed parameter version of this mechanism has been programmed up, and its predictions are used as the expectations variables.

We have stressed in our empirical work that the degree of forward-looking behaviour in wage setting depends upon the institutional setting in which bargains are struck. We could find no role for forward terms in our analysis of German wage bargaining, and we could find no evidence of any structural change. Hence we are prepared to use our wage equation for that country in all our analysis. We did find a role for forward-looking behaviour in the UK and France, and in those two countries we have implemented a forward-looking wage equation. The Italian case is more interesting. The all pervasive backward indexation associated with the *Scala Mobile* left little room for forward expectations, and our wage equation for Italy contains a strong backward measure for the 1970s. However, during the 1980s there is a clear role for forward-looking wages. We have programmed up two versions of our Italian wage equation.

We wish to evaluate the prospects for monetary union in Europe, and in order to do this we have to be able to evaluate the response to policy changes and to external events. It is not sufficient to presume that individuals will assume that monetary union will work, or that the structure will not change. We therefore undertake our analyses on three different versions of our model. The first version has forward-looking expectations, but these are generated in line with our instrumenting regression. Hence they reflect the past successes and failures of the authorities, and their historical credibility, rather than some assumed level of credibility and success under a monetary union. These results can be compared to those using the same wage equations but with model consistent expectations. Macroeconomic stability in response to shocks may be enhanced by forward-looking behaviour. This is particularly true in a world where the behaviour of the authorities is known to have changed. These two models represent the structural changes that have taken place in the 1980s in Italy and contain the post-1982 Italian wage equation with an expected inflation term. A third model has been constructed that contains the alternative Italian wage equation that represents the backward indexation without a forward-looking expected inflation term.

The analysis of monetary union with forward-looking wages

We have attempted to evaluate the responses of a potential monetary union to a series of external and internal shocks. We have assumed that a full monetary union is in place, and that the European Central Bank targets European-wide inflation and GDP. We examine the effects of a fiscal expansion of 1 per cent of GDP in each of the four major European economies in turn. We have not imposed fiscal stabilising rules because the worst case asymmetric shock is one where one country undertakes a fiscal expansion financed by issuing debt. This is possible in a monetary union, and the Maastricht Treaty attempts to lay down rules for preventing this happening. Fiscal deficit stabilising rules applied one country at a time are reported in Barrell and in't Veld (1992), and they considerably reduce the deviations of inflation and output from base. However, we feel it is useful to analyse the 'worst possible' case here.

We also examine the effects of a sustained fiscal expansion in the US. Once again we assume that the deficit is financed by issuing bonds. This would mean that debt is expanding, and obviously eventually some solvency constraint would have to operate. We have maintained the assumption that solvency constraints do not bite in order that our experiments with internal and external shocks are comparable. Our final shock involves a sustained 50 per cent increase in oil prices. This is an external supply shock, and its effects will differ significantly depending upon the expectations assumptions made and upon the structure of labour markets.[9]

There are a number of ways of evaluating the outturns of our counter factual runs. The utility derived (or lost) along any path depends upon the structure of the policymakers' utility function. We report two different aggregate measures of losses in utility. The first index assumes that deviations from base of output levels and inflation have equal effects. The index is

$$MI = \sum_{t=1}^{n} [(\dot{p} - p_b)^2 + (\dot{y} - y_b)^2]$$

where $\dot{p}$ is inflation, y is output and a subscript b indicates the base value for the variable is used. A higher value of the index implies greater losses in utility. However, as we have stressed elsewhere (Barrell 1992) the desire for monetary union reflects a desire for low inflation, and it is possible that policymakers' utility functions have changed. We also report deviations of the price level from base in order to evaluate the three different regimes.

Internal fiscal shocks
In each case we have increased government spending by 1 per cent of base GDP in 1991. This expansion is maintained, and deficits accumulated. Chart 3.1 plots the effects of these expansions on GDP under the assumption of model consistent expectations in each of our countries.   In the first years of the simulation, the fiscal expansion is partially crowded out and output is between 0.5 and 0.9 per cent above base. In the following years the expansion is crowded out further. However, a sustained fiscal expansion leads to an accumulation of public debt, rising interest payments and fiscal deficits. In later years this debt expansion can offset the crowding out and leads to further deviations of output from base. However, even in a monetary union a continued fiscal expansion of this sort could produce solvency problems, and hence would have to be reversed.[10]

Chart 3.1

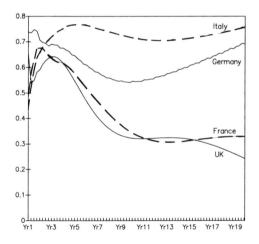

Table 3.3a reports the index and the deviation of the price level from base for a sustained fiscal expansion in Germany. There is no difference between the model versions as we could find no role for forward-looking inflation in our German wage equation, nor evidence of any structural change in wage bargaining. There are, however, slight differences between the outturns for the two models, as data consistent expectations produce slightly higher

Table 3.3 Fiscal expansions (1% of GDP)

	Year 1	Year 2	Year 3	Year 4	Year 5	Year 10
(a) Germany						
(i) Effects on price level (% deviations from base)						
Model I	0.05	0.22	0.38	0.53	0.67	1.01
Model II	0.05	0.22	0.38	0.53	0.67	1.01
(ii) Effects on utility index						
Model I	2.10	3.92	5.62	7.14	8.44	12.55
Model II	2.10	3.91	5.60	7.12	8.40	12.51
(b) France						
(i) Effects on price level (% deviations from base)						
Model I	0.07	0.36	0.83	1.40	1.97	3.56
Model II	0.07	0.39	0.96	1.63	2.28	3.74
(ii) Effects on utility index						
Model I	1.48	3.33	5.05	6.70	8.11	11.35
Model II	1.48	3.33	4.99	6.51	7.71	10.13
(c) Italy						
(i) Effects on price level (% deviations from base)						
Model I	0.06	0.19	0.32	0.46	0.61	1.32
Model II	0.05	0.19	0.31	0.45	0.61	1.32
Model III	0.06	0.18	0.30	0.43	0.58	1.29
(ii) Effects on utility index						
Model I	1.26	3.14	5.25	7.49	9.71	19.02
Model II	1.26	3.14	5.26	7.49	9.71	19.00
Model III	1.26	3.14	5.27	7.53	9.79	19.42
(d) UK						
(i) Effects on price level (% deviations from base)						
Model I	0.06	0.24	0.48	0.74	0.95	1.08
Model II	0.06	0.24	0.48	0.75	0.97	1.08
(ii) Effects on utility index						
Model I	1.44	2.99	4.55	5.82	6.70	8.30
Model II	1.44	3.00	4.56	5.82	6.68	8.26

Utility index $\quad \text{MI} = \Sigma[(\pi - \pi_b)^2 + (y - y_b)^2](x100)$

Model I $\qquad$ With data-consistent expectations generating mechanism
Model II $\qquad$ With model-consistent expectations
Model III $\qquad$ As II, but with pre-1982 wage equation for Italy.

increases in output in France and Italy, and hence in Germany. The fiscal expansion leads to higher inflation and after ten years the price level is 1.0 per cent above base. The index gives equal weight to deviations of output and inflation from base, and is 12 per cent above base after ten years.

The speed and scale of response to an internal fiscal shock differs under the alternative versions of the model for France, because of the differences in the expectation generating process. The first row in table 3.3b reports the outcome using the version of the model which generates the forward-looking inflation term in the wage equation in line with the auxiliary instrumenting regression.[11] The second row relates to the version of the model that uses the same wage equations, but with model consistent expectations. After five years the index has risen more with the data consistent expectation generating mechanism than with model consistent expectations. The price level, however, has risen less rapidly over the first five years. The higher index with data-consistent expectations is due to the greater deviation of output from base. The higher inflation under model consistent expectations leads to more rapid crowding-out of the fiscal expansion. This outweighs the larger deviation of inflation from base and results in a smaller loss in utility. With data consistent expectations a sustained fiscal expansion leads to lower inflation, at least in the first five years, which may be a reflection of higher inertia in the French price system.

After ten years, the price level is 3.56 per cent above base, while under model consistent expectations it is 3.74 per cent above base. The index, which gives equal weight to deviations of inflation and output from base, is slightly higher though, because there is less crowding out in the first years of the simulation. However, after fifteen years the deviation of output from base under model consistent expectations is slightly larger than under data consistent expectations.

Table 3.3c reports the index and price level under a sustained fiscal expansion in Italy. The first two lines compare the differences caused by the expectations generating mechanism. There is hardly any difference between the two model versions. In the first model expectations are based on current and past inflation and capacity utilisation, and under the assumption of monetary union with the authorities targeting European-wide aggregates of GDP and inflation, this proves a close proxy for model consistent expected inflation. After ten years the price level is 1.32 per cent above base, the same in both models. The index is much higher than in the other European countries at 19 per cent above base after ten years. The reason for this is that hardly any crowding out occurs in Italy. Output remains persistently above base in these simulations and is even rising after ten years (see chart 3.1). A sustained fiscal expansion leads to a debt expansion and rising deficits. Of course, in reality this cannot be sustained and must be reversed at some stage.

This simulation merely shows what could happen if financial markets were myopic, which is equivalent to the absence of a solvency constraint from the model.

The comparison with the third model version, which contains the pre-1982 Italian wage equation, is more interesting. This wage equation does not contain an expected inflation term and no unemployment term. Instead of expected inflation it contains a lagged inflation term, reflecting the almost complete indexation that took place under the *Scala Mobile* scheme. The inflation response in this model after a sustained fiscal shock is somewhat slower and less rapid crowding out of the fiscal expansion occurs. Output is further above base and the loss in utility is greater after ten years. This slower inflation response is caused by the absence of an unemployment effect in the wage equation as described in the previous section. In the post-1982 model the fiscal expansion reduces unemployment and this leads to higher wage claims and forms an extra stimulus for inflation.

The responses to a fiscal expansion in the UK are not very different between the two models. The results are reported in table 3.3d. Model consistent expectations lead to a slightly faster inflation response but the differences are negligible. The expectations generating mechanism produces an unbiased estimate of next period's inflation and the first model seems to be a close proxy of the model consistent version. This conclusion holds for all the simulations considered here under the assumptions of monetary union.

External symmetric shocks
Our US fiscal shock is quite expansionary on a global scale. In a world without Ricardian equivalence government debt is net wealth, and as long as a government is solvent it can expand world wealth. The second shock considered here is a permanent 50 per cent rise in the oil price. The effects of oil price shocks are notoriously difficult to model, and responses vary depending upon the reaction of wages to prices. This is particularly important when we compare a backward-looking inflation expectations generating run to model consistent runs.

Tables 3.4 to 3.7 report our indices and deviations of the price level from base. A US fiscal shock is most expansionary in the UK but the price effects are modest. The tables clearly show that the data consistent expectations generating mechanism is a close proxy for model consistent expectations.

The oil price shock is more illustrative. A permanent 50 per cent rise in the oil price leads to a 5-7 per cent rise of the price level after ten years. The output response however, is quite different. For Germany, France and Italy, output falls below base. However, for the UK, GDP rises above base, although the differences from base are small over the first ten years. The significant reductions in output in Germany, France and Italy are reflected in much greater

Table 3.4 Effects of external shocks on Germany

	Year 1	Year 2	Year 3	Year 4	Year 5	Year 10
US fiscal expansion (1% of GDP)						
(i) Effects on price level (deviations from base)						
Model I	0.01	0.05	0.06	0.07	0.08	0.22
Model II	0.01	0.05	0.06	0.07	0.08	0.22
(ii) Effects on utility index						
Model I	0.03	0.04	0.04	0.05	0.06	0.13
Model II	0.03	0.04	0.04	0.05	0.06	0.14
Oil price shock (50% increase)						
(i) Effects on price level (deviations from base)						
Model I	0.89	1.69	2.25	2.73	3.18	5.55
Model II	0.89	1.64	2.24	2.72	3.17	5.56
(ii) Effects on utility index						
Model I	1.09	2.99	5.19	7.22	9.11	17.37
Model II	1.10	3.09	5.43	7.52	9.41	17.59

Notes: see table 3.3.

Table 3.5 Effects of external shocks on France

	Year 1	Year 2	Year 3	Year 4	Year 5	Year 10
US fiscal expansion (1% of GDP)						
(i) Effects on price level (deviations from base)						
Model I	0.02	0.07	0.09	0.07	0.02	0.00
Model II	0.03	0.09	0.11	0.09	0.02	0.01
(ii) Effects on utility index						
Model I	0.00	0.03	0.12	0.23	0.33	0.46
Model II	0.00	0.03	0.13	0.24	0.33	0.47
Oil price shock (50% increase)						
(i) Effects on price level (deviations from base)						
Model I	0.68	1.96	2.90	3.50	3.88	5.27
Model II	0.77	2.30	3.35	3.94	4.24	5.46
(ii) Effects on utility index						
Model I	0.80	2.68	4.80	7.00	9.24	17.53
Model II	0.96	3.23	5.81	8.45	11.11	20.71

Notes: see table 3.3.

Table 3.6 Effects of external shocks on Italy

	Year 1	Year 2	Year 3	Year 4	Year 5	Year 10
US fiscal expansion (1% of GDP)						
(i) Effects on price level (deviations from base)						
Model I	0.04	0.07	0.08	0.10	0.13	0.34
Model II	0.04	0.07	0.08	0.10	0.13	0.34
Model III	0.04	0.07	0.08	0.10	0.13	0.34
(ii) Effects on utility index						
Model I	0.02	0.02	0.02	0.02	0.02	0.07
Model II	0.02	0.02	0.02	0.02	0.02	0.07
Model III	0.02	0.02	0.02	0.02	0.02	0.07
Oil price shock (50% increase)						
(i) Effects on price level (deviations from base)						
Model I	1.10	1.94	2.46	2.97	3.46	5.90
Model II	1.10	1.93	2.45	2.96	3.46	5.97
Model III	1.09	1.93	2.50	3.04	3.57	6.14
(ii) Effects on utility index						
Model I	0.81	1.06	1.34	1.61	1.92	4.23
Model II	0.82	1.07	1.36	1.63	1.92	4.22
Model III	0.80	1.05	1.35	1.65	1.99	5.00

Notes: see table 3.3.

Table 3.7 Effects of external shocks on the UK

	Year 1	Year 2	Year 3	Year 4	Year 5	Year 10
US fiscal expansion (1% of GDP)						
(i) Effects on price level (deviations from base)						
Model I	0.04	0.06	0.07	0.05	0.04	0.17
Model II	0.04	0.06	0.07	0.05	0.03	0.17
(ii) Effects on utility index						
Model I	0.03	0.18	0.44	0.73	1.02	1.93
Model II	0.03	0.14	0.44	0.74	1.02	1.92
Oil price shock (50% increase)						
(i) Effects on price level (deviations from base)						
Model I	0.58	1.33	2.12	2.93	3.71	6.93
Model II	0.58	1.34	2.13	2.94	3.73	7.00
(ii) Effects on utility index						
Model I	0.22	0.43	0.72	0.97	1.17	1.97
Model II	0.22	0.42	0.68	0.91	1.11	1.90

Notes: see table 3.3.

losses in utility than in the UK. For France, the inflationary response is faster under model consistent expectations. The fall in output is also larger, and this is reflected in the higher index. The model that contains the wage equation with backward indexation for Italy produces the most significant set of differences. This model produces higher inflation than the model with expected inflation and unemployment terms in the wage equation.

Conclusion

Our empirical work suggests that some labour markets in Europe may have changed in the 1980s. Italian wages have become more forward-looking, and this may well reflect the increased credibility of the anti-inflationary stance. As Layard, Nickell and Jackman (1991, p.139-40) stress, slower dynamic responses can lead to a more flexible economy. Our simulation results suggest that a European Central Bank operating with a conservative monetary feedback rule can successfully stabilise the rate of inflation in Europe, and the divergences in inflation caused by external shocks will not be particularly great. Our results do not depend upon bargainers believing that the central bank will be successful in combatting inflation. This belief, embedded in model consistent runs, does help speed up the process of adjustment, but our alternative data consistent expectations mechanisms are not associated with significantly higher inflation. Even if bargainers in labour markets do not act as if they believe a monetary union will remain in place it appears we can still rely on the stabilising effects of successful policies.

If we had repeated our experiments without monetary union in place but with similar monetary rules then the results would not have been greatly different. Whitley in Chapter 5 of this book summarises similar simulations under a number of policy regimes, and our conservative feedback rule for interest rates is generally stabilising. However, it is possible that the monetary authorities in, say, the UK and Italy might find it difficult to adopt such a rule unless they are in a monetary union. Experience over the last two decades does indeed suggest that this would be the case. It may be politically easier for them to allow an independent European Central Bank to operate such a feedback rule.

Notes

1 The most commonly cited studies are those by Giavazzi and Giovannini (1988) and Giavazzi and Pagano (1988).

2 This work is summarised in Barrell (1990b) and has been extended in Anderton, Barrell and McHugh (1992).

3 The best known are probably Nickell (1984) and Layard and Nickell (1985).

4 The relation between indexation and inflation dynamics is discussed at length in Barrell (1990b).

5 Further details are given in Anderton and Barrell (1992).

6 If expectations are consistent, and therefore on average correct, then actual one period ahead inflation is a good proxy for expectations. However, following Pagan (1984) we have instrumented this variable. Our relationships including expectations have to be estimated by Instrumental Variables, and we have used the Wald variable deletion test advocated by Godfrey (1988, p.200-203), as our basic stability test.

7 This section can be seen as an extension and elaboration of Barrell (1990a) in that we have undertaken a set of analysis with forward-looking behaviour in the labour market.

8 More formally our terminal condition is that $\log CED_{T+1} - \log CED_T = \log CED_T - \log CED_{T-1}$ where T is the terminal date

9 In each case we have undertaken runs over a twenty year period, and hence our forward-looking long rates and prices reflect this. We report results only for the first five years in any detail.

10 In Barrell and in't Veld (1992) we show how a solvency constraint can be imposed in the model. There the tax rate is used as an instrument to target the deficit, and a sustained shock to government spending as described above leads to an increase in direct taxes and the deficit returns to base within 5-7 years.

11 These contain lagged inflation terms and current and lagged capacity utilisation and can be seen as fixed parameter learning equations.

4

Wage Regimes in a United Europe
A Simulation Study on QUEST

Gustav Adolf Horn and Rudolf Zwiener

Introduction

The process of establishing a European market with a single currency requires numerous adjustments of key economic relations. To level competitive advantages there has to be a tendency of convergence from nationally divergent to uniform European economic behaviour. Wage formation will certainly be a major issue in the course of such a convergence process.

The importance of a uniform European wage formation is fairly obvious. If in one country wages react systematically differently to economic changes compared to others, there will be a systematic divergence of competitiveness. In an economic and monetary union changes in competitiveness can no longer be compensated for by realignments of exchange rates or movements within the ERM bands. If the economies of the Community countries are similar in all other respects, it could be argued that only policy reactions or the convergence of the wage bargaining process could prevent systematic divergencies of competitiveness.

This chapter illustrates the implications of uniform wage behaviour for the competitiveness and the shock absorption capability of the major European economies. The shocks considered are a worldwide oil price shock and a joint European fiscal shock. For the purpose of this exercise the countries are assumed to have fiscal and monetary reaction functions which are the same for all countries. Hence we implicitly assume that there already exists convergence of monetary and fiscal policy in Europe. Thus a difference of wage formation cannot be offset by policy action. The common exchange rate of European currencies against the dollar is determined by uncovered interest parity, allowing for a risk premium related to the current balance position.

The simulations are run on the Quest model under different assumptions about wage formation across the Community.[1] The main change in the assumptions of the model will be that wages are formed in the German way. It is shown that this could have improved the competitiveness of economies like Italy and the UK dramatically. The first sections deal with a short description of the presently-prevailing wage mechanism in Europe as they are modelled in the DIW- QUEST version. Special consideration will be given to their specific nominal and real rigidity properties. In the next section it is assumed that the German wage function would apply for all major European economies. Then the implications for the GNP path and the reactions on shocks are described.

European wage paths

Wage regimes
In the standard version of QUEST, wage behaviour in the European countries is modelled in accordance with a common structural framework. The coefficients are estimated separately for each country. They imply an almost complete indexation for consumption price changes within one year after they have occurred. The short-run labour productivity effect on nominal wages is constrained to be the opposite of that on prices. An error-correction mechanism which ensures that real wages have a long-run elasticity of one with respect to changes in labour productivity is included in the value-added price equation.

These constraints are such that the response of wages to common shocks in the models of the European countries is already similar and cannot be the cause of major differences in GDP and prices. Indeed, the results of simulations on the EC version of QUEST, imposing the average coefficients on all European wage functions, show that such a convergence of wage behaviour could only be responsible for a closing of the GDP gap by 2 per cent at most over the period 1988-93. The main difference between the countries lies in the short-run dynamics of the wage–price system.

The DIW version of QUEST differs from the standard version in that the wage functions have been reestimated with as few constraints on short-run responses as possible. The constancy of real unit labour costs in the long run was not rejected in cointegration tests and the corresponding error correction term was included in the wage rate equations. Differences between countries are again caused by the different effects which unemployment has on wage rate changes, but also by different speeds of indexation and the pass through of labour productivity improvements.

Our analysis will focus on two issues related to wage formation. First, the impact of the modified wage functions on the GNP path in different European countries will be analysed. Second, we will focus on its reaction to shocks. As an example for a supply shock we will take a permanent oil price increase of 50 per cent above the baseline. We will use a coordinated European fiscal expansion of 1 per cent of respective national GNP as a demand shock.[2] The results give some insight on how the alternative wage formation process may affect the competitiveness of the respective economy. Thus we can draw conclusions if some economies may benefit or lose from convergence.

For the following analysis we measure the competitiveness of an economy by its labour unit costs. Given the fact that intermediary unit costs and capital unit costs are more or less the same for all market economies, since goods and capital can easily be traded, labour costs remain the most important cost component which may differ between national economies and thus will indicate a cost advantage. Given a system of constant exchange rates like the EMS or even a joint European currency, exchange-rate movements will no longer affect competitiveness between European economies. Exchange-rate movements affect the competitiveness of the EC countries only with respect to international trade outside the EC.

A German wage regime

By definition, our measure of competitiveness is determined through wage and labour productivity movements. This means a wage settlement is neutral with respect to competitiveness if nominal wages move according to the inflation rate and labour productivity growth, and is the same as in competing economies. Any higher wage contract would lead to a cost disadvantage. Wage bargaining then serves best to maintain competitiveness if there is a close relationship to labour productivity growth. Looking at the estimates of European wage functions (see tables 4.1 and 4.2) one can observe that the German wage function fulfills this criterion better than those of the other countries. The elasticity of wages with respect to productivity growth is relatively high for Germany. Therefore wage bargaining there tends to stabilise competitiveness in periods when productivity growth varies. This leads to the conclusion that the replacement of the original wage functions in this case must enhance competitiveness of the other European economies. This should be particularly so in Italy and Great Britain, where nominal wages respond more rapidly to inflationary surges.

In analysing the shock the reaction of wages to inflationary pressures is also of major importance. Since German wages react more sluggishly, and to a lesser extent to inflation, than most other European countries, we should face, at least in the short run, smaller deviations from baseline if there is a German wage regime in Europe. However both supply and demand shocks influence productivity. An oil price shock will initially diminish productivity. In this case the expected reaction is unambiguous. With German wage functions nominal wage rises caused by inflation should be smaller than with the original wage functions. The sluggish productivity growth impact will then partly offset the inflation effect and wage settlements should be comparatively lower. The situation is slightly more complex in the case of a fiscal shock, which initially raises productivity growth. With German wage functions nominal wages will react

Table 4.1 Results of the cointegration tests

Country	Dependent variables	Explanatory variables	NOB	CRDW	DF	ADF	Model
US	w-p	PR	52	0.30	2.23**	1.39	DF
UK	w-p	C,PR	72	0.39	2.86	2.92*	ADF
Italy	w-p	C,PR	72	0.53	3.36*	1.22	DF
France	w	WED, PR	72	0.22	3.05*	2.12	DF
Germany	w-p	PR	52	0.42	2.06*	3.00*	ADF

NOB - number of observations
WED - tax wedge
w - wage rate per employee (nominal)
p - consumer expenditure deflator
C - constant; PR - labour productivity
CRDW - Durbin-Watson test for stationarity
DF - Dickey-Fuller test
ADF - augmented Dickey-Fuller test
Model - choice of DF or ADF
All variables in logs
* significant at 10 per cent level
** significant at 5 per cent level

less to the induced inflation but more to the productivity rise. Hence it is not clear *a priori* whether the wage reaction to a fiscal shock will be as strong with German wages as it would be with the original wage function.

In the DIW version of QUEST the reactions of wages to unemployment are quite similar across European countries expect for France. There we found a very small elasticity, so that French nominal wages, *ceteris paribus*, will increase more for the oil-price shock and less for the fiscal shock under German wage conditions.

These considerations are in line with theoretical approaches which conclude that nominal wage rigidity, that is, a sluggish reaction to inflation as it is shown by German wage settlements, is of advantage in absorbing supply shocks. Firms facing higher production costs due to higher import prices then face relatively lower costs if nominal wages react sluggishly.

In the long run the equations imply that there are quite uniform wage movements in Europe. Our cointegration test (reported in table 4.1), using an error

Table 4.2 Estimation results
Dependent variable: nominal wage rate per employee (growth rate), 1975I-1987IV

Country	C	$\hat{W}(t\text{-}j)$	$\hat{P}(t\text{-}j)$	U	$\hat{PR}$	EC	R	DW
US	1.36	-	-	-0.03	0.16	-0.34	0.60	1.90
	(8.0)			(-7.7)	(2.3)	(-7.7)		
UK	-0.73	0.43	0.28	-0.01	-	-0.15	0.53	1.84
	(-2.2)	(-3.4)	(1.3)	(-1.8)		(-2.3)		
Italy	-0.70	-	0.67	-0.02	-	-0.15	0.54	2.28
	(-2.0)		(4.0)	(-2.2)		(-2.2)		
France	-	-	0.76	-0.003	-	-0.01	0.97	1.56
			(9.5)	(-4.3)		(-6.5)		
Germany	-0.94	-	0.47*	-0.02	0.33	-0.19	0.58	2.16
	(-2.3)			(-2.6)	(2.4)	(-2.4)		

$\hat{}$ - quarterly growth rates
C - constant
W - nominal wage rate per employee
P - consumer price level
PR - labour productivity
U - unemployment rate
EC - error correction term as specified in table 4.1
* Sum of contemporaneous and lagged coefficients

correction approach which includes (except for France) wages, prices and labour productivity could not be rejected. Thus long-run adjustments are already almost the same for all European economies. Nominal wages have a long-run elasticity of one for both price and productivity movements. Hence differences resulting from the changes of the wage function should be of short-term nature only.

The simulation design
To simulate the macroeconomic effects of a modified wage bargaining process, several additional assumptions have to be imposed. In an economically more united Europe national economies must reach agreements on the way monetary and fiscal policy take place. Thus we have incorporated some rules into the model which reflect some sort of economic policy convergence.

One major issue concerns the effects on the exchange rate mechanism. The QUEST model in its original version does not incorporate an endogenously determined exchange rate mechanism. Assuming a currency union among European countries does mean that there is no exchange-rate adjustment between European countries any longer. But since the convergence of the bargaining process affects the competitiveness of Europe with respect to the rest of the world this must be mirrored by adjustments of a European exchange rate in relation to all other currencies. Thus it is necessary to establish an appropriate mechanism.

We use the assumptions outlined by Whitley in this volume. Our exchange-rate regime is equivalent to a currency union but not a monetary union. The dollar-D-Mark rate is determined by the following rule for quarterly models:

$$e_t = e^e_{t+1} + ((r-r^b) - (r^*-r^{*b})) + g[(CB/GDP) - (CB^b/GDP^b)], \qquad (4.1)$$

where e denotes the exchange rate, e^e the expected exchange rates, r are short-term interest rates, CB is the current balance where b are the baseline values, and $*$ denotes US rates. We take 0.1 as value for g. Hence the actual exchange rate is determined by the expected rate for the next period, the deviation of the interest-rate differential between Europe and the US from baseline and a risk premium. The latter is defined as the percentage point deviation of current balance to GDP from baseline. Equation (4.1) is basically an uncovered interest-rate parity (UIP) path.

The determination of the expected exchange rates is demanding. To avoid the enormous informational as well as computational input which is required by model-consistent forward-looking expectations, we have constrained our analysis to a somewhat less stringent expectation path. This may be even more realistic than the alternative approach. We used a two-stage process to extract an expectational path which is based on some model reactions. Substituting e^e_{t+1} in (4.1) one gets :

$$e_0 = e_T + \sum_{t=0}^{T-1} [((r-r^b) - (r^*- r^{*b})) + g(CB/GDP - CB^b/GDP^b)_t] \qquad (4.2)$$

The initial jump which is due to forward-looking expectations for the exchange rate then depends on the cumulative interest-rate differential and the cumulative risk premium over the simulation period. As a first step we calculate (4.2) by running a simulation with exchange rates held fixed. The result is then plugged into the model and the simulation is run again, this time with exchange rates following the UIP path outlined in (4.1). The procedure described above does not lead to model-consistent expectations since there are no adjustments during the simulation period. However, at the beginning of the simulation the expectations on profitability changes of foreign financial assets are perfectly compatible with model reactions. The major difference to model consistent expectations is that actual reactions do not change during the simulation period.

In a one-market Europe with unlimited capital mobility, interest rates must converge. Thus we have assumed that interest rates all over Europe are basically equal to the German interest rates. They only differ by a risk premium which is computed as in (4.1). This reflects potential perceptions of financial investors that assets of firms with a low performance on world markets may be somewhat riskier than others.

In such a setting the determination of German interest rates is of major importance. The above framework amounts to the assumption that the Bundesbank will be the leading force for the determination of money market conditions. As a monetary reaction function the following rule has been selected:[3]

$$(r - r^b)_t = 0.25 [100 (1.5 (P - P^b) + 0.4 (\log y - \log y^b)]$$
$$+ 0.75 (r - r^b)_{t-1} , \qquad (4.3)$$

where P is the inflation rate and y nominal GNP. Equation (4.3) constitutes an anti-inflationary monetary policy. In order to get relative smooth effects we imposed a damping factor of 0.25.

The final convergence requirement refers to fiscal policy. It seems realistic to assume that despite the unification process there will still be some independence left for future national governments. Therefore we impose a spending rule which leaves room for each government to practise a nationally oriented stabilisation policy.

$$(G - G^b) / yr^b = -0.2 (\log yr - \log yr^b), \qquad (4.4)$$

where G is real non-wage government spending and yr real GNP. The other components of government spending follow the rules as set in the original model version.

We have run for each wage regime two sets of baseline simulations using the framework of rules outlined above. In the first set wage equations in each country remain as originally specified. In the second set they are replaced by the German wage equation. The differences between base simulations are used to assess the impact of different wage functions on competitiveness. After that an oil price shock and a fiscal shock were imposed and the difference is used to analyse the change in shock absorption behaviour induced by a convergence of wage bargaining processes in a more closely related European Community.

Convergence to a German wage function

Baseline simulation in Europe

As a first approach a baseline simulation is run which shows economic developments in the European countries resulting from the same type of wage adjustment as in Germany. To examine this question we replaced the wage equations in the models of France, UK and Italy by the German wage equation, using the estimated German coefficients. Although this is a very artificial procedure, all models could be simulated and solved.

Our *a priori* hypothesis is that Italy and Great Britain would show much lower wage increases using the German equation, whereas for France we expect lower wage increases than under the (original) wage equation. The results conform with our expectations. After five years nominal wages in Italy are 44 per cent below their original baseline level using the German wage equation, in the UK they are 29 per cent lower and in France the difference is very small. Differences in real compensation per employee are much smaller: -9 per cent for Italy and -5 per cent for the United Kingdom after five years. This shows that a major disinflation process would be induced by a German wage bargaining process and that following German wage patterns makes it easier to avoid a wage–price spiral. At the same time, employment rises in both countries: 3.8 per cent for Italy and 2.3 per cent for the United Kingdom after five years.

The lower wage and price increases in Italy and the United Kingdom imply an important impact on the international competitiveness of these countries. Using constant exchange rates, Italy's export prices are 22 per cent below the baseline level after five years, and the United Kingdom's 20 per cent. The level of real exports of goods and services is consequently 19 per cent (Italy) and 21 per cent (United Kingdom) higher than otherwise (chart 4.2). This dominates GNP development in both countries. Chart 4.1 shows a steady gain in real production for Italy and the United Kingdom.

Using constant exchange rates inside Europe and a flexible exchange rate mechanism for countries outside the EMS does not change these results in principle. The EMS currencies devalue mainly because of lower interest rates in Europe as a consequence of lower inflation rates. Growth gains for Italy and the United Kingdom are lower in the long run, since higher import prices to some extent reinflate the economy.

However, the simulation results suggest that growth rates in Germany would be lower if the other European countries had the same (German) wage behaviour, for then Germany itself would not achieve such a strong level of competitiveness as under disparate wage behaviour and production levels are then mainly due to a lower trade surplus. This result indicates that the German wage bargaining process with its relatively close links to productivity growth is one reason for Germany's competitive advantages on foreign markets. Germany's position with respect to intra-EC trade is partially strengthened by its wage bargaining process. If the wage function converges in the EC countries, Germany would lose this advantage and consequently show lower growth rates. But the results are not very dramatic. During a five-year period Germany's average growth rate would be just 0.2 per cent lower on average. On the other hand Italy and the United Kingdom would improve their average growth rates by 1.5 per cent and 0.9 per cent, while for France growth is not influenced in the long run. This overall growth in Europe would have been higher if wages had followed the German adjustment mechanism because Europe as a whole improves its competitiveness towards the rest of the world by the modified wage bargaining process. In addition, the devaluation of the EC currency reinforces the expansive export push. Thus lower inflation rates induce additional indirect improvements via lower interest rates.

Because imports are influenced by both competitiveness and internal growth the results differ from country to country. For the United Kingdom the gain in competitiveness dominates the growth effects, so real imports drop. For Germany both factors (lower growth and lower competitiveness) offset each other. For France (which has similar growth and a loss of competitiveness) real imports rise. Italy differs from the United Kingdom during the first years. Then growth effects dominate the competitiveness effects and real imports rise. During the last years of the simulation period the competitiveness effect prevails (chart 4.3).

The simulation results stress the point that having different wage formation processes in the European countries without the possibility of an exchange-rate realignment creates differences in competitiveness between countries. Politicians in Europe do not like to realign exchange rates in the EMS very often. But the option is always there and there have been some realignments. Introducing a common currency for all these countries abolishes exchange-rate adjustments. If wage behaviour in Europe does not converge but remains unchanged, Germany will benefit and other countries except France will lose, facing relatively higher inflation and lower production. Since the outcome clearly is not a sustainable one, changes of wage formation are likely to occur. The overall net effects on growth and employment in Europe then would be adverse according to the simulation results.

Oil price shock

The oil price shock was chosen so that the price of oil was increased by 50 per cent in the first year of the simulation and afterwards kept above baseline by the same amount. Charts 4.4–4.7 compare the simulation results as a deviation from base with flexible exchange rates both with the original wage equations in the

European models and with a base where the German wage equation is used. The oil price shock can be considered as an example of a supply shock. Our analysis shows how the degree of shock absorption varies with modified wage equations.[4]

The reaction of monetary policy in such a setting is very important. We assumed that real long-term interest rates are exogenous, but nominal short-term interest rates are influenced by inflation and nominal GNP growth in Germany. This is a simple type of reaction function for the German Bundesbank. The simulation results show that wage reactions to the import price shock are much lower using the German wage equation in other European countries (charts 4.4 and 4.5), hence inflation and real compensation per employee in European countries are also lower. At first glance nothing else really seems to change. Production in the UK as an oil exporting country is not as much affected as production in other countries. France, Germany and Italy show the same loss in real GNP (slightly higher in Italy). There is a slightly lower GNP growth in Europe using the German wage equation. The results have to be interpreted very carefully because the base differs significantly between the two sets of simulations with the consumers' expenditure deflator much lower with the German wage function, and hence the impact of a nominal oil price shock must be greater. If the outcome with respect to GNP nevertheless remains more or less the same, one may conclude that growth losses are in fact diminished with the changed wage function. With the 'German' wage adjustment process in Europe, Germany itself loses competitiveness against its neighbour countries. Therefore German exports are lower. Consequently the risk premium for Germany increases, leading to comparatively higher interest rates. Using the flexible exchange rate mechanism therefore leads to an appreciation of the EMU currencies compared with a situation when original wage functions are used. In the end, all European economies face a small growth loss due to the higher interest rates.

Fiscal shock

We also consider the effects of a permanent fiscal shock in all European countries. Such a fiscal shock increases real GNP, employment, wages, prices and interest rates as expected. Using the German wage equation in the other European countries leads to higher wage increases if exchange rates are constant, because of the relatively high productivity reaction. Thus the productivity effect mentioned in the previous section dominates the more sluggish price effect. Therefore foreign currency markets expect an even higher appreciation of the European currencies leading to a higher initial jump in the exchange rate.

The simulation results do not yield such a clear picture under a flexible exchange rate system. The strong appreciation of the EMU currencies has a dampening effect on wages. Only French wage development is still very much above that path which would have been followed using the original wage equation. In Italy, UK and Germany wage increases are now below the path using the original country wage equations (charts 4.8 and 4.9). The main reason lies with the exchange-rate adjustments. Chart 4.12 shows the impacts of the shock on exchange rates. In the case of the oil price shock the joint exchange rate of the European countries does not move much against the US dollar. The United States and Europe are both influenced by an oil price shock in a similar way, and hence there is no reason for large variations of their bilateral exchange rates. In case of a common fiscal shock in Europe things are different. The depreciation of the US dollar is the consequence of higher nominal interest rates in Europe, whereas the US interest rate stays more or less on the baseline.

The effects of the fiscal shock on growth are small and the magnitude and time pattern of the multipliers for the European countries are much the same. Using the German wage equation all over Europe does change the peak from the first year of the shock to the second and third year. But the long-run values are not different. Thus in the case of a fiscal shock the wage equations are not really of importance.

A European wage regime

Since the inflation rates in the countries participating in the exchange rate mechanism of the European Monetary System have converged so remarkably and wage setting is seen as the main determinant of inflation, it is sometimes assumed that the wage formation process itself must have become very similar across Europe. In particular, it is argued that the parameters of the wage equations should adhere more to the 'German standard'.

The empirical evidence for such a change in behaviour is rather thin, if not contrary to the assertion. Certainly after the German unification, wage changes in West Germany seem to be more in line with those generated by an average of European wage functions than with those generated by the German wage function over the period up to 1987. The argument that changes in wages have been responsible for the convergence of inflation rates is also not very convincing. Artis and Nachane (1990) found no evidence that wages in Germany and its EMS partners were cointegrated before 1987. At the same time, their tests did confirm the cointegration of inflation rates and suggested that German inflation rates have been a determinant of inflation rates in the other countries, except for the UK. The shift towards counter-inflationary policies and the credibility which participation in the ERM has lent to the outcome of such policies in terms of expectations seems to have contributed more to the convergence of inflation rates than changes in wage bargaining behaviour.

Another point is whether convergence to German behaviour would actually be beneficial for the Community. The most competitive country under EMU does not necessarily have to be the same as the country that proved to be most competitive under flexible exchange rates. In the *One Market, One Money* (EC Commission, 1990) report it was shown that the costs of the loss of the exchange-rate instrument are larger, the slower the indexation of wages and the less flexible the response to labour market disequilibrium. With EMU the Community countries lose the ability to adjust the bilateral exchange rates against other EC currencies and have a common exchange rate against other currencies. The common exchange rate can still be used to cushion the effect of shocks on the Community, but not to compensate for the divergencies between countries. This loss will be greater for a country with slow indexation such as Germany, although it may be compensated by a more flexible response to changes in labour productivity and unemployment. So, it not only matters whether wages converge, but also to which form of wage bargaining they converge.

As long as the economic responses to a shock in the Community countries are not similar, it may also be important whether monetary policy reacts mainly to German variables, as in the current EMS, or to some Community average. All the wage functions used here imply some trade-off between growth and inflation. Monetary policy reacts to a desired shift of this trade-off. Since even in the standard version of the model the unemployment effects on wages differ between countries, it is interesting to investigate whether reacting to Community variables would give results which are different from reacting to German variables. Simulations on the EC version of QUEST suggest that this is hardly the case. In describing the results of the simulations it is helpful to concentrate on the exchange-rate response. The rise in oil prices as a supply-side shock calls for a small depreciation in the DIW version and for an even smaller appreciation in the EC version. The initial appreciation becomes almost 2 per cent when monetary policy reacts to Community averages, involving the UK as an oil producer. For the fiscal shock which applies more symmetrically to all European countries, the difference in the exchange response is much smaller. In the EC version, reacting to Community averages only calls for a quarter point more appreciation than the 2.75 per cent triggered within a German-dominated EMU.

Conclusions

In future, united Europe wage adjustments will become more important. With the aim of transforming the EMS into a single currency zone for the common market, exchange-rate adjustments are no longer feasible. We have simulated with a common flexible exchange rate against all other currencies, whereas inside Europe the exchange rates are fixed. There is also dominant German monetary policy which affects short-term interest rates all over Europe. This simulated world is not so far away from what is going on in reality. In such a situation the type of wage adjustments in the European countries is of major importance for their competitiveness. If wage adjustments remain as they are, some countries will lose employment in a united Europe. The overall net effect for Europe is positive with a German-type wage adjustment type. The 'advantage' of the German wage adjustment process lies in its nominal rigidity and particularly its relatively strong reaction on productivity changes. These results include an important message for a future European wage process. It should react flexibly to changes in competitiveness. It is particularly in that respect that the German wage formation process has advantages relative to that of other European countries.

One has to bear in mind, however, that the German wage function has changed after unification with East Germany, at least temporarily. Due to the rapid adjustments agreed within Germany, wage movements are more loosely related to productivity than previously. This may cause some harm to Germany's competitive advantages. This is a road to convergence to European behaviour, but not the intended one.

Notes

1 The simulations for this project have been run on the QUEST model, which has been made available to the DIW by the Commission of the European Communities. Any errors, ommissions or misunderstandings are the responsibility of the authors. We thank Andries Brandsmaa for his very helpful comments and his simulations with the EC version of Quest.

2 We increased real non-wage government consumption spending by 1 per cent of GNP. The rest of government spending is then determined endogenously.

3 Real long-term interest rates have been kept to their original baseline. The model failed to converge when we did not make this assumption.

4 More detailed tables are available from the authors.

Chart 4.1 German wages in Europe: GNP deviation from base

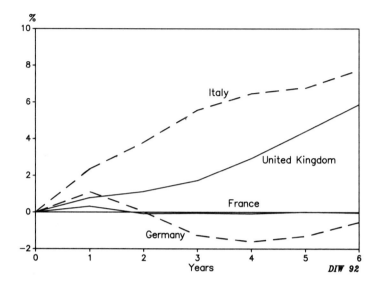

Chart 4.2 German wages in Europe: real exports deviation from base

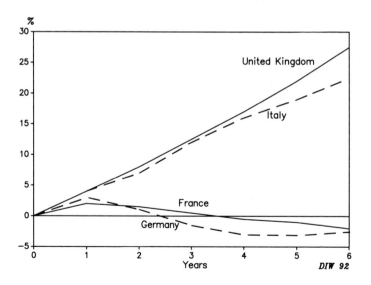

Chart 4.3 German wages in Europe: real imports deviation from base

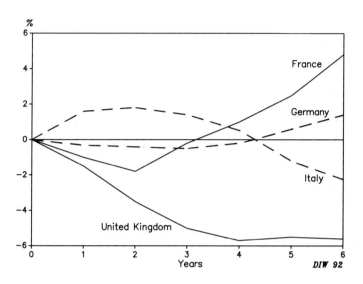

Chart 4.4 Oil price shock: compensation per employee – deviation from base (flexible exchange rate)

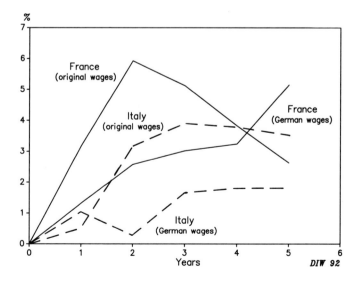

Chart 4.5 Oil price shock: compensation per employee – deviation from base (flexible exchange rate)

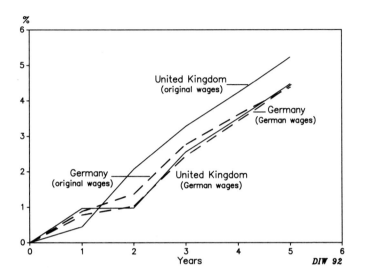

Chart 4.6 Oil price shock: GNP deviation from base – flexible exchange rate

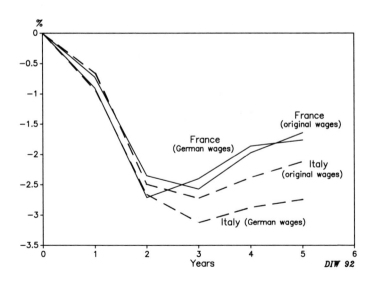

Chart 4.7 Oil price shock: GNP deviation from base – flexible exchange rate

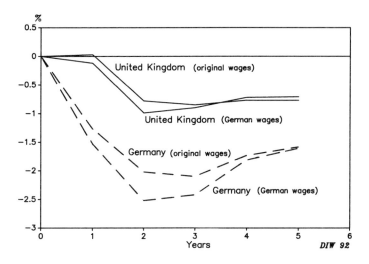

Chart 4.8 Fiscal shock: compensation per employee – deviation from base (flexible exchange rate)

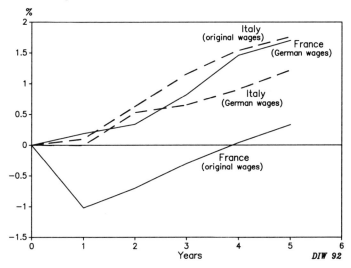

Chart 4.9 Fiscal shock: compensation per employee – deviation from base (flexible exchange rate)

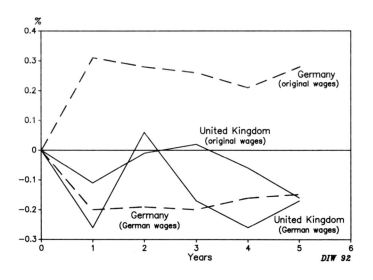

Chart 4.10 Fiscal shock: GNP deviation from base – flexible exchange rate

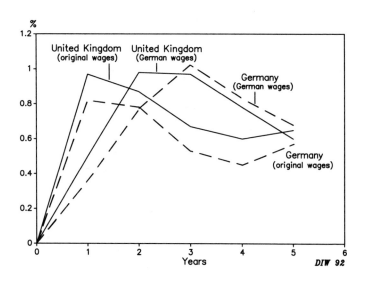

Chart 4.11 Fiscal shock: GNP deviation from base – flexible exchange rate

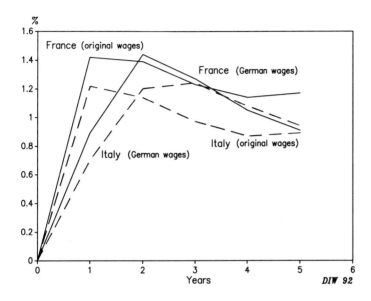

Chart 4.12 Exchange rate (US/$ rate): deviation from base

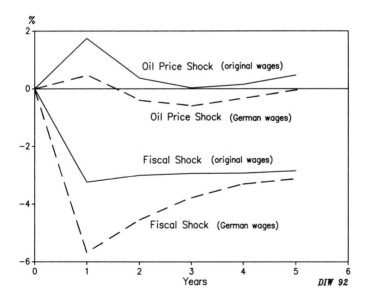

5

Aspects of Monetary Union – Model-based Simulation Results

John D. Whitley

Introduction

An earlier comparative paper on the multicountry models included in the modelling network financed by SPES dealt with comparative diagnostic simulations (Whitley, 1992). The obvious next step is to use the multicountry models to explore various alternative policy options facing Europe. The modelling groups involved in the earlier exercise agreed to use their models to simulate EMS and EMU-style regimes and explore the implications of these regimes for output, employment and inflation in the face of an internal fiscal shock (increased government spending) and an external shock (higher world oil prices). Some benchmark is obviously necessary in order to compare the EMS and EMU regimes so that policy reactions under an 'independent' policy or floating exchange-rate regime have to be specified. The method of analysis used is deterministic simulation rather than the stochastic approach used with MULTIMOD in the *One Market, One Money* report (EC, 1990) and Minford in this volume, and discussed by Masson, also in this volume. Thus the analysis is limited here to discussion of specific single shocks and cannot therefore be used to judge the overall robustness of a policy regime which examines the effects of random disturbances affecting all variables simultaneously. This was beyond the scope of our resources. Nor does the study attempt to derive optimal rules for the authorities under these regimes, as do for example, Currie and Wren-Lewis (1990). The policy rules chosen are simply stylised representations of the possible setting of policy which ignore issues of credibility, reputation and so on. The main emphasis is on evidence of the loss of the exchange-rate instrument in the EMS and EMU regimes and in the transmission effects of shocks across the European economies, using asymmetric and symmetric deterministic shocks.

*Valuable comments and suggestions have been made by Peter Richardson, Geoff Meen, Gustav Horn and by participants at the Warwick Conference. Discussions with Ray Barrell have been particularly illuminating. However all errors and omissions of interpretation are the property of the author.

A major objection to the use of macroeconometric models to simulate alternative policy regimes is that they may not correctly take into account economic agents' changed perception of the policy rules and hence their resultant behaviour. This problem of the Lucas critique (Lucas, 1976) can be tackled by distinguishing between the expectations formation of economic agents and their underlying structural behaviour. Two key areas where forward expectations may be particularly relevant are in financial and foreign exchange markets and in labour and goods markets, where expectations of future inflation impacts on current wage and price setting. Although there is some evidence of amended wage and price behaviour historically under EMS (Anderton *et al.*, Chapter 3) the models do not take account of any revision to wage and price behaviour as a result of the EMS or EMU policy regimes. An attempt is made to incorporate exchange-rate expectations however.

The earlier paper on diagnostic simulations was obliged to assume fixed nominal exchange rates throughout as not all the models contained exchangerate equations. Since the exchange rate is a key element in the comparison of EMS- and EMU-style policy regimes with a free float it is necessary to incorporate endogenous exchange-rate behaviour in the policy-related simulations. In order to achieve maximum comparability it was decided to adopt a common modified UIP approach to exchange-rate determination. This includes an explicit role for forward-looking expectations. However the implementation of forward-looking exchange-rate behaviour in large-scale macroeconometric models is by no means a straightforward process. Computational problems were likely to delay the comparative programme and previous experience has shown that the solution of large-scale models with an exchange-rate equation which contains a unit root requires certain well-behaved responses from the remainder of the model in order to modify this root in full-model solutions (Fisher *et al.*, 1990). In practice the necessary stock or flow equilibrium conditions may not be satisfied by the model and hence a solution under forward consistent expectations may not be possible; for example, a bond financed fiscal expansion may lead to a debt explosion. Hence we adopt a treatment of the exchange rate which approximates the behaviour of the UIP model without actually needing to solve the model in a forward-looking mode (although as we note below this requires some important simplifying assumptions).

Experience has shown that comparative model exercises are best carried out by an independent third party. This tends to avoid different interpretations which may occur if experiments are conducted by the modellers themselves, even if they have all agreed on a common approach. Furthermore it is often the case that a first examination of the results reveals flaws in the simulation design which are relatively easy to rectify if the simulations are compared by the independent party but difficult to organise if repeated simulation rounds by the individual models are to occur. The SPES programme has not provided the resources to operate along the best-choice option of the independent party (which *inter alia* requires the models to be easily accessed by the third party). This has inevitably meant that there have been differences in interpretation of the 'rules' for the simulations between the modelling groups, but of greater importance is the fact that with hindsight the simulation design might have been altered in some respects.

The first section of this chapter sets out the agreed approach and raises issues of simulation design. It is followed by a consideration of the empirical results and the final section draws some conclusions.

The models included in the SPES-financed comparative programme are those of the EC's model (QUEST) as operated by the Deutsches Institut für Wirtschaftsforschung (DIW); the model developed by the National Institute of Economic and Social Research and jointly maintained with the London Business School (NiGEM); the model used by OFCE/CEPII (MIMOSA); the Oxford Economic Forecasting model (OEF) and OECD's Interlink model. All, with the exception of MIMOSA, were able to complete the comparative policy exercises. Although we attempt to discuss differences between models in the various policy scenarios, in the light of differences in their properties previously noted in the diagnostic simulation exercise, it should be noted that some of the models have been respecified in various ways between the two comparative exercises, hence exact comparison is not possible.

Simulation results are presented for a six-year horizon, reflecting the longest common horizon for the major four European economies. This simulation horizon is rather short for models with forward-looking expectations, but a compromise had to be adopted to suit all the modellers involved in the network.

Simulation design

The basic design of the rules for domestic fiscal and monetary policy under the various regimes is similar to that used in the *One Market, One Money* report with MULTIMOD. Each G7 country sets monetary policy in the independent policy regime (freely floating exchange rate) in line with an interest-rate reaction function which attributes a relatively large weight to inflation. Fiscal policy is a simple countercyclical rule for government spending. Common versions of these reaction functions are applied to each model with parameters also constant across the different countries within each model. Exchange rates are determined by a common exchange-rate equation which is based on the UIP approach modified by a risk premium.

Under EMS the exchange rates of the major four European economies are linked to one another and the overall monetary policy is set by Germany (using the same interest-rate reaction as under independent policy). The German exchange rate continues to float against the non-EMS currencies. Monetary policy in the other three European economies is governed by the need to maintain parity with the D-Mark. Full credibility is assumed and there is no possibility of realignment. This form of EMS is very similar to the EMU regime except for the role of the risk premium on exchange rates and comparison of EMS and EMU can be considered as equivalent to a comparison of an asymmetric and symmetric EMU.

Under EMU all countries are assumed to adopt the same policy reaction for the nominal short-term interest rate, and it is assumed that the reaction depends upon the weighted average of deviations from base of inflation and output in Europe as a whole rather than on individual country outcomes. This corresponds to an 'indifferent' EMU in the terminology of Currie (1992b) where Germany pays attention to broader European macroeconomic outcomes. We examine two alternative fiscal policy rules under EMU. The first is the standard countercyclical fiscal rule and the second is a rule which adjusts government spending in response to changes in the budget deficit (in order to reflect the emphasis on the public sector deficit in the Maastricht agreement). The first rule therefore implies an absence of policy coordination within EMU whereas the latter is more consistent with a coordinated response.

These alternative regimes are compared for two shocks. First we examine the impact of an increase in government expenditure of 1 per cent of GNP (in practice this is an *ex ante* adjustment to the fiscal policy rule). Second we look at the response to a world oil price shock of 50 per cent (approximately $10 per barrel).

We now describe the fiscal, monetary and exchange-rate rules in more detail.

Fiscal policy
The rule is $(G-G^b)/y^b = 0.2\ [(y^b-y)/y^b] + A$ where G is general government expenditure; y is GNP and the superscript b refers to base solution values. The variable A reflects the *ex ante* shock to fiscal policy. In practice we find that the *ex post* change in government spending is very similar to the *ex ante* change under the fiscal policy rule, hence the countercyclical response is weak. A larger endogenous reaction occurs under the oil price shock but this does not prevent substantial changes in the general government fiscal balance from occurring.

Under EMU we also examine a general expenditure rule which adjusts expenditure to shift the budget deficit towards its base value in the reaction term, using an integral control term.

$$(G - G^b)\,/\,y^b = \beta_i[\{1\,/\,12 \sum_{j=0}^{11}(GBR_i, t - j)\} - 3.0\,GDR_{i,t-j}]$$

where *GBR* is the ratio of the government deficit to GDP, *GDR* is the ratio of government debt to GDP and β_i are scaling factors which vary across countries to reflect the size of government spending and the units in which GDP is measured. The values chosen for β_i are as follows: Germany, 1.0; France, 1.6; Italy, 227.0; UK, 135.0. The parameter on government debt was chosen empirically to bring about the necessary deficit correction by the end of the simulation period.

Monetary policy

For countries in a floating rate regime, monetary policy is often assumed to target a nominal aggregate. Standard approaches are either money supply targeting or nominal income targets. We follow the approach used in the EC exercise which derives an interest-rate reaction function in terms of inflation and output deviations using parameter estimates from money demand functions in MULTIMOD. We have chosen to adopt this rule in order to ensure comparability. It differs from a nominal income rule by using an inflation target which has a higher weight than output. Thus

$$(r - r^b) = \alpha[100(2(\pi - \pi^b) + 0.4(\log y - \log y^b))] + (1 - \alpha)[r - r^b]_{t-1}$$

where *r* is the nominal interest rate, π the inflation rate (defined in annual terms) and *q* represents domestic output whilst a '*b*' subscript denotes the base value of the variable.

The equation includes a partial adjustment mechanism, allowing inertia in interest-rate responses in order to avoid potentially excessive instrument instability. The parameter α is a damping factor and is chosen so as to ensure that mean lags are eqivalent across the different periodicities of the model (Interlink is a semi-annual model, MIMOSA uses annual data, whilst the others are based on quarterly data). The equation implies a strong response of interest rates to inflation. In the long run a rise of 1 percentage point in inflation generates a 2 percentage point increase in nominal short-term interest rates. This interest-rate rule applies to all G7 economies under independent policy and to Germany and non-EMS countries under the EMS regime. Under EMU the same form of reaction function is assumed for the major four European economies but with the difference that the output and inflation variables are now weighted averages of the individual country outcomes, using GNP weights. Thus

$$(r - r^b)_i = \alpha\{100[2(\overline{\pi} - \overline{\pi}^b) + 0.4(\log \overline{y} - \log \overline{y}^b)]\} + (1 - \alpha)(r - r^b)_{i-1}$$

where $\overline{\pi} = \sum_{i=1}^{4} w_i \pi_i$ and $\overline{y} = \sum_{i=1}^{4} w_i y_i$, with *i* representing individual country outcomes and w_i GNP weights.

Exchange rate

The exchange-rate rule assumed for each country and each model is a modified UIP equation:

$$e_t = e_{t+1}^e + (r - r^*)_t + \gamma\ CB / GDP_t$$

where e refers to exchange-rate expectations, $r\text{-}r^*$ to the nominal interest rate differential and CB/GDP is the ratio of the current balance to GDP (representing the risk premium). The parameter γ is imposed at 0.1. This risk premium is appropriate in a flow portfolio model of the exchange rate. Not all of the models possessed a capital account, and hence it was not possible to use a stock portfolio approach in our comparison.

This form of equation is used to govern the exchange-rate reaction under independent policy and under EMS for Germany. Under EMS we assume no realignment for the other major four European economies so that interest rates are dependent on the German rate subject to the risk premium and exchange rates are linked to the D-Mark. We invert our exchange-rate equation in order to determine interest rates (see Barrell, 1990a, for a justification):

$$r_i = r_g - \gamma CB / GDP$$

where r_i are the nominal interest rates for the UK, France and Italy and r_g is the short rate for Germany. Thus the approach differs from that of *One Market, One Money* where the interest-rate reaction function under EMS is modified to give a high weight to exchange-rate changes and where there is some allowance for the possibility of realignment. Under EMS for Germany and under EMU for all countries the bilateral dollar exchange rate can fluctuate and consequently the *effective* exchange rate can also change.

The exchange-rate equation is not used directly in the models because of the difficulties in implementing forward-consistent expectations within the time scale possible for the comparative project. Instead we use the properties of the UIP approach to approximate the exchange-rate jump and its subsequent path.

The exchange-rate equation implies, substituting for e_{t+1}^e, (see Barrell and Gurney, 1990),

$$e_0 = e_\tau + \sum_{t=0}^{\tau}(r - r^*)_t + \sum_{t=0}^{\tau}\gamma A_t$$

where e_0 is the exchange rate in the first period and e_τ is the value at the terminal date. We implicitly assume that e_τ is the value in the base solution.

The initial jump in the exchange rate then depends on the cumulative interest differential and the cumulative risk premium and this can be calculated from a simulation where the exchange rate is held fixed. The exchange rate in subsequent periods follows the UIP path and is determined endogenously using the rule:

$$e_i' = e_{i-1} - (r - r^*)_i - \gamma A_i$$

for $e_i \dots e_n$. This exchange-rate path may then generate a different outcome for inflation and hence interest rates from the original path but we do not iterate to obtain a consistent UIP path of interest rates and exchange rates.

The form of risk premium in the exchange-rate equation is consistent with a terminal condition in the stock of net assets (as long as the shock does not change the equilibrium stock of net overseas assets). In forward-looking models the terminal condition is an approximation to the equilibrium path — the main problem lies in knowing what the appropriate terminal condition should be. In this instance we expect the equilibrium to be associated with a given stock of net assets. The equation should ensure a return to balance of the current account except insofar as this is not modified by a change in the interest-rate differential. Under a demand shock we expect the current account to weaken and interest rates to rise. In principle one might expect inflation and output to return to their base level following a demand shock in which case the interest-rate changes would be temporary. In this event the exchange rate would be dominated in the long run by asset equilibrium. However in practice the models do not ensure that the interest rate returns to base by the end of the simulation period and the exchange-rate path is dominated by changes in interest differentials rather than by current balance and asset stock considerations. Hence the real exchange rate tends to appreciate following a demand shock and there is no tendency for the current balance to be corrected; in principle wealth effects could serve this purpose but these feedbacks are weak and slow-acting in practice. In model solutions over a finite period the problems would be avoided by the use of a terminal condition (possibly involving the current balance itself). The lack of a terminal condition is a defect in our study. It is also a problem that the initial nominal exchange-rate jump in a UIP model depends in part on the length of period for which interest rates are above base. We have used a common six-year solution period in order to standardise across the models although this is probably an unrealistically short horizon for a forward-looking model.

The risk premium in the exchange-rate equation should be defined as a *relative* current balance term, reflecting the riskiness of different assets. This is only of practical importance in the oil shock simulation. Here we define the risk premium as relative to the US current balance, if the exchange rate is the bilateral dollar rate, or relative to the G7 countries if the effective rate is used.

Simulation experiments

Government spending shock

In this simulation general government spending is increased by 1 per cent of GNP throughout, in each of the four major European economies in turn. This is an *ex ante* shock to the government spending reaction function.

We first set out some *a priori* expectations. Under independent fiscal and monetary policy single country considerations suggest an appreciation of the nominal exchange rate as in the standard Mundell-Flemming framework. This will tend to counteract some of the expansionary output effects from the fiscal expansion and reduce some of the inflationary impact so that the net effect on output and inflation is uncertain. Spillover effects whereby higher demand in the other European countries feeds back to the country initiating the fiscal shock can provide some output compensation. In the long run if output returns to base we would also expect the real exchange rate to do likewise. For those models which do not generate as much inflation from a demand expansion as others, the interest-rate response and exchange-rate appreciation will be less and the output response correspondingly stronger. Our earlier comparative study found little evidence of complete crowding out of output over the medium term under fixed exchange rates. Under EMS we would expect to observe a greater degree of (negative) spillover from a German fiscal expansion than under independent monetary and fiscal policy, since the exchange rates and interest rates of the UK, France and Italy will move in line with those of Germany. The impact on Germany itself is likely to be very similar to that under independent policy. Fiscal expansion in the non-German EMS countries will be characterised by the absence of the crowding out effect of higher exchange rates and interest rates so that the output response should be greater than under independent policy.

Under EMU, interest-rate responses for a German fiscal expansion are likely to be moderated compared with EMS (since the reaction function uses a weighted average of output and inflation across the major four European economies) and hence the output response should be greater. Fiscal policy in the other EMU countries can shift the community average inflation and output and hence change their effective exchange rates and interest rates, and hence the output response should be less than under EMS interest-rate targeting.

We first describe the results by model and then proceed to analyse the differences between models.

NiGEM

Under independent policy setting the nominal exchange rate appreciates by around 1 per cent for a single-country fiscal expansion with the size of the appreciation varying across the four European economies (chart 5.1). The exchange rate remains higher by this amount throughout the six-year solution period and lower inflation means that the real exchange rate also appreciates in each case (hence the current balance deterioration remains uncorrected, since no terminal condition is imposed). Evidence from simulations over longer horizons shows that the real exchange rate eventually returns to base. *Ex post*, interest rates rise modestly in Germany but are largely unaltered for the other three European economies when they initiate a demand shock. This arises since the downward pressure on inflation from higher exchange rates more than offsets the upward pressure on inflation from the demand shock, hence only output exerts upward pressure on interest rates. In Germany the short-run output multiplier of just over 0.6 is higher than for the other European economies but falls away over time. In contrast in a six-year model run there is little crowding out in France, Italy and the UK (chart 5.2), but as the model is forward-looking longer simulation periods are associated with greater short-run crowding out.

Following a fiscal expansion in one country the exchange rates of the other three European economies fall and their interest rates rise. It is the balance of these effects which largely determines the degree of output spillover to the other economies. Thus, although exchange-rate spillovers are greatest for a German fiscal expansion, so are those of interest rates and hence there is relatively little expanding country-specific sensitivity in the size of the output spillover. Furthermore, the average spillover on GDP is very small so that, for example, on average a 1 per cent increase in GDP in the home country is only associated with a 0.1 per cent change elsewhere (in some cases there are small negative spillovers, for example the UK and France under a German fiscal shock). This limited nature of spillovers and hence feedback effects to the home country suggests that analysis of the output response can be largely explained by the same sort of mechanisms as would normally pertain to single-country analysis.

In Germany initially higher private domestic demand accompanies the increase in government spending but, although consumption remains higher throughout the simulation, fixed investment falls below the base simulation from the second year. It is this response together with lower exports following the increase in the real exchange rate that produces the crowding out of output in the simulation. Not only is the export loss smaller in the simulation for an expansion in France but investment remains higher throughout so that the output multiplier persists at around 0.5 over the six-year period. However there are very slow dynamics in the equations for France and hence six years is too short a period to usefully draw conclusions about medium- to long-run properties. Similar qualifications apply to the simulation for Italy. Here there is a sharp exchange-rate appreciation which lowers inflation and results in an initial rise in real interest rates. Hence private domestic demand hardly increases at first and the overall rather flat response of GDP is due to a recovery of private domestic demand as the real interest 'jump' disappears, offset by falling exports as demand adjusts to the higher real exchange rate. There are some signs of instability in the consumption response. This feature was observed in Whitley (1992) and was attributed there to the rudimentary treatment of personal sector determination. The step increase in the real interest rate in the UK simulation dampens the investment response and the lack of any induced rise in personal consumption means that the short-run output multiplier is low, the crowding out over time arising from lower export demand and a fall in investment. The flatness of the consumption response arises as the increase in long-term interest rates changes bond yields and equity prices and hence personal sector wealth.

Under EMS the response of output following a fiscal expansion in Germany is much the same as under the independent policy rules. However the responses for the other three European economies initiating the fiscal shock are different. Under EMS, interest rates in France, Italy and the UK do not adjust to domestic inflation and output divergencies but are constrained to follow German interest rates and exchange rates subject to a risk premium. Hence interest rates are virtually unchanged and the effective nominal exchange rate only rises to reflect the general appreciation of the German exchange rate against other non-European currencies. The main change therefore is that the export loss present under independent policies now disappears giving higher output growth in response to a fiscal shock, but at the cost of higher inflation. In the case of France domestic consumer spending is lower under EMS than under independent policy as a consequence of the higher inflation but fixed investment is higher. A similar pattern arises for Italy but not for the UK where personal consumption is higher than under EMS despite higher inflation, as long-term interest rates are lower.

Spillover effects now become asymmetric under EMS (chart 5.7). Fiscal expansion singly in France or Italy or in the UK does not spill over much to the remaining European economies in EMS since the transmission mechanisms through interest rates and nominal exchange rates are closed off, leaving only the operation of trade flows. In contrast a fiscal shock in Germany has far greater spillover effects to the other economies, both relative to the spillovers initiated by these economies and to the spillovers generated by a German fiscal shock under independent policy. Of particular note is that expansionary fiscal policy in Germany now lowers output elsewhere by obliging the other countries to adopt higher interest rates and exchange rates. Furthermore these negative spillovers are quite substantial. They are most marked for France and the UK where the medium-term output responses are respectively as large as, and greater than, the increase in German output. For example, after three years German output has risen by 0.29 per cent under EMS but UK output has fallen by 0.33 per cent. The higher spillovers to the UK reflect a marked decline in fixed investment where there is a higher elasticity with respect to interest rates. In contrast domestic expenditures are less sensitive to interest rates in France and Italy, and spillovers are relatively weak.

An EMU-style policy regime where interest rates respond to average inflation and output deviations changes the results for a German fiscal shock relative to EMS, raising domestic output and inflation. The impact of fiscal shocks in the other three economies is to reduce output below EMS levels, but only modestly.

The asymmetry between EMS and EMU in response to a German shock emerges because the exchange-rate appreciation that was generated under EMS rules is reduced. Hence the export loss is reduced and lower interest rates under EMU result in higher private domestic spending than under EMS. Furthermore the strong negative spillover from a German fiscal expansion is now considerably reduced in size.

In France, Italy and the UK, a domestic fiscal expansion can now lead to an appreciation of the nominal exchange rate (higher interest rates) to the extent that it raises average community inflation and output, and this effect tends to lower the increase in domestic output compared to the same simulation under EMS rules. As a consequence of EMU domestic shocks can now spill over to a greater degree to the other economies. These spillovers are relatively small but larger and of an opposite direction than under independent policy setting.

There is a radical difference in the results under EMU when the deficit targeting rule is adopted. Under the standard fiscal policy spending rule the government deficit worsens by 0.6-0.8 per cent of GNP (but by nearly 1 per cent for Italy). The deficit targeting rule is designed to bring the deficit almost back to base within the six-year period by adjusting government spending. This still permits the level of spending to remain higher than under the base but reduces it substantially below the level implied by the *ex ante* fiscal shock. These simulations tend to produce almost complete crowding out of output with most of the adjustment taking place within the first two years. These results are extended and explained further in Barrell and in't Veld (1992).

There are no striking differences in the outcomes for the current balance or the general government deficit under the alternative policy regimes (apart from the deficit balance alternative). The main exception is for Italy where without solvency constraints the government deficit appears to be unstable under independent policy setting. Nor are inflation differences particularly marked.

In the case of Germany there is little difference under EMS but slightly more inflation under EMU. In France there is a fall in inflation under independent policy but higher inflation under EMS. Inflation also falls under independent policy for Italy but rises under EMS and EMU where the inflation pressures are stronger. The inflation response is almost non-existent under independent policy for the UK, with demand and inflation higher under EMS and EMU.

OECD model

Fiscal expansion in Germany in the OECD model is characterised by a large initial increase in output followed by gradual crowding out (chart 5.3). Nominal interest rates remain higher throughout but the nominal exchange rate returns towards base by the end of the simulation period, after jumping by around 1 per cent at the beginning of the simulation (chart 5.1). There are two main mechanisms of crowding out in Germany: lower exports, as domestic inflation lowers competitiveness towards the end of the simulation period despite the return to base of the nominal exchange, and lower investment following the rise in domestic interest rates. There is a cyclical response in both investment and exports but crowding out is very rapid.

In contrast output in France rises gently in the first three years of the simulation before gradually easing back towards the level obtained in the first year. Here inflation rises more sluggishly and hence the response of interest rates is delayed more than in the case of Germany. As a consequence fixed investment rises quite strongly and this largely explains the difference in the level and path of output compared with Germany. Similar comments apply to Italy but here both the investment cycle and the fall in exports are more damped. The increase in output for the UK accelerates in the second year of the simulation but then is crowded out quite rapidly. Once more it is the behaviour of fixed investment which dominates the path of demand, the strong cyclical response being shorter-lived than in the case of France. The increase in private consumption is larger in the UK than for any of the other three economies. Spillover effects of the single-country fiscal expansion to the other major European economies are very modest. Short-run output spillovers are always positive but where inflation also spills over it generates a rise in interest rates which reduces private investment and the increase in exports arising from fiscal expansion elsewhere.

Given our assumptions it is no surprise that a German fiscal expansion under EMS has almost identical effects in that country to those under independent fiscal policy. Spillovers to France, Italy and the UK are of greater quantitative importance than under independent policy and, apart from a minor initial boost, output falls in these economies following a German fiscal expansion when the EMS is in place. As the output effects in Germany become crowded out so the negative spillovers produced by high interest rates diminish in size and hence are not as persistent (nor as large) as are found for NiGEM.

A fiscal expansion in France and the UK induces a higher output gain than under independent policies, for the same reasons as noted for NiGEM, that is, the reduction in the size of the exchange-rate appreciation and in the rise in domestic interest rates. In the case of France the output response under EMS now also shows little indication of crowding out as the strong investment response is maintained throughout the simulation period. In the UK the behaviour of investment is also an important factor but the increase in investment is accompanied by higher private consumption. Somewhat surprisingly exports still fall by very much the same amount by the end of the simulation period as under independent policies.

The results for Italy under EMS are at greater odds with those for France and the UK for there is very little difference in output response as compared with the independent policy regime until the very end of the simulation horizon. This can be explained by the fact that the export volume response to exchange rates is very weak in the OECD Italian sector and that interest rates also have a small effect on private domestic demand. Finally we note that the spillover effects of a fiscal expansion in France, Italy or the UK are negligible under EMS.

Responses under EMU for the OECD model are almost indistinguishable from those under EMS for France, Italy and the UK but output (and inflation) are higher for Germany in the short run. Although domestic interest rates rise by less than under EMS and hence result in higher private investment and consumer spending, the effective exchange rate appreciates by more. The spillover output effects of a German fiscal expansion under EMU become minor.

The effects on inflation under the three policy regimes are very similar for Germany. France, Italy and the UK, however, experience higher inflation under EMS for a fiscal policy shock than under independent policy. Inflation in all three regimes is higher than for NiGEM. Changes in the current balance in the OECD simulations are very similar across the three policy regimes with a deficit of between 0.6-1.0 per cent of GDP recorded at the end of the simulation period (the lowest deficit is for Italy and the largest for France). In general the deficits appear to be stable but an exception is the UK where there are some signs that the deficit is increasing.

Changes in the government fiscal deficits are much larger than for NiGEM (often three times as large) and vary considerably across the different policy regimes. The UK has the smaller increase in the deficit of between 1-1½ per cent of GDP, with Germany and France just under 2 per cent and Italy between 2-2½ per cent of GDP. Furthermore the deficits of Germany, France and Italy show clear signs of accelerating over time — the simulation period being too short to conclude that there is an instability problem. Results for the OECD model under EMU with deficit targeting were not available. One might expect that this alternative would lead to substantial output crowding out.

DIW-QUEST

Output effects in the DIW-QUEST model tend to be relatively large, with responses of around 1 per cent of GDP after three years (chart 5.4) under independent fiscal policy, compared with the other models in this exercise. These increases are despite fairly substantial exchange-rate appreciation, especially for Italy. The strong inflation effects raise domestic interest rates *ex ante* and this results in the sizeable appreciation of the exchange rate. It appears, however, that the use of nominal rather than real GNP in the interest-rate reaction function may be partly responsible for these results. However the appreciation in turn reduces inflation so that, *ex post*, interest rates do not rise much, or even fall. Although the initial real exchange-rate appreciation is reduced over time the real exchange rate remains well above base after six years. In the case of Germany there is a strong initial increase in consumption and fixed investment demand which offsets the lower level of exports. As real exchange-rate appreciation diminishes the export loss is reduced but investment tends to fall away leaving the difference in the level of output at around ½ per cent. Output responds by much more in France (with a peak GDP effect of 1.4 per cent) where the exchange-rate appreciation is much smaller and where the investment response does not fall away. In common with Germany, interest rates fall in the first two years thus further stimulating economic activity consistent with no increase in inflation. The smaller exchange-rate appreciation for France stems from the fact that a fiscal expansion is far less expansionary in France on the DIW-QUEST model than it is for the other countries. In the case of Italy the substantial exchange-rate appreciation leads to an initial fall in exports which is gradually offset by higher consumption and fixed investment. The appreciation of the exchange rate lowers inflation initially thus enabling a cut in interest rates (nearly 2 percentage points after two years). This is an important mechanism in stimulating investment and as interest rates subsequently rise so the investment response falls away.

There is considerably more crowding out of output for a fiscal expansion in the UK. In the short run the lower level of exports partly offsets higher domestic demand. There is a pronounced investment cycle which explains some of the profile of the output response. There are no major differences in the responses of the current account and the government deficit across the four countries; these tend to stabilise at ½ and ¾-1 per cent of GNP respectively.

EMS-style policy with German leadership tends to flatten out and stabilise the output response. German fiscal expansion results in higher short-term output gains than under independent policy resulting from a smaller degree of exchange-rate appreciation. With little change in the export reduction over the simulation period the gradual decline in the output response is almost entirely attributable to fixed investment. Under independent policy for France there is only a very small exchange-rate appreciation and the EMS result is hardly any different (since some appreciation still occurs). In contrast, the absence of the substantial initial appreciation, experienced under independent policy for Italy under EMS, prevents the cyclical response of output observed in the former case, giving as a result a fairly steady step increase in GDP with consumer spending the main endogenous demand contribution. A similar result holds for the UK but here there is an additional contribution from fixed investment.

Output effects under EMU differ most from those under EMS for Germany and the UK, with much less difference for France and Italy. In Germany fiscal expansion is now far more powerful in its immediate impact on output with only a modest effect on inflation. The GDP response peaks at 1.5 per cent after two years. The absence of the initial fall in exports under EMU (the exchange rate no longer appreciates) means that the powerful multiplier—accelerator effects on investment and consumption dominate the early part of the simulation period. Gradually, however, interest rates rise in response to higher output and this causes a decline in investment accompanied by a fall in exports. The export decline is common to all four countries and is associated with a fall in total OECD demand at the end of the simulation period. This appears to be associated with the synchronicity of the investment cycle in all four European economies as a result of German fiscal expansion. In consequence GDP falls below base by the final year of the simulation and the simulation response appears unstable (the solution period is too short to confirm this). There is now a small depreciation under EMU for France in contrast to the appreciation under EMS, and this raises exports initially, but the synchronised investment cycle eventually results in lower OECD demand and hence lower French exports. A similar phenomenon takes place for Italy where, in common with France and Germany, short-term interest rates appear to be the main factor causing the fall in investment both domestically and in other European countries. The investment and export decline is particularly severe for the UK towards the end of the simulation period and results in GDP falling well below its base level in the final year of the simulation.

Spillover effects from fiscal expansion in the DIW-QUEST model differ substantially across the alternative policy regimes (chart 5.9). Under both independent policy and EMS, fiscal expansion in one country tends to raise output elsewhere, but by a relatively small amount. However, under EMU the spillovers appear exceptionally large and lead to output declining in the other European economies, often by more than in the originating country. The mechanisms appear to be that higher output in the short run under EMU, together with higher inflation than EMS, induces a substantial community-wide rise in interest rates towards the end of the simulation period. This then reduces investment in all four economies simultaneously and hence reduces total world demand, thus leading to a further adverse effect on output through lower exports. The UK and Germany appear to be most vulnerable to these adverse spillovers. Under a German fiscal expansion UK output falls by over twice that of German output in the final year of the simulation period. Under a French fiscal shock both Germany and the UK experience a substantial fall in output after six years but French output remains well above base, and a similar result holds for Italy. When the UK initiates a fiscal expansion, output falls in all four economies at the end of the simulation period but by far more in Germany than elsewhere. These results appear to owe a great deal to the strong multiplier—accelerator mechanisms in DIW-QUEST which induce the rise in interest rates.

A deficit financing rule with EMU in place has very large effects in the DIW-QUEST model. In order to return the deficit ratio to GNP back to base, government spending needs to be reduced below base levels. The powerful accelerator effects in the model then produce large reductions in output below base in the final three years of the simulation period. The own country output reductions after six years range from 5 per cent for Germany, 3 per cent for the UK, 2 per cent for Italy and 1 per cent for France. The spillover effects are substantial. The German fiscal expansion now reduces UK domestic output by 2.7 per cent after six years; a French expansion lowers output in Germany by 3.4 per cent, in the UK by 2.5 per cent and by 1.5 per cent in Italy compared with the own-country reduction of 0.8 per cent. Similarly an Italian expansion lowers output in the UK and Germany by more than in Italy.

OEF

Fiscal expansion in the OEF model leads to a step appreciation of the exchange rate by around 2 per cent for Germany and Italy, 1 per cent for France and nearly 3 per cent for the UK under independent policy setting. The consequent initial increase in domestic output ranges from 0.7 per cent in the UK to around 0.8 per cent for Germany, France and Italy (chart 5.5). In the medium term, output in France and Italy stabilises around 0.7 per cent, whereas there is marked crowding out of the initial effect in Germany and the UK. In general inflation falls initially, but then rises accompanied by a short-term fall in interest rates. The real exchange rate remains high throughout, giving a steady adverse influence on output from export demand. In the case of Germany the main source of endogenous demand in this simulation comes from private consumption, the fall in exports accounting for the crowding out of output. Consumer spending increases more strongly in the UK simulation where higher real personal wealth is an important contributor, and there is also a strong cyclical investment response, whereas in France and Italy the investment response is sustained. The current account deteriorates by around ½ per cent of GNP in Germany and the UK but by much less in France and Italy (around 0.2 per cent of GNP). The general government fiscal deficit also increases by more in the case of Germany, by more than twice that in Italy and France (with the UK somewhere in between).

Unlike the other models a fiscal expansion in Germany under EMS increases output by more than under independent policy, although it is difficult to locate the reasons why this result arises. Output is higher under EMS than under independent policy for the UK and Italy in the short run but only marginally so for France where higher investment under EMU is counterbalanced by lower private consumption, following higher inflation. In the case of Italy higher fixed investment and exports combine to increase output in the short run but higher inflation under EMS tends to reduce export demand in the last three years of the simulation. The UK results are largely the product of higher export demand under EMS, in the absence of the exchange-rate appreciation under independent policy.

One variation in simulation design with the OEF model is that the EMS dollar exchange rates are not allowed to vary under EMU. In the case of Germany interest rates are now determined by community-wide aggregates and hence increase by less than under EMS. This produces a larger induced investment and consumption response and hence higher output (exports are also higher). Fiscal expansion elsewhere produces very similar results to EMS. Current balance and government deficit implications are quite close across the three policy regimes (chart 5.8) but deficits are typically far smaller than for the other models (for example, the current account only deteriorates by 0.2 per cent of GNP for France and Italy with a government deficit increase of around 0.3 per cent of GNP).

Cross-model comparisons
Model responses under independent policy are strongly influenced by the size of the initial exchange-rate appreciation accompanying the fiscal expansion. The exchange-rate jump is itself determined by the path of interest rates and the current balance. Given that the models share a common interest-rate reaction function and that the current balance effects are quite similar across the models, the exchange-rate response is therefore a product of output and inflation consequences of the fiscal shock. It is no great surprise that the exchange-rate appreciation is most marked for the DIW-QUEST model for this tends to generate both large government expenditure multipliers and relatively large inflationary pressure which in turn raise interest rates. What is more interesting is that the strengths of the underlying multiplier-accelerator mechanisms on domestic demand in DIW-QUEST are more than sufficient to

counteract the adverse export consequences of a higher real exchange rate so that DIW-QUEST generates relatively large output response along with gently declining inflation. Where appreciation is greatest (Germany and Italy), the impact effect on output is smaller but subsequent induced increases in economic activity are substantial. Although NiGEM has a smaller exchange-rate appreciation than DIW-QUEST, it also has a much smaller multiplier under constant exchange rates and hence generates both a weaker impact effect on output and a smaller medium-term effect. Inflation tends to fall, especially in the case of a French expansion. Evidence from extending the model solution period to twenty years reveals that the real exchange rate does tend to return to base eventually, but accompanied by a sustained current account imbalance with a small permanent rise in output. The simulation horizons in the other models are too short to deduce whether the same long-run response occurs but they all share the same real exchange-rate appreciation over the common six-year simulation period. The OECD model exhibits a relatively smaller initial exchange-rate jump, which is similar across the four economies (although the subsequent path differs). This, however, reflects more marked current balance effects rather than weaker inflationary pressure. The OEF model tends to exhibit relatively large impact output multipliers, despite a relatively larger initial appreciation.

In general the rise in interest rates following a fiscal expansion is not particularly large and this reflects a low inflationary response in the models (see Whitley, 1992, table 2). There is some consensus across the models, despite the different estimates of the magnitude of the output and inflation responses to the fiscal shock, for crowding out tends to be present far more for Germany and the UK and is of little importance for France and Italy.

We would expect, *a priori*, that a German fiscal expansion under EMS with German leadership should not be very different from a fiscal expansion under independent policy, any difference being due to the feedback from changed activity levels in the other EMS countries tied to German interest rates and exchange rates. In contrast fiscal expansion in the non-German EMS countries should be more expansionary since the rise in interest rates and hence real exchange-rate appreciation is far more limited. This *a priori* expectation is fulfilled for NiGEM and OECD but not so clearly for DIW-QUEST and OEF. In the case of OEF output is higher under EMS for Germany with little difference for France and Italy in the long run. In DIW-QUEST it is where a French fiscal expansion takes place that there is little difference between EMS and independent policy, principally due to the relatively small appreciation that occurs under independent policy in France. Elsewhere EMS tends to flatten out the output response. The profile, but not the average level of output, is different for Germany under EMS, reflecting the feedbacks from the other countries.

Under EMU with spending targets we might expect, *a priori*, that fiscal expansion in Germany should be more powerful in raising domestic output but that expansion in the other countries may be less effective in that, insofar as they raise aggregate European output and inflation, they will induce an interest-rate response. Generally the simulation results support this prediction although the differences between output under EMS and EMU for France, Italy and the UK tend to be relatively small (this is also the case for a German fiscal expansion in the OEF model). The DIW-QUEST model is an outlier for a German and UK fiscal expansion where output under EMU is initially greater than under EMS and then is rapidly crowded out.

EMU results under the assumption of deficit targeting were only available for two of the models (NiGEM and DIW-QUEST) and they do show important qualitative and quantitative differences from EMU under spending targets. In NiGEM there is little increase in output in the medium term from a fiscal expansion, thus implying that independent fiscal policy is powerless whereas in the DIW-QUEST model the net effect is to lower domestic output — the latter results are due to the synchronisation of the economic cycle in the European economies induced by the common monetary policy.

Under independent policies inflation tends to fall for NiGEM but rise for the other models. There is a higher degree of consensus that fiscal expansion increases inflation under EMS, the main outlier being NiGEM for Germany. There is little difference in inflation under EMU compared with EMS, the main exception being Germany where inflation tends to be higher under EMU. DIW-QUEST is also an outlier here for inflation consequences are very substantial in the short to medium term given the output consequences of the common monetary policy.

The potential spillover effects from a single-country fiscal expansion to economic activity in the other European economies is of particular relevance when evaluating the different policy regimes. Estimates of these spillovers are available for three of the models (NiGEM, OECD and DIW-QUEST).

There is some consensus over the size and direction of spillover effects for the NiGEM and OECD models. They suggest that the output spillovers to the other economies are quite modest (but usually positive) for a single-country fiscal expansion. However, spillover effects become asymmetric under EMS. Now there is very little effect on the other economies following a fiscal expansion in France, Italy or the UK but a German fiscal expansion generates lower output elsewhere as a consequence of the transmission of higher exchange rates and interest rates. Furthermore these spillover effects are quantitatively important. EMU also generates negative output spillovers for a fiscal expansion but in general these are of a modest size. Spillovers under EMU with deficit targeting also tend to be negative, but given the crowding out of domestic output, also tend to be short-lived. The DIW-QUEST model gives somewhat different results. Spillover effects tend to be larger in all three regimes, being typically positive under independent policy. They remain positive under EMS for fiscal expansion of France, Italy and the UK and show the asymmetry for a German fiscal expansion. However this asymmetry is most marked in the case of the UK where the output reduction is almost one half of the size of the increase in German output. In contrast output in France is hardly affected and output in Italy gains by almost as much as the UK loses. Spillover effects on output under EMU for DIW-QUEST tend to be exceptionally large and negative as the common monetary policy produces a synchronised investment cycle which results in output losses in the other European economies far larger than those in the country initiating the fiscal shock.

Oil price shock
In this simulation we assume an increase of 50 per cent in the world oil price, affecting all the European economies simultaneously. In a single-country context this can be classed as an adverse supply-side shock, but in a multi-country framework it also depends on the adjustment of oil producers. The OECD model assumes the extra oil revenues are respent by OPEC producers by the end of three years; adjustment is somewhat slower for OEF and NiGEM. If the response is quantitatively small then we would expect to observe lower output under independent policies accompanied by an increase in the price level (but not the rate of inflation, since monetary policy is not accommodating). We review the model responses in each policy regime.

Independent policies
In the study on diagnostic simulation responses with these models (Whitley, 1992) it was observed that, under a monetary policy of fixed real interest rates and fixed nominal exchange rates, there was general agreement that output was adversely affected when oil prices rose but that there was considerable divergence between the models as to whether this negative effect diminished or increased over time. There remains some disagreement when we simulate the oil shock on the present versions of the models, allowing for the common monetary and fiscal reactions under endogenous exchange rates. The OECD model suggests fairly small output effects but output falls more substantially in the NiGEM, DIW-QUEST and OEF models.

In NiGEM the effective nominal exchange rates of the major four European economies appreciate following an oil price shock (chart 5.10) as the higher rate of inflation induces interest-rate increases of between ½-1 per cent. The initial nominal appreciation varies between 1 per cent for Germany to nearly 3 per cent for France, and an equivalent real appreciation is observed throughout the simulation period. The current accounts of Germany, France and Italy all worsen at first (chart 5.11) but then as world trade picks up later on (as a result of higher OPEC demand) those of Germany and France return to base. The Italian deficit persists however. The UK suffers no short-run adverse effects on the current balance and this improves throughout the simulation period, with the difference from base reaching 1 per cent of GNP after six years.

In the simulations on NiGEM (see table 5.3) GDP falls by around 1 per cent in the medium term for Germany following a sharp fall in fixed investment (some 5 per cent) and a 1 per cent fall in personal consumption, although government consumption rises by a similar amount. Output in France falls by nearly half as much again as in Germany, where lower exports and higher interest rates initially induce a sharp fall in consumer spending. Private demand is less sensitive in Italy and hence the output decline is more modest. UK domestic demand is strongly reduced, despite lower interest rates than for the other countries but the effect is cushioned by the reduction in imports.

There is no common pattern of exchange-rate change for the OECD model under independent policies. The exchange rates of the UK and France appreciate by around 1 per cent initially, that of Germany *depreciates* by the same order of magnitude, and Italian exchange rates are hardly altered in the short run. This appears to be associated with the more marked deterioration in the current balance in Italy which offsets the rise in domestic interest rates in respect of the influence on the exchange rate. The contribution of improved current balance and higher interest rates results in the UK appreciation, the French appreciation being more difficult to explain.

The short-run output responses in the OECD model (table 5.3) are a reduction of around 0.2-0.3 per cent (slightly more for France). The German path of output and inflation is somewhat cyclical, making it difficult to infer the level of medium-term response. Output is lower in the UK, partly through trade feedbacks and partly on account of the exchange-rate appreciation but output reductions are more severe in France and Italy where investment plays a more major role. Inflation rises in all four economies but only returns to its base level within the six-year period for Germany and Italy. By the sixth year the consumer price level has increased by between 1½-3 per cent.

Considerable adverse domestic output effects are uniformly observed for the DIW-QUEST model (where the simulations could only be conducted over a five-year period) but the fall in output is far less marked in the UK. This difference is due to the exchange-rate response. In the UK the large exchange-rate appreciation against the dollar (8 per cent) and other European currencies results in only a small increase in domestic inflation. This leaves lower exports (due to weakened competitiveness and lower world demand) as the main source of lower domestic output. In Italy and Germany the output decline is quite marked over both short and medium term with output some 2 per cent below base after five years (at a peak output is nearly 3 per cent lower in Italy).

In both cases the exchange-rate response is modest and the differing effects in the short run are dominated by higher domestic interest rates which reduce consumption and investment expenditure. In the longer term the adverse output effects are maintained by the fall in world trade. France exhibits an exchange-rate appreciation of nearly 6 per cent after three years which reduces export demand, but higher interest rates have a weaker effect on consumption demand than for Germany and Italy, and it is the investment cycle and reduction in exports which dominate the decline in output. With the exception of the UK, inflation rises sharply at first in DIW-QUEST and then declines leaving the price level some 3-4 per cent higher by the end of the simulation period.

Finally, we turn to the results from the OEF model. These are not fully comparable with the results from the other models since the dollar exchange rate is not permitted to change except in the UK. This reflects the prior view that an oil shock should have a comparable exchange-rate effect across the other three main European currencies. The results for Germany, France and Italy are therefore quite similar to those reviewed in Whitley (1992). Output declines in all four European economies but hardly at all in France where there is little response of the endogenous demand components to higher domestic interest rates. In Germany and Italy both private consumption and investment fall as higher inflation raises interest rates initially. These adverse effects are much larger for Italy and produce an overall fall in output which has not stabilised after six years (by which time it has reached 2 per cent). In contrast the decline in output peaks in Germany in the third year at 1.9 per cent and 1 per cent after six years (however it has not stabilised by this point). In the UK the exchange-rate appreciation moderates inflationary pressure so that interest rates do not rise as strongly. Lower consumption and fixed investment together with lower exports are then the prime explanations for the peak decline of 1 per cent in domestic output after three years.

EMS

EMS-style policies neither reduce the degree of dispersion in the output reaction to the oil price shock in NiGEM nor change the individual country responses with France remaining an outlier due to very slow dynamics. The EMS countries all experience an appreciation of between 1-2 per cent against the US and Japan. Although nominal interest rates rise by ½ per cent initially and 1 per cent after two years, real interest rates fall at first and then rise modestly. Total and manufacturing world trade rise in the medium term by much the same as under independent policy, although the impact effect remains adverse. Output continues to fall relatively sharply in France due to the very strong adverse private consumption response (higher real interest rates) whereas the net trade effect in the UK (principally lower imports) continues to leave a small decline in domestic output. Although there are considerable short-run divergencies in inflation responses there is consensus that domestic inflation settles down around 0.5-0.6 per cent per annum over the medium term.

The decline in output under EMS for the OECD model is less severe than under independent policy, in particular UK output is now hardly affected by the oil price shock. The level of German output is, however, little different. All the European currencies experience an initial nominal exchange-rate depreciation before adjusting back to the baseline simulation; by construction the profile follows that for Germany, as do interest-rate paths. The combination of lower interest rates and exchange rates under EMS results in an improvement in exports and private sector domestic demand which explains the relatively higher output levels under EMS for France, Italy and the UK. Private consumption is little changed for France and Italy and the private demand improvement comes principally from fixed investment, but in the UK consumers' expenditure is boosted under EMS (although still below the baseline simulation) despite higher inflation. France also experiences higher inflation under EMS but in Italy the inflation pass-through merely becomes more rapid. The difference in exchange-rate paths under EMS is not sufficient to alter the level of current account deficits which, apart from the UK, remain persistent over the six-year period.

The model responses from DIW-QUEST suggest a slightly greater degree of both short- and medium-term convergence in output under EMS for the non-UK EMS countries with a common initial exchange-rate depreciation of just under 2 per cent which then adjusts back towards the baseline. However the output decline remains substantial, given that total OECD demand falls by some 3 per cent throughout under independent policy. The fall in output in the UK is larger than under independent policy but remains smaller than the reduction in the other economies. Exports gain relative to the situation under independent policy from the smaller exchange-rate appreciation but the substantial European-wide rise in interest rates results in a substantial fall in private consumption and lower investment. These results further illustrate the strong inflationary response of DIW-QUEST for this is the key factor producing the strong fall in output through higher interest rates.

Given the assumed invariance of the exchange rate to the oil price shock for the non-UK European countries under independent policy in the OEF model there is very little change when EMS policy rules are invoked. The main difference relates to the UK where interest rates move initially but are subsequently lower than under independent policy. Hence the medium-term output effect of higher oil prices is now negligible for the UK. This coincides with the conclusion for France.

EMU

There is almost no change in the relative responses between the EMU countries relative to EMS for NiGEM, France remaining an outlier. Under EMU with deficit targets NiGEM produces a more substantial output decline in Germany, France and Italy (table 5.3) as government consumption now falls to correct the deficit and hence generates a further fall in demand.

In the case of the OECD model, output still declines in France and Italy but to a greater degree and there is also now a consistent fall in output in Germany and the UK. Hence there is some evidence for greater convergence of output under EMU. However, it is not possible to draw the same conclusion for inflation. One reason for the trend towards greater output convergence is that effective exchange rates do not change as much under EMU and this therefore eliminates the divergencies between the country results that arise precisely due to their differing estimates of the output effects of the exchange-rate changes. In addition there is a greater agreement between estimates of output change due to variations in interest rates (Whitley, 1992) so that higher interest rates under EMU do not increase the divergence between output in the European economies. The output decline in Germany remains smaller than that in France or Italy given that exports do not fall to the same extent as in these countries whereas the UK result is explained by the lower sensitivity of private domestic demand.

The reactions for DIW-QUEST are quite different to those under EMS and result in greater short-run divergence between the four economies. The changes principally relate to Germany and the UK where the short-run output effects are now boosted but at the cost of a greater medium-term reduction. The EMU countries now experience in common a substantial exchange-rate depreciation relative to the dollar but otherwise differ quite considerably. The UK and Germany have higher exports initially as world demand is higher at first and this explains the difference in output response from that under EMS. However, subsequently depreciation is eroded by higher inflation and the output loss is more marked as lower exports induce a sharp decline in domestic demand. The lack of homogeneity in the French sector of the DIW-QUEST model partially explains the relative insensitivity of the results to the EMU assumption. In the case of Italy higher exports in the short run due to the exchange-rate depreciation under EMU are offset by lower private domestic demand due to the higher level of interest rates. There is no evidence that the DIW-QUEST simulations of output response have settled down by the end of the simulation horizon.

In the absence of any relative change against the dollar under EMU (by assumption) the OEF results are almost identical to EMS. There is a tendency towards a smaller output reduction under EMU than occurs under EMS.

Cross-model comparisons

The evidence from the oil price simulation does not suggest that there is a greater degree of convergence of output response across the European economies under EMS or EMU than under independent setting of monetary and fiscal policy. Nor is there any uniform tendency in the size of the output and inflation responses across the various regimes. Under independent policy differences arise, both across models and across countries, from the differences in inflation response to an oil price shock and these translate into differing profiles of interest rates and exchange rates. The main differences across the policy regimes are in the behaviour of interest rates and exchange rates and although there are common responses under EMU the simulation results tend to be dominated by differences in the sensitivity to interest rates and exchange-rate shocks in the different models. The DIW-QUEST results are a clear outlier whereas differences in simulation design mean that the exchange-rate implications of the different regimes are not fully taken into account in the OEF model.

Under independent monetary and fiscal policies the UK and French exchange rates tend to appreciate relative to the other European currencies but NiGEM also generates an appreciation for Germany and Italy. The current account effects in the models appear to be relatively insensitive to the choice of policy regime. The models generate an improvement in the UK balance and deterioration elsewhere for an oil price shock as a general result, but in many cases the current balance returns to base by the end of the simulation period. The DIW-QUEST model tends to generate much larger current account changes than in the other models. In particular, France stands out as being more obviously different than either Germany or Italy where the terms of trade effect is more adverse.

Conclusions

This comparative exercise has attempted to use the multicountry models to examine alternative policy regimes. This has involved extending the models to include exchange-rate adjustment. Although some models already contain forward-looking exchange rates (NiGEM) it was not practical to expect the other models to adopt a similar endogenous treatment within the timescale of the project. Consequently a second-best solution to exchange-rate determination was applied which, although suffering from some problems, does appear to capture some of the basic features of the UIP approach. Although there are important model differences which dominate the simulation results (for example, the very large multipliers of DIW-QUEST) there appears to be some consensus that a non-fiscal expansion under a German-led EMS is more powerful than when independent monetary policies are pursued, since the countries originating the fiscal shock are sheltered from the resulting interest-rate and exchange-rate crowding out effects. However, a German fiscal expansion results in lower activity in the other European economies. An EMU regime where independent fiscal policy is still possible has little different effect on output for France, Italy and the UK but reveals asymmetry in Germany where monetary policy is weaker, as it adjusts to community-wide outcomes. Attention to the government deficit, however, under EMU requires almost complete reversal of the expansionary fiscal shock in NiGEM, leaving output almost unchanged. The same policies in DIW-QUEST produce a highly cyclical output response. The results from NiGEM suggest that negative output spillovers are most marked for a German fiscal expansion under EMS but are stronger for a fiscal expansion in the other countries under EMU. However spillover effects in most cases are small — the exception is DIW-QUEST whose spillovers under EMU are implausibly large.

Under EMS and EMU expansionary fiscal policies are observed to be more inflationary than under independent monetary policy, since the countries originating the fiscal shock can no longer export inflation through exchange-rate appreciation. There is, however, little evidence of higher inflation under EMU than under EMS, suggesting that a strong German-led monetary policy is not much more powerful in constraining inflation than an equivalent feedback rule based on European-wide outturns which would be in place under EMU. The diversity of the output responses to an oil price shock across the models makes it difficult to draw any general conclusions about convergence under the different policy regimes. There is no tendency for EMU to reduce the recessionary effect of higher oil prices on European output levels or to moderate inflationary pressures.

This exercise is only a first step towards a complete examination of economic reactions under different policy regimes. No account has been taken of possible credibility and reputation effects on expectations and possible repercussions for wage and price behaviour. Nor does it fully represent an EMU with fully-coordinated economic policy. Nevertheless we would argue that it reveals certain features which can be used as a benchmark in a fuller study.

Table 5.1 GDP responses under the various regimes for a government spending shock (per cent difference from base)

Model		NiGEM				DIW-QUEST		
Country		GE	FR	IT	UK	GE	FR	IT	UK
(i) Independent policy								
Year	1	0.66	0.49	0.33	0.42	0.27	1.01	0.25	0.51
	2	0.50	0.49	0.36	0.37	0.43	1.37	1.07	0.98
	3	0.36	0.53	0.36	0.31	0.75	1.27	1.34	1.11
	4	0.32	0.56	0.36	0.27	0.67	1.08	1.12	0.80
	5	0.31	0.55	0.36	0.24	0.54	1.04	0.79	0.49
	6	0.31	0.53	0.37	0.24	0.53	1.10	0.65	0.48
(ii) EMS								
Year	1	0.69	0.56	0.43	0.50	0.61	1.05	0.93	0.89
	2	0.52	0.61	0.56	0.53	0.67	1.28	1.02	1.11
	3	0.34	0.63	0.58	0.51	0.50	1.26	0.89	1.09
	4	0.28	0.65	0.58	0.46	0.42	1.19	0.80	0.96
	5	0.28	0.66	0.56	0.41	0.51	1.13	0.74	0.87
	6	0.29	0.66	0.53	0.36	0.59	1.14	0.73	0.83
(iii) EMU								
Year	1	0.76	0.53	0.41	0.47	1.25	1.14	1.02	1.10
	2	0.61	0.53	0.56	0.44	1.47	1.40	1.06	1.58
	3	0.54	0.55	0.53	0.42	1.21	1.29	0.84	1.41
	4	0.53	0.59	0.53	0.39	0.73	1.18	0.68	1.07
	5	0.48	0.60	0.52	0.35	0.40	1.13	0.58	0.69
	6	0.45	0.60	0.50	0.31	-0.41	0.89	0.33	-0.26
(iii) EMU -deficit target								
Year	1	0.92	0.56	0.47	0.46	1.78	1.76	1.65	1.64
	2	0.15	0.26	0.41	0.22	1.99	1.98	1.72	2.16
	3	0.04	0.18	0.21	0.14	0.40	1.05	0.51	1.09
	4	0.18	0.26	0.15	0.11	-1.91	0.21	-0.62	-0.42
	5	0.02	0.18	0.09	0.05	-3.75	-0.27	-1.38	-1.81
	6	0.00	0.14	0.02	0.02	-4.97	-0.79	-1.95	-3.44

Model		OECD				OEF		
Country		GE	FR	IT	UK	GE	FR	IT	UK
(i) Independent policy								
Year	1	0.53	0.46	0.60	0.49	0.80	0.79	0.80	0.65
	2	0.20	0.60	0.58	0.62	0.56	0.83	0.59	0.76
	3	-0.01	0.63	0.53	0.44	0.38	0.81	0.58	0.77
	4	0.16	0.55	0.46	0.28	0.41	0.79	0.75	0.60
	5	0.13	0.47	0.40	0.24	0.40	0.79	0.74	0.45
	6	-0.05	0.36	0.34	0.27	0.27	0.75	0.72	0.37
(ii) EMS								
Year	1	0.54	0.47	0.63	0.49	0.89	0.82	1.00	0.78
	2	0.17	0.61	0.63	0.68	0.73	0.88	0.98	1.02
	3	-0.04	0.69	0.53	0.61	0.54	0.86	0.96	1.01
	4	0.16	0.66	0.45	0.51	0.49	0.81	0.75	0.87
	5	0.11	0.60	0.43	0.44	0.44	0.79	0.74	0.72
	6	-0.06	0.52	0.42	0.38	0.31	0.75	0.54	0.61
(iii) EMU								
Year	1	0.59	0.49	0.62	0.50	0.98	0.82	0.80	0.78
	2	0.40	0.66	0.63	0.71	0.77	0.86	0.98	1.00
	3	0.08	0.71	0.55	0.62	0.59	0.86	0.77	0.96
	4	0.11	0.67	0.49	0.49	0.57	0.81	0.75	0.82
	5	0.19	0.61	0.46	0.42	0.51	0.79	0.74	0.68
	6	0.05	0.52	0.45	0.37	0.39	0.73	0.54	0.58

Table 5.2 Price level responses under the various regimes for a government spending shock – government spending increased by 1% of GDP (per cent difference from base)

Model		NiGEM				DIW-QUEST		
Country	GE	FR	IT	UK	GE	FR	IT	UK
(i) Independent policy								
Year 1	0.02	-0.01	-0.17	-0.11	0.00	0.00	0.00	0.00
2	0.17	0.24	-0.01	0.11	-0.05	-0.16	0.33	0.15
3	0.34	0.52	0.26	0.51	0.00	-0.21	1.29	0.75
4	0.50	0.90	0.65	1.08	0.11	-0.07	2.81	1.76
5	0.65	1.38	1.18	1.79	0.25	0.24	4.74	3.02
6	0.79	1.94	1.84	2.55	0.43	0.69	6.94	4.36
(ii) EMS								
Year 1	0.04	0.14	0.04	0.05	-0.05	0.00	0.00	0.00
2	0.15	0.25	0.16	0.22	-0.05	-0.16	0.33	0.15
3	0.17	0.28	0.27	0.40	0.05	-0.05	0.96	0.60
4	0.16	0.38	0.39	0.57	0.11	0.14	1.52	1.01
5	0.15	0.48	0.53	0.71	0.14	0.31	1.93	1.26
6	0.14	0.56	0.66	0.76	0.18	0.45	2.20	1.34
(iii) EMU								
Year 1	0.05	0.12	0.02	0.03	0.00	0.00	0.00	0.00
2	0.20	0.18	0.12	0.17	0.45	0.09	0.62	0.51
3	0.27	0.18	0.21	0.30	1.11	0.34	1.48	1.45
4	0.33	0.26	0.31	0.43	1.64	0.51	2.07	2.28
5	0.38	0.33	0.43	0.53	1.95	0.61	2.38	2.73
6	0.41	0.39	0.55	0.60	1.90	0.50	2.37	2.73
(iii) EMU - deficit target								
Year 1	0.07	0.14	0.05	0.05	0.00	0.00	0.00	0.00
2	0.23	0.30	0.21.	0.22	0.47	-0.07	0.78	0.54
3	0.20	0.39	0.40	0.45	1.31	0.35	1.93	1.75
4	0.20	0.57	0.63	0.73	1.59	0.61	2.28	2.44
5	0.21	0.77	0.90	1.02	1.09	0.63	1.57	2.07
6	0.19	0.96	1.19	1.30	-0.38	0.43	0.12	0.74
Model		OECD				OEF		
Country	GE	FR	IT	UK	GE	FR	IT	UK
(i) Independent policy								
Year 1	0.20	-0.01	-0.08	-0.16	-0.22	-0.19	0.00	-0.06
2	0.64	0.26	0.33	0.11	-0.59	-0.15	0.83	0.14
3	1.10	0.73	0.88	0.68	-0.83	0.01	2.01	0.59
4	1.69	1.40	1.52	1.56	-0.79	0.34	3.43	1.29
5	2.48	2.28	2.22	2.69	-0.59	0.86	4.98	2.18
6	3.37	3.37	2.99	3.98	-0.31	1.55	6.59	3.15
(ii) EMS								
Year 1	0.23	0.12	0.20	0.05	-0.21	0.01	0.23	0.04
2	0.44	0.27	0.41	0.27	-0.37	0.04	0.83	0.20
3	0.46	0.47	0.55	0.57	-0.24	0.16	1.18	0.45
4	0.59	0.67	0.64	0.88	0.04	0.33	1.42	0.70
5	0.79	0.88	0.70	1.13	0.20	0.52	1.55	0.89
6	0.89	1.09	0.77	1.29	0.28	0.69	1.61	0.97
(iii) EMU								
Year 1	0.24	0.06	0.11	-0.02	-0.11	0.01	0.23	0.04
2	0.57	0.14	0.25	0.17	-0.15	0.04	0.71	0.20
3	0.69	0.31	0.38	0.46	0.06	0.15	1.01	0.43
4	0.77	0.49	0.49	0.75	0.29	0.33	1.20	0.68
5	0.94	0.68	0.58	0.96	0.43	0.51	1.32	0.84
6	1.05	0.89	0.68	1.08	0.48	0.68	1.39	0.92

*Table 5.3 GDP responses under the various regimes for an oil price shock –
50% increase in world oil price (per cent difference from base)*

Model		NiGEM				DIW-QUEST		
Country		GE	FR	IT	UK	GE	FR	IT	UK
(i) Independent policy									
Year	1	-0.40	-0.41	-0.27	-0.24	-0.93	-0.89	-0.52	-0.90
	2	-0.70	-0.95	-0.51	-0.41	-1.78	-2.63	-2.27	-0.48
	3	-1.05	-1.38	-0.74	-0.68	-2.12	-2.69	-2.92	-0.17
	4	-1.03	-1.53	-0.81	-0.71	-1.94	-1.49	-2.58	-0.34
	5	-0.96	-1.54	-0.79	-0.61	-1.90	-1.26	-1.97	-1.06
	6	-0.96	-1.51	-0.77	-0.53				
(ii) EMS									
Year	1	-0.44	-0.38	-0.22	-0.25	-1.26	-0.72	-0.65	-0.03
	2	-0.81	-1.00	-0.46	-0.58	-2.02	-2.35	-2.49	-0.78
	3	-1.13	-1.40	-0.69	-0.85	-2.10	-2.57	-2.72	-0.85
	4	-1.05	-1.47	-0.77	-0.78	-1.73	-1.97	-2.38	-0.77
	5	-0.95	-1.43	-0.76	-0.61	-1.59	-1.64	-2.12	-0.77
	6	-0.95	-1.41	-0.76	-0.50				
(iii) EMU									
Year	1	-0.38	-0.33	-0.20	-0.17	0.10	-0.27	-0.14	1.15
	2	-0.59	-0.84	-0.37	-0.34	0.76	-1.83	-2.08	1.74
	3	-0.89	-1.21	-0.59	-0.57	-0.35	-2.70	-2.66	0.78
	4	-0.86	-1.32	-0.69	-0.59	-1.89	-2.31	-2.71	-0.64
	5	-0.89	-1.37	-0.74	-0.57	-2.82	-1.85	-2.77	-1.77
	6	-0.96	-1.41	-0.81	-0.55				
(iii) EMU - deficit target									
Year	1	-0.43	-0.38	-0.14	-0.16				
	2	-0.83	-1.02	-0.24	-0.37				
	3	-1.48	-1.59	-0.69	-0.66				
	4	-1.14	-1.66	-0.90	-0.53				
	5	-1.11	-1.74	-1.02	-0.47				
	6	-1.37	-1.91	-1.24	-0.47				
Model		OECD				OEF		
Country		GE	FR	IT	UK	GE	FR	IT	UK
(i) Independent policy									
Year	1	-0.26	-0.36	-0.19	-0.17	-0.49	-0.08	-0.60	-0.31
	2	-0.47	-0.76	-0.60	-0.47	-1.55	-0.27	-1.57	-0.88
	3	-0.01	-0.74	-0.57	-0.50	-1.88	-0.39	-1.73	-1.09
	4	-0.19	-0.68	-0.42	-0.30	-1.54	-0.36	-1.69	-0.90
	5	-0.50	-0.63	-0.55	-0.20	-1.43	-0.25	-1.85	-0.63
	6	-0.31	-0.57	-0.64	-0.24	-1.04	-0.15	-1.99	-0.47
(ii) EMS									
Year	1	-0.28	-0.28	-0.13	-0.05	-0.49	-0.08	-0.60	-0.38
	2	-0.38	-0.42	-0.40	-0.04	-1.59	-0.35	-1.57	-1.23
	3	0.16	-0.33	-0.31	0.08	-1.96	-0.47	-1.93	-1.33
	4	-0.11	-0.38	-0.25	0.07	-1.58	-0.36	-2.07	-0.80
	5	-0.48	-0.37	-0.46	-0.11	-1.35	-0.17	-1.66	-0.26
	6	-0.26	-0.37	-0.50	-0.22	-0.93	-0.05	-1.62	-0.09
(iii) EMU									
Year	1	-0.32	-0.28	-0.16	-0.09	-0.44	-0.08	-0.60	-0.33
	2	-0.60	-0.56	-0.50	-0.23	-1.42	-0.27	-1.38	-0.95
	3	-0.22	-0.54	-0.48	-0.24	-1.80	-0.34	-1.73	-1.08
	4	-0.12	-0.51	-0.37	-0.16	-1.54	-0.33	-1.88	-0.86
	5	-0.40	-0.49	-0.48	-0.20	-1.43	-0.22	-1.66	-0.62
	6	-0.37	-0.47	-0.58	-0.27	-1.12	-0.15	-1.81	-0.45

Table 5.4 Price level response under the various regimes for an oil price shock – 50% increase in world oil price (per cent difference from base)

Model		NiGEM				DIW-QUEST		
Country		GE	FR	IT	UK	GE	FR	IT	UK
(i) Independent policy								
Year	1	0.85	0.39	0.85	0.34	0.00	0.00	0.00	0.00
	2	1.50	1.21	1.66	0.85	1.63	3.23	4.54	0.09
	3	2.05	1.88	2.18	1.22	2.79	2.06	5.86	0.31
	4	2.54	2.45	2.66	1.54	3.25	1.30	5.06	1.11
	5	3.07	2.98	3.13	1.88	3.64	1.57	4.30	2.06
	6	3.61	3.43	3.57	2.27				
(ii) EMS								
Year	1	0.84	0.54	0.98	0.42	0.00	0.00	0.00	0.00
	2	1.55	1.62	1.86	1.01	1.53	4.30	4.36	2.44
	3	2.04	2.52	2.41	1.45	2.52	3.88	5.74	3.60
	4	2.49	3.32	2.92	1.87	3.02	2.75	5.60	4.60
	5	2.99	4.00	3.42	2.34	3.51	1.65	5.27	5.62
	6	3.50	4.57	3.89	2.87				
(iii) EMU								
Year	1	0.86	0.56	0.99	0.45	0.00	0.00	0.00	0.00
	2	1.61	1.70	1.89	1.09	2.87	6.04	6.44	4.13
	3	2.15	2.63	2.46	1.62	5.69	6.35	9.70	7.77
	4	2.63	3.42	3.18	2.12	7.65	4.99	10.65	10.86
	5	3.13	4.09	3.68	2.63	8.71	3.21	10.68	12.58
	6	3.62	4.65	4.14	3.13				

Model		OECD				OEF		
Country		GE	FR	IT	UK	GE	FR	IT	UK
(i) Independent policy								
Year	1	0.67	0.71	0.92	0.54	1.10	0.58	1.15	1.07
	2	0.75	0.90	1.39	0.88	2.63	1.55	2.04	2.05
	3	1.12	1.35	1.85	1.19	3.54	2.19	2.85	2.75
	4	1.52	1.94	2.29	1.46	3.85	2.48	3.81	3.20
	5	1.57	2.41	2.41	1.75	3.92	2.53	4.72	3.58
	6	1.68	2.80	2.33	2.15	4.05	2.53	5.54	3.95
(ii) EMS								
Year	1	0.62	1.15	1.22	0.97	1.10	0.58	1.15	1.07
	2	0.75	1.80	1.75	1.49	2.63	1.55	2.08	1.98
	3	1.29	2.27	2.01	1.97	3.52	2.19	2.82	2.62
	4	1.80	2.61	2.26	2.39	3.82	2.45	3.59	3.05
	5	1.89	2.89	2.30	2.65	3.86	2.48	4.54	3.53
	6	2.03	3.06	2.29	2.77	3.97	2.29	4.59	4.04
(iii) EMU								
Year	1	0.43	1.02	0.97	0.80	1.09	0.58	1.15	1.07
	2	0.32	1.52	1.29	1.25	2.61	1.55	2.14	2.04
	3	0.51	1.92	1.52	1.61	3.52	2.20	3.04	2.74
	4	0.92	2.34	1.82	1.91	3.88	2.49	3.91	3.20
	5	1.15	2.64	1.98	2.24	3.98	2.56	4.79	3.60
	6	1.40	2.85	2.05	2.44	4.13	2.58	5.65	3.98

Chart 5.1 Initial exchange-rate jump; fiscal policy simulations

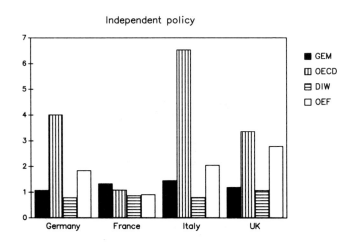

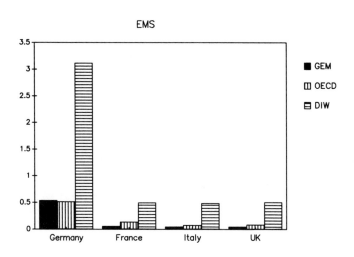

Chart 5.1 continued

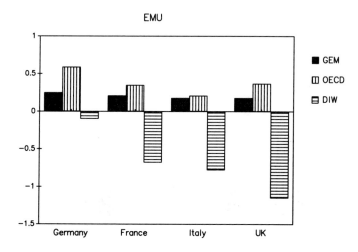

Chart 5.2 Output under the various policy regimes, NiGEM model, per cent difference from base

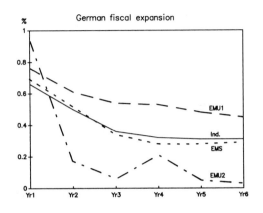

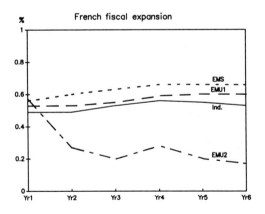

Chart 5.2 continued

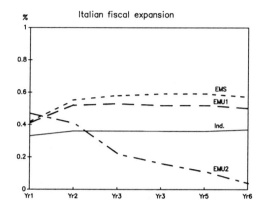

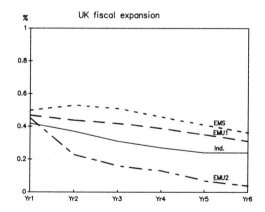

Chart 5.3 Output under the various policy regimes, OECD model, per cent difference from base

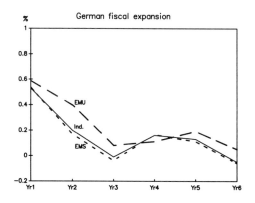

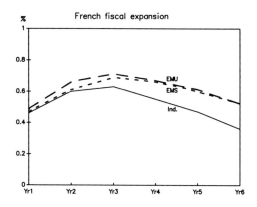

Chart 5.3 continued

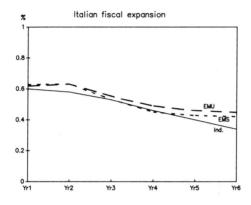

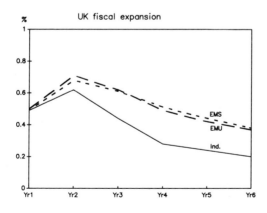

Chart 5.4 Output under the various policy regimes, DIW model, per cent difference from base

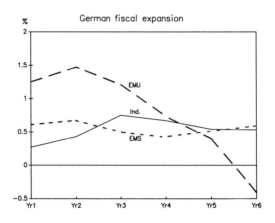

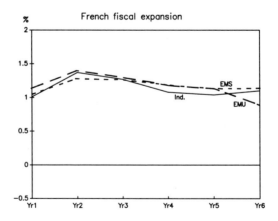

Chart 5.4 continued

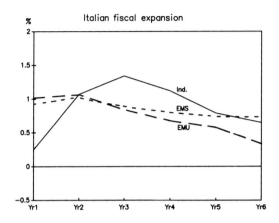

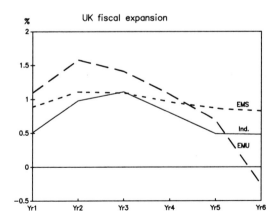

Chart 5.5 Output under the various policy regimes, OEF model, per cent difference from base

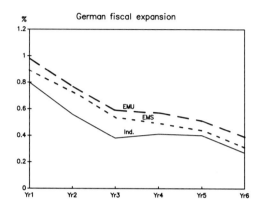

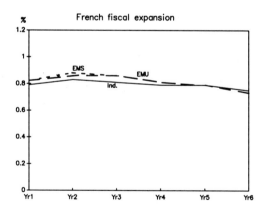

Chart 5.5 continued

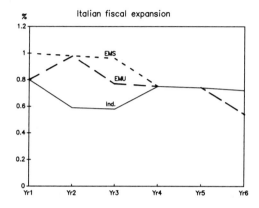

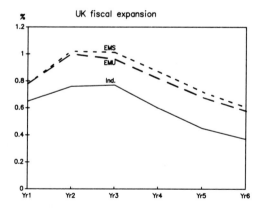

Chart 5.6 Price level response, fiscal policy simulations (after 6 years, per cent difference from base)

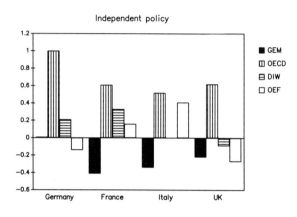

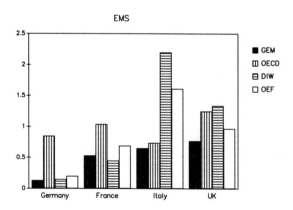

Chart 5.6 continued

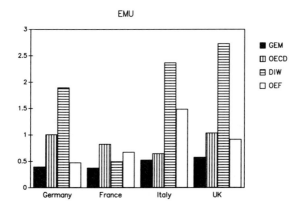

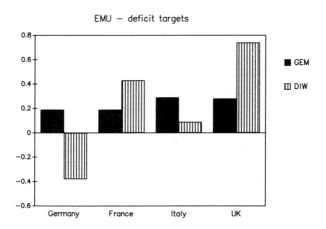

Chart 5.7 Spillover effects on output, fiscal policy simulations, NiGEM model

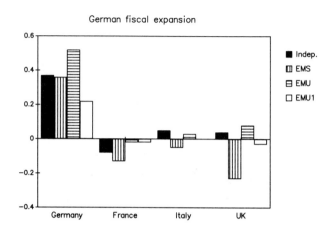

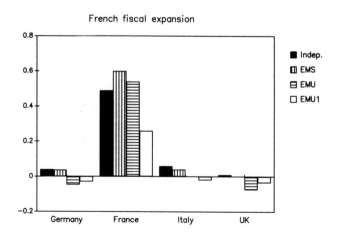

Chart 5.7 continued

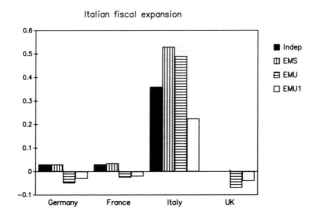

Italian fiscal expansion

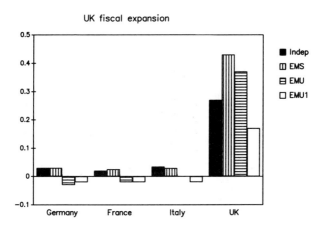

UK fiscal expansion

Chart 5.8 Current balance and government deficit independent monetary policy - fiscal shock, per cent of GDP, year six

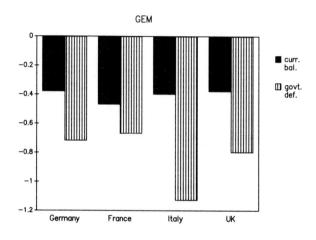

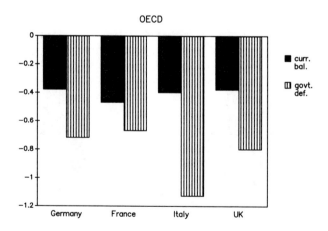

Chart 5.8 continued

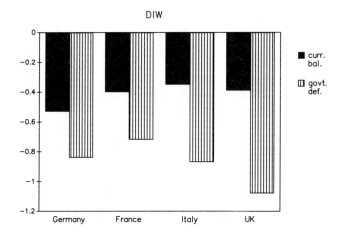

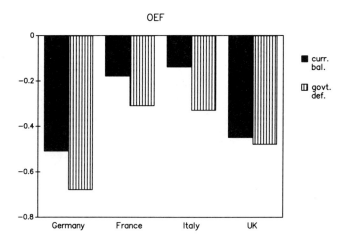

Chart 5.9 Spillover effects on output, fiscal policy simulations, DIW-QUEST model

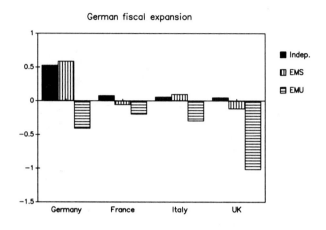

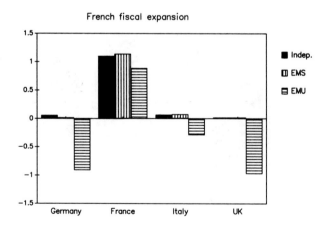

Chart 5.9 continued

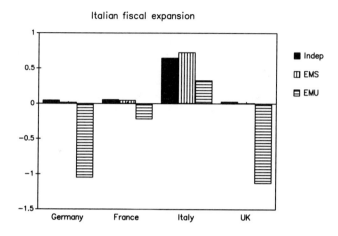

Italian fiscal expansion

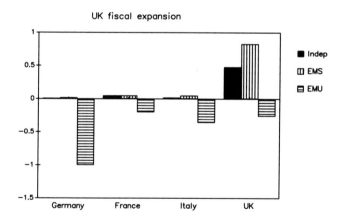

UK fiscal expansion

Chart 5.10 Exchange rates for the oil price shock, per cent difference from base

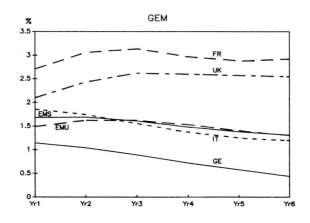

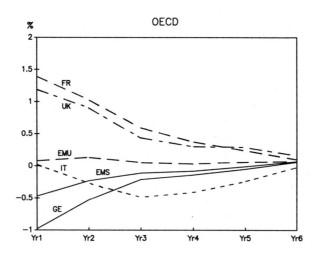

Chart 5.10 continued

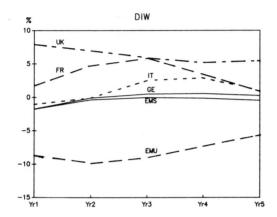

Chart 5.11 Current blance under an oil shock, independent monetary policy

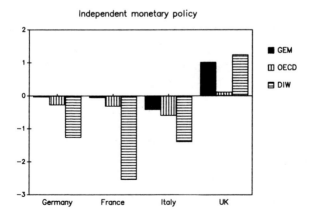

6

Policy Collaboration and Information Exchanges with Risk Averse Policymakers: the Case for Making Strategic Model Choices

A.J. Hughes Hallett

Introduction

The uncertainty which surrounds the specification and estimation of an econometric model is a major reason why policymakers are so reluctant to rely on such models and, if it is hard to establish which economic paradigm is right, there is bound to be disagreement about which model should be used. Policymakers rightly resist the idea that they should implement policies which may need frequent revisions because of a failure to perceive the economy's true responses, or because the policies are based on conflicting views of those responses. This chapter examines whether information exchanges, about models and about their policy implications, can help overcome that problem.

In an influential paper, Frankel and Rockett (1988) point out that uncertainty and disagreement pose an important difficulty for macroeconomic policymaking. They show that policymakers who are unable to agree on the model will still be able to agree on a coordinated policy package that each believes will increase their welfare. Yet, because of the uncertainty about the 'true' model, those policies can easily turn out, *ex post*, to decrease welfare. That is more a matter of uncertainty than the failure to agree *per se*, since disagreement can only follow if there is substantial uncertainty about the true model. Frankel and Rockett themselves concluded that 'the ..... bargaining solution is as likely to reduce welfare as increase it. But more definitions of cooperation should be investigated'.

Concentrating on just the policies obscures an important difficulty. If the major problem is model uncertainty, and if disagreements spring from that uncertainty, then it is hard to see how alternative ways of putting a policy package together can do much to reduce the underlying uncertainty about the way the economy works. On the other hand, alternative bargains can always be constructed which are robust against different strengths of belief about different views of the world (Holtham and Hughes Hallett, 1992). That means we can deal with disagreements, but not the underlying uncertainties. To deal with the latter, we have to look at the scope for collaboration over the choice of models. That will have the effect of combining different information about how the world works; and a strategic use of that information may help reduce the impact of uncertainty in much the same way that policy coordination can reduce the adverse spillovers between countries. Indeed no one has yet considered the relative importance of the strategic use of model information (including information exchanges) as compared to just collaborating on the policies themselves. That is the task of this chapter.

Pascal, the mathematician, used to argue that one cannot prove whether God exists or not, but that it is certainly worthwhile to act as if one knew He did exist. The reason is that, if you are right, the gains (a place in heaven) are huge but the costs, if you are wrong, are pretty small (denying oneself certain pleasures from time to time). The alternative, acting as if God did not exist, is inferior because the gains, if you are right, are small (some extra freedom) while the losses if you are wrong are immense (eternal damnation). We exploit the same principle here, taking the view that governments need to expect gains *ex post*, as well as *ex ante*, before adopting new policies. But, since they will never be able to prove whether any particular model is true or not, we must allow policymakers to make strategic choices from the available economic models with the aim of minimising the downside risks, while retaining what they can of the potential gains. If there is genuine uncertainty about the 'true' model, then model selection inevitably becomes part of a wider bargaining process which aims to pick out the best *combination* of both model and policy package. Indeed we must expect that, if governments are really concerned about uncertainty, they will make allowances for that uncertainty in their policy choices – perhaps by using simple rules or by picking robust policy-model combinations. And there is scope to do so; Ghosh and Masson (1988) report that taking explicit account of model uncertainty may actually increase the benefits of coordination.

There are two ways in which governments can allow for model uncertainty in their calculations. One possibility is to construct a compromise model (an average of the available models, each weighted by the perceived probability of being 'correct'), or to optimise the expected utility (weighted by the same prior probabilities) of the outcomes predicted by each model. The other possibility is to play explicit non-cooperative or cooperative (bargaining) games across the set of available models. The latter approach makes model choice a strategic matter; the former is passive as regards model selection. In this chapter we take the strategic approach because disagreement and uncertainty about which model(s) should be used must also mean disagreement or uncertainty about the prior probabilities to be assigned to them. As a result, an expected utility approach can offer no extra generality since each agent will be working with his own private utility calculations contingent on projected utility calculations for the other players, and the problem of model choice becomes strategic once again. Secondly, it is not clear how to set the prior probabilities when averaging models, or utilities, and we wish to avoid results which are dependent on arbitrary probability assignments. Thirdly, averaging models or utilities has the effect of 'pulling the results towards the middle', so that the overall perform-ance is unlikely to be very different from that of the original models. Frankel and Rockett failed to find any improvements, and Holtham and Hughes Hallett (1987) found cases where averaging models actually makes things worse. That is not at all surprising since we are dealing with multiplicative uncertainties. Certainty equivalent procedures are hardly likely to work well.

Of course there is also the possibility of using a learning model in which policymakers revise both their policies and their models in the light of past errors. The difficulty here is that the policymakers' errors depend on the policies and models chosen and, conversely, what they learn depends on what they have been doing. That implies the learning process, the policies and the model revisions all have to be chosen jointly. That kind of approach has proved extraordinarily difficult to implement in practice.[1] Perhaps the only thing which can be done is to model particular situations – and some experiments along those lines have now been undertaken by Ghosh and Masson (1991). Even then only very simple models can be used. However the main reason for not adopting such an approach is that, in the short term, policymakers will not be able to distin-guish a random (information) shock from a systematic (model) error. Policymakers are hardly likely to start a comprehensive revision of their models on the basis of just one or two disappointments. But they will be interested in making policy revisions and perhaps a revision to the priors which govern their choice of model. That forms the basis for our approach.

The decision framework

If both policies and models are subject to choice the following decision strategies are available:

Strategy A:
Policymakers make no attempt to agree on which model or model combination to use, or to coordinate their choice of policies. (This is the standard free-for-all strategy).

Strategy B:
Policymakers exchange information or bargain over the model, leading to some

agreement on which model (or model combination) should be used, but they make no attempt to cooperate on the policy choices (a risk averse non-cooperative approach, not examined elsewhere in the literature).

Strategy C:
Policymakers do not exchange information or discuss which model(s) should be used, but their policy choices are coordinated explicitly. (That is, they bargain on policy values, but do not discuss the justification for their particular proposals. This is the classic approach: see Frankel and Rockett 1988, and Holtham and Hughes Hallett, 1987.)

Strategy D:
Policymakers attempt (through an exchange of information) to agree on both the choice of model (or model combination) and their policies. In this case the bargain covers the joint selection of both models and policies (extending the Holtham/Hughes Hallett, 1992, treatment to allow strategic choices between models).

Strategy E:
No model is chosen. Policymakers use simple, model free rules in order to prevent the uncertainties and disagreements damaging their policy choices. (This is the strategy recommended by Feldstein, 1988).

How can policymakers take account of rival models and uncertainty? Let y^A represent the vector of deviations of player A's target variables from their ideal values at time t. Then $y^{A'} = (y_1^{A'}....y_T^{A'})$ will be the vector of target 'failures' over the decision periods $1...T$. Similarly let $x^{A'} = (x_1^{A'}...x_T^{A'})$ be the vector of deviations of player A's instruments from their ideal values. We can now define a loss function:

$$w_A = (y^{A'} C^A y^A + x^{A'} E^A x^A) \tag{6.1}$$

where C^A and E^A are positive definite symmetric matrices. This loss function will be minimised subject to a set of linear constraints:

$$y^A = R_{AA} x^A + R_{AB} x^B + s^A \tag{6.2}$$

where R_{AA} and R_{AB} are matrices containing submatrices of dynamic multipliers, and s^A represents the sum of non-controllable (random exogenous) influences on y^A. If the instrument values of the other player, B, are treated as given, the first order conditions yield a set of linear reaction functions (Hughes Hallett, 1986a):

$$X^A = -(R'_{AA}C^A R_{AA} + E^A) - R'_{AA}C^A(R_{AB}x^B + s^A) \qquad (6.3)$$

Meanwhile country B will have its own loss function $w_B = (y^{B'}C^B y^B + x^{B'}E^B x^B)$ and face the constraints $y^B = R_{BA}x^A + R_{BB}x^B + s^B$. Hence a reaction function for B, analogous to (6.3), can be solved simultaneously with (6.3) to yield the Nash equilibrium values x^A and x^B. [2] This equilibrium is, in general, not optimal even among the set of possible non-cooperative outcomes. But it is an equilibrium in the sense that, given each player presumes the other policymaker will continue what he is currently doing, then no-one has any incentive to change his instrument values. It is therefore the solution concept most commonly used in this literature. Cooperative outcomes, on the other hand, can be calculated by minimising the 'collective' loss function:

$$w = aw_A + (1-a)w_B \qquad\qquad 0 < a < 1 \qquad (6.5)$$

subject to the constraints represented by (6.2) and its counterpart for y^B.

If there is model uncertainty, then there are rival values of the policy multipliers which might be used in these calculations. For example we might use multipliers R_{AA}, R_{AB} and R_{BA}, R_{BB} (and s^A, s^B), computed either from model A or from model B, to evaluate and compare the optimal non-cooperative and co-operative policies in welfare terms (wA, wB).

Model disagreement, on the other hand, appears when player A uses model A (say) to describe the constraints on his targets while player B uses model B to define the constraints on y^B. In that case (6.2) and its counterpart for y^B will be replaced by the mixed set of constraints:

$$\begin{bmatrix} y^A \\ y^B \end{bmatrix} = \begin{bmatrix} R^A_{AA} & R^A_{AB} \\ R^B_{BA} & R^B_{BB} \end{bmatrix} \begin{bmatrix} x^A \\ x^B \end{bmatrix} + \begin{bmatrix} s^A \\ s^B \end{bmatrix} \qquad (6.6)$$

where the superscript on each R matrix indicates whose model was used to derive the dynamic multipliers which that matrix contains. Substituting these constraints for y^A and y^B in w_A and w_B yields non-cooperative and cooperative policies under disagreement, and simulating those policies through models A and B respectively will give the outcomes expected by each player in turn.

Experimental design

In Holtham and Hughes Hallett (1987) we drew a distinction between *ex ante* and *ex post* robustness. The former has to do with model disagreements among the participating decision makers, while the latter is associated with model uncertainty. A cooperative policy bargain would be robust *ex ante* if, irrespective of the model our opponents might choose, our model predicts a gain (for us) over non-cooperative policymaking, while at the same time our opponents' model predicts that they will also make a gain irrespective of the model we might use. If, in addition, no losses are to be expected across the range of alternative or possible 'truths', then we could say the policy bargain was robust *ex post*. However, what actually happens may turn out to be better or worse than those expectations, depending on how far away from the truth the two maintained models really are.

In order to minimise the sensitivity of the expected policy outcomes to model errors or disagreements, we have to examine the *ex post* robustness of policies derived from different choices of model and policy regime. The standard way to do that is to compute expected outcomes when the policy packages which are optimal for each model, or combination of models, are evaluated according to each of the other models in the sample (Chow, 1981, Hughes Hallett and Rees, 1983, Becker *et al.*, 1986). This is the only practical way of simulating, *ex ante*, what could happen if the world behaved differently from the maintained model(s). It is, of course, an act of considerable faith to suppose that the available models represent all the possible states of the world. The difficulty here is not the expense of adding extra models, but the fact that we can never know which other specifications should be included.

In this chapter the *ex post* robustness of optimal cooperative and non-cooperative policymaking is examined using a group of four models drawn from the group of twelve that reported to the Brookings model comparison seminar in 1986 (Bryant *et al*, 1988), and which also used the Frankel-Rockett(1988) and Holtham-Hughes Hallett (1987) studies. The properties of those models, and the differences between them, are documented extensively in Bryant *et al.* and supporting references. That discussion will not be repeated here. In any case, the overall policy responses are complicated functions of so many similarities and differences in specification within and between the countries modelled that it effectively becomes impossible to lay any particular result unambiguously at the door of any given model. If it were easy to do that, model choice would not pose much of a problem. Instead we work from the Brookings comparison exercise which analysed the results of simulating a set of standardised macroeconomic policy actions taken in the United States, for the US economy and for the rest of the OECD (ROECD). Those standardised simulations were performed on each of the models in turn and then parallel results were generated for policy actions taken in the ROECD. In what follows we use matrices of dynamic multipliers from the Brookings exercise and treat them as invariant to the level of economic activity. Strictly speaking this procedure only approximates the properties of a non-linear model, but most investigators agree that the errors are small in terms of policy choice. Finally each model uses the same standardised baseline so that the differences in optimised policies due to model variations do not become confused with changes due to different definitions of the baseline position.

The four models used in the exercises reported here were MCM, LINK, EC and MINIMOD. These are four of the most widely used empirical multicountry models. MCM and LINK were selected because they represent the least risk choices for cooperative and non-cooperative policymaking (respectively) in the Frankel-Rockett and Holtham-Hughes Hallett results on model uncertainty. The next best performer was the EC model, and the best of the rational expectations models was MINIMOD.

For the sensitivity analysis, a benchmark objective function has to be specified as a standard of comparison. We have made no attempt to infer 'as if' parameters for this objective function from the actual values of policy instruments in the recent past, as Oudiz and Sachs (1984) do. That would only be legitimate if there were just one model which the policymakers believe since the 'as if' parameters will be dependent on the model used to generate them. Since our purpose is to estimate the size of the gains from cooperation across a range of models, the 'as if' procedure would bias the results towards one model and might exaggerate the differences between models and their projected outcomes.

A 'plausible' parameterisation of a standard quadratic utility function was used for each country across all models. Each country sets its own priorities and ideal values. The arguments in the hypothesised utility functions were: GNP growth, the rate of consumer price inflation, the (nominal) exchange rate, and the balance of foreign trade. Government expenditures and the rate of growth of the money supply (M1) are the policy instruments. Deviations of either instrument from a constant growth path are penalised to prevent excessive movements. Further details on the models' specifications and properties will be found in Bryant *et al.* (1988), and the summary of their policy responses in Holtham and Hughes Hallett (1987).

The impact of model uncertainty and disagreement on policy performance

Policymakers happen to agree on the choice of model
Tables 6.1 and 6.2 show the payoff matrices under non-cooperative and cooperative policy regimes. Each column shows the expected value of the US and ROECD loss functions using the optimised policies from the indicated

Table 6.1 Pay-off matrix for optimal non-cooperative (Nash) results: maintained model

	LINK	EC	MCM	MINI
LINK	551.4	858.5	5580.0	6203.5
	750.6	720.3	8403.8	6103.3
EC	688.8	480.4	4778.6	3503.2
	873.7	766.5	9463.6	3360.7
REALITY				
MCM	484.8	428.6	678.5	1086.6
	701.1	571.7	1345.6	1474.5
MINI	477.4	326.7	1565.7	1003.9
	601.6	414.2	3253.6	1085.7
MINIMAX	688.8*	858.5	5580.0	6203.5
	873.7	766.5*	9463.6	6103.3

Notes: The cell in the upper row relating to each model is the loss-function value for the United States; the lower row is loss-function value for ROECD. Columns are maintained model; rows denote the model corresponding to reality.

Table 6.2 Pay-off matrix for cooperative (a=½) results: maintained model

	LINK	EC	MCM	MINI
LINK	366.3	860.6	819.7	2104.4
	470.7	851.7	958.3	2142.3
EC	1283.7	382.2	1028.9	3452.9
REALITY	2497.9	492.0	1318.0	3587.7
MCM	16807.6	7707.2	323.6	10263.8
	9741.5	22475.5	450.8	5497.7
MINI	1206.1	1991.5	751.7	294.3
	1787.6	3668.0	1013.9	482.8
MINIMAX	16087.6	7707.2	1028.9*	10263.8
	9741.5	22475.5	1318.0*	5497.7

maintained model, when the 'true' state of the world is given by the model named in each row. The diagonal elements therefore show outcomes when the maintained model is correct; the other elements show the outcomes under various model errors.

No cooperation:

Suppose that policymakers have diffuse priors – they are not dogmatic – and suppose that they are risk averse and wish to use a minimax criterion for selecting the model and policy combination. If they do not wish to cooperate but assume, at least to start with, that their opponents will believe the same model as they do, the US policymakers would select the LINK model and its associated policy package, while the ROECD would prefer the EC model. Policymakers would inevitably tend to disagree, therefore.

Cooperation:

Suppose, instead, that policymakers have a prior commitment to cooperation and are looking for the best model on which to proceed. The MCM model clearly dominates on the minimax outcome criterion (table 6.2). It is in fact the only model which predicts gains from coordination in all cases, or indeed yields a positive expected return from coordination when each model is assigned an equal prior probability of being 'correct'. Moreover the MCM model continues to dominate when the range of possible 'truths' is extended to the set of ten models considered by Holtham and Hughes Hallett (1987).

A comparison of tables 6.1 and 6.2 shows that cooperative policymaking clearly entails greater downside risks for the US than does non-cooperative policymaking,[3] and that the losses risked may be quite a lot larger than the coordination gains one could hope to make if the chosen model turns out to be 'correct'.

The downside risks for the ROECD follow exactly the same pattern, but they turn out to be more serious than for the US. Nevertheless the maximum losses risked with non-cooperative policies based on the LINK model are less, for both countries, than the maximum losses risked under cooperation based on any model. That illustrates our first major finding: although non-cooperative policies cannot secure all the gains available through cooperation, they do not carry the risk of such large downside losses either.

Policymakers do not agree on the model

Tables 6.1 and 6.2 presented only submatrices of the 64 possible outcomes which could arise when policymakers are uncertain about which model(s) they should use.[4] Tables 6.3 and 6.4 complete the story by showing the results of explicit disagreement under non-cooperative and cooperative policymaking respectively.

Table 6.3 The pay-off matrix for non-cooperative policies with disagreement over the models

Maintained models	Reality									
	LINK		EC		MCM		MINI		MINIMAX (a)	
	W/US	W/RO	W/US	W/RO	W/US	W/RO	W/US	W/RO	W/US	W/RO
US=LINK RO=MCM	259.2	488.3	501.9	481.6	1502.5	2190.3	1238.8	1419.0	1502.5*	9463.0
US=EC RO=MCM	305.6	565.6	281.5	446.1	1807.5	2844.7	1294.9	1633.0	1807.5*	9463.0*
US=MINI RO=MCM	325.1	547.4	277.0	450.3	727.9	1253.2	590.1	869.9	6203.0	9463.0
US=MCM RO=LINK	3915.2	630.2	5214.0	1004.0	10975.0	7405.4	4805.7	2237.7	10975.0	7405.4*
US=EC RO=LINK	365.0	496.9	315.1	372.8	3683.7	6834.7	2731.4	2803.1	3683.7*	6834.7*
US=MINI RO=LINK	346.6	458.5	300.8	367.2	2322.7	4212.4	1873.0	2000.1	6203.0	4212.4*
US=MCM RO=EC	379.5	628.5	266.3	490.9	935.0	3719.0	527.5	861.3	5580.0	3719.0*
US=LINK RO=EC	358.2	697.0	462.5	564.3	2465.7	6166.9	1659.9	1809.3	2465.7*	6166.9*
US=MINI RO=EC	336.8	621.3	192.8	485.2	1333.9	3958.1	534.7	850.4	6203.0	3958.1*
US=MCM RO=MINI	346.2	446.5	320.9	429.0	758.2	2944.6	700.5	828.7	5580.0	6103.0
US=LINK RO=MINI	269.2	423.6	476.0	322.7	2032.4	4125.6	1659.8	1527.6	2032.4	6103.0
US=EC RO=MINI	368.8	453.9	278.2	318.3	2316.9	5166.1	1652.9	1664.6	2316.9*	5166.1

Notes: (a) The minimum loss which each country could sustain by maintaining the model named in the row descriptor (from tables 6.1 and 6.3). * denotes the maximum loss is supplied by model disagreement.

Table 6.4 The pay-off matrix for cooperative ($\alpha = \frac{1}{2}$) policies with disagreement over the models

	Reality									
	LINK		EC		MCM		MINI		MINIMAX (a)	
Maintained models	W/US	W/RO	W/US	W/RO	W/US	W/RO	W/US	W/RO	W/US	W/RO
US=LINK RO=MCM	297.9	511.1	555.8	483.6	1934.9	3181.5	2015.7	2149.3	16087.6	1318.0
US=EC RO=MCM	335.8	575.3	310.4	475.5	3580.0	5061.0	3464.0	3780.0	7707.2	5061.0*
US=MINI RO=MCM	333.6	553.3	258.6	462.1	3792.0	4437.0	887.0	1241.0	10263.8	4437.0*
US=MCM RO=LINK	406.2	534.3	430.4	493.8	2630.0	5085.0	5297.0	5534.0	5297.0*	9741.5
US=EC RO=LINK	421.4	593.0	391.7	495.6	4063.0	8514.0	7961.0	8105.0	7061.0*	9746.5*
US=MINI RO=LINK	367.2	510.7	333.7	442.0	2886.0	5454.0	4808.0	5015.0	10263.8	9741.5*
US=MCM RO=EC	423.9	604.9	329.2	476.2	1879.0	4663.0	1950.0	2185 0	1950.0*	22475.5
US=LINK RO=EC	471.9	747.1	680.9	616.6	3640.7	8671.1	3239.0	3211.1	16087.6	22475.5
US=MINI RO=EC	368.0	577.1	229.7	430.2	2241.0	5234.0	1872.0	207.0	10263.8	22475.5
US=MCM RO=MINI	357.0	453.6	342.2	445.5	1618.0	3050.0	1242.0	1373.0	1681.0*	5497.4*
US=LINK RO=MINI	329.3	457.2	566.5	359.7	2551.6	5619.4	2528.3	2363.7	16087.6*	5619.4*
US=EC RO=MINI	445.1	460.3	361.5	345.6	2994.0	6915.0	4343.0	4314.0	4343.0	4314.0

Notes: see table 6.3.

No cooperation:

Disagreement over the model evidently adds significantly to the risks which policymakers face in a non-cooperative environment. Under a 'minimax' criterion, 14 out of 24 entries in the final double column of table 6.3 show that disagreement produces a worse outcome with a given pair of maintained models, than would agreement to adopt either model from that pair. Interestingly disagreement produces all these bad outcomes from the case where MCM is 'true'. In fact, contrasting table 6.3 with table 6.1, the outcomes when either LINK or EC represent reality are uniformly better under disagreement than under agreement; those when MINI represents reality are roughly the same either way, while those when MCM represents reality are all rather worse under disagreement. So the incidence of risk is very unevenly spread across alternative states of the world, but fairly evenly spread over the different combinations of the maintained models. Hence our second finding is that, if policymakers fail to make any allowance for potential model errors, they will have rather little to control over the risks generated by uncertainty *either* about the 'true' model or about which model their opponents are likely to choose. The fact that model disagreement may, in some cases, produce better results *ex post* illustrates the practical importance of mixing information to produce policy responses which are closer to reality.

Cooperation:

Turning now to the cooperative case (table 6.4), disagreement over the model appears to offset some of the risks of model uncertainty; the entries in the columns of table 6.4 are smaller than the corresponding rows of table 6.2 for LINK, EC and MCM (but not MINI). This happens because mixing the constraints, as in (6.6), introduces the characteristics and information of another possible model. The resulting combination of two models necessarily produces results 'closer' to the various alternative realities than either of those models could have done individually. Consequently we find that model disagreement exaggerates the risks facing policymakers less under cooperation than under non-cooperation – only 8 out of 24 of the maximum losses due to model errors now arise through disagreement, compared to 14 out of 24 in table 6.3. That is our third finding.

Minimax model selection criteria:

The minimax approach to model selection requires some justification. As a criterion it is only one way of handling multiplicative uncertainty and it reflects a highly risk averse attitude. It is, however, the recommended decision criterion in the presence of rival models (see Chow, 1981, Becker *et al.*, 1986). It is also the criterion used by previous authors in the field so that comparisons between their policy bargains and our model choice approach must first be made on a minimax basis.

Nevertheless some policymakers might prefer to optimise their expected welfare outcomes, recognising that models other than their own choice may be true. Frankel and Rockett, for example, suppose that players would assign probabilities to each model being correct and then pick policies to maximise their own expected welfare. Note that this does not mean constructing a consensus model, using probability priors on a first order certainty equivalent basis in order to give a closed form solution. Instead it requires policymakers to maximise $\Sigma P_i U(Y_i)$, where $U(.)$ denotes policymaker i's utility function, P_i the (*ex ante* assigned) probability that model i is true, and Y_i the set of target variable values obtained by applying certain policies to model i. One might expect this approach to be superior to each policymaker picking just one model and sticking to it. But the situation is more complicated than that because an expected utility criterion does not in fact imply any extra generality. There are several points to make here. First Frankel and Rockett's calculations show that the success rate of policy cooperation over no cooperation fell from 60 per cent and 85 per cent for the US and Europe, to 60 per cent and 20 per cent when an expected utility criterion was substituted for a single model-by-model optimisation process. Hence the *ex post* probability of (model) error may be worse, at least for one player, and there is no point in pressing ahead with the expected utility approach in such cases.

Second, an expected utility approach provides no extra generality once it is recognised that agents will generally disagree about their subjective probability priors, implying that there will be uncertainty about which priors correctly describe the relative frequency that each model is 'right'. That puts us back to square one. Holtham and Hughes Hallett (1992) show that exactly the same selection strategies will be played as in the minimax case since model j will just be replaced by agent j's probability weighted average of the available models (for each j in turn). That produces the usual pair of pay-off matrices and we have to choose between them in the usual way – including allowing once again for the possibility of policy and model bargains. In other words, no extra generality is obtained because disagreement/uncertainty do not require each player to pick just one model. Instead they imply that each player will assign different (and uncertain) probability weights to the available models.

A third point is that, if the aim is to reduce the frequency of *ex post* losses, we have to be able to identify the chances of a type I error (rejecting a good model selection/policy bargain) and a type II error (accepting a bad selection/ bargain). Only then can we choose to maximise the probability of a correct decision (Holtham and Hughes Hallett, 1992, table 1). Simply maximising expected utilities cannot get us that far, unless the usual pay-off matrices are subsequently examined as well. A minimax criterion is also helpful here because it avoids results which are dependent on arbitrary prior probability assignments.

Strategic model choices and information exchanges

Policymakers agree to agree (or agree to differ) on the choice of model
No cooperation:
Taking the results of tables 6.1 and 6.3 together we find that allowing policymakers
to choose their models on a rational (risk averse) basis, but giving them no
opportunity to exchange information about those choices, would lead the US
to maintain the LINK model and the ROECD to adopt the MINI model, since
(in complete ignorance of the other's intentions) the US could then limit its
losses to 2465 at worst and the ROECD would limit its losses to 6103. Both
countries would risk larger losses if they *unilaterally* adopted any other models.

This is therefore the outcome of *Strategy A*: policymakers make no attempt
to agree on the best model or model combination or to coordinate their policy
choices. But it produces results which fall a long way short of what they could
achieve under *Strategy B* where policymakers can agree on which model (or
models) to use, or where they exchange enough information to allow them to
predict the choices made by other policymakers. For example, if both the US
and the ROECD could agree to use LINK in a non-cooperative environment
they could limit their maximum losses to just 688 and 873 respectively; that
is a third or less of the losses recorded under Strategy A. They might do this
by reading through the outcomes in a pay-off matrix constructed from tables 6.1
and 6.3 together, to find a model choice which generates a sufficient Pareto gain
over Strategy A. Even better, they could look for an optimal bargain, in terms
of the choice of model or model combination compared to strategy A, while
retaining a non-cooperative choice of policies.

Even if explicit bargains on the choice of model are not possible (for
example, a search cannot be organised, or agreement cannot be reached because
one country has very strong priors on a particular type of model), information
exchanges sufficient to enable policymakers to make predictions about the
choices made by others may be enough to reduce the problems of disagreement
and the risk of serious performance losses. For example if the US knew or could
predict that the ROECD would choose MINI as its model, then the US would
pick LINK expecting a maximum loss of 2032 (and one of 6103 for the ROECD).
But if the ROECD knew or deduced that the US would pick LINK, then it would
choose LINK too (reducing its maximum loss risked to 873 and that for the US
to 688). Similarly, if either country knew or predicted that the rival would use
the EC model, then it would choose the same, implying a maximum loss of 859
for the US and 767 for the ROECD. However this second example is not
produced by playing a model choice game starting from ignorance of the
opponent's intentions (Strategy A), and it produces a smaller product of gains
over Strategy A than does the LINK model solution. Hence the LINK version
of Strategy B corresponds to a Nash (or, as it happens, Harsayni) model bargain
and is the natural outcome of playing a bargaining game across alternative

model choices. For that reason we use the LINK model bargain to represent Strategy B from now on.

The implication of all this is that a policymaker sophisticated enough to worry about the effects of model uncertainty is unlikely to pick one of the (high-risk) disagreement solutions – or, to make the same point another way, the incentives to go for an information exchange about models and information sets, but to continue to pick policies in a non-cooperative manner, are really quite large. That is our fourth and most important finding.

Cooperation:

Repeating the same arguments on the results in tables 6.2 and 6.4 shows that both US and the ROECD would want to use the MCM model since their maximum losses (in ignorance of each other's intentions) would be limited to 5297 and 5061. Alternative model choices lay them open to the risk of much greater losses. This is the outcome generated by *Strategy C*: policymakers make no attempt to agree on a model or a combination of models, but they do try to cooperate on the choice of policies. That means they would have to bargain on policy values without saying what mechanisms were thought to generate those policies or why those particular policies were being proposed for a bargain. That of course is exactly the 'black box' approach adopted by Frankel and Rockett (1988) and it has equally disastrous results in terms of downside risks.

Once again the choice of model is important here and one must expect policymakers to choose their models to reduce the policy risks faced. If they do so, the results change dramatically. Consider an information exchange which allows policymakers to choose a model bargain together with a policy bargain. Alternatively, suppose there are information flows sufficient for them to make reasonable projections of their opponent's potential outcomes and then simulate a bargaining game across those outcomes. Either approach leads to *Strategy D*. A bargaining game here would lead to agreement on the MCM model with the US and ROECD expecting maximum losses of 1028 and 1318 respectively – about one quarter of the losses expected under Strategy C. Strategy D therefore produces better results than the best non-cooperative outcomes when disagreement is possible and there are no information exchanges, but worse outcomes than when policymakers can 'agree to agree, or to disagree, on the model choice' but do not cooperate on the policies. Thus our fourth conclusion also carries over to coordinated policies: model disagreement exaggerates the risks, and a powerful way of reducing those risks is to cooperate on picking a suitable model.

Simple (fixed) policy rules

Our final strategy (*Strategy E*) is to follow policies which are fixed independently of any particular model specification. This is an obvious way of trying to avoid the inevitable uncertainties and errors associated with any particular model specification since the true model can never be known exactly. Many authors have argued that highly developed decision rules, such as those being operated here, are not robust enough to be reliable when there is a substantial uncertainty about the true economic responses or planning priorities. Fixed policy rules, they argue, give nearly as good a performance on average, but without the attendant downside risks.[5]

Fixed rules also simplify matters. Not only do policymakers avoid any complicated decision procedures designed to reduce the possible risks from model errors or model disagreements, they do not even have to maintain any formal model or information gathering network.

Table 6.5 sets out the results of applying fixed policy rules to each of our four models. The instruments have been set to the ideal values of the previous exercise: government expenditure in the US falls by 1 per cent of GNP each year (from 20 per cent to 15 per cent, to eliminate the US budget deficit); government expenditures in ROECD remain at their historical value of 22 per cent of GNP; and monetary growth is assumed to be constant at 5 per cent in the US and at 6 per cent in ROECD. This is a scenario of fiscal conservatism and neutral monetary growth. It is not the only possible fixed rule scenario, but it is the obvious one since it represents the optimal policy when the priorities on reaching the targets are reduced (Hughes Hallett, 1979). Hence other fixed rules do not perform any better under the standardised objectives and baseline which have been used throughout these comparisons.

Table 6.5 Objective function values for the fixed rule policies

REALITY	MCM	EC	LINK	MINI
w*/US	1924.2	938.2	1005.7	1150.6
w*/RO	1753.9	924.1	1047.6	1095.0

The objective function values in table 6.5 show significant losses compared to the minimax non-cooperative outcomes under information exchange or model agreement; compare table 6.5 with the outcomes of Strategy B and with table 6.1 respectively. (For ease of reference, the minimax outcomes obtained for Strategies A-E are collected together in table 6.6). On the other hand, fixed rules appear to perform much better when there is no information exchange or attempt to agree on (a pair of) models; compare the minimax outcomes under Strategy A. The same thing happens with cooperative policies; fixed rules perform well when there is no information exchange (compare Strategy C) but poorly when compared to exchanges of information or agreement on the choice of models (Strategy D). Naturally enough, the potential gains from coordination when we get the model right are not obtained. Fixed rules therefore eliminate the downside risks of model disagreements and uncertainty fairly effectively, but at the cost of not being able to capture any of the upside gains when the model turns out to be right.

Table 6.6 A summary of the best Minimax solutions under five different strategies of information exchange and policy selection

Strategy	w*/US	w*/RO	Models used
A	2465	6103	US=LINK/RO=MINI
B	688	873	US=LINK/RO=LINK
C	5297	5061	US=MCM/RO=MCM
D	1028	1318	US=MCM/RO=MCM
E	1924	1754	Model free policy rules

Strategy A: no attempt to exchange information (bargain) on the models or to cooperate on policies.

Strategy B: exchange information (bargain) on choice of models but no cooperation on policies.

Strategy C: no attempt to exchange information (bargain) on the models, but cooperate on policies.

Strategy D: exchange information (agree) on choice of both models and policies.

Strategy E: 'optimal' fixed rules.

The fact that these outcomes are more robust than either the non-cooperative or the cooperative results shows that policy conflicts, whether fully exploited in the non-cooperative case or partially resolved in the cooperative case, greatly increase the risks faced by policymakers. But, by the same token, these results do not constitute grounds for adopting fixed rules since table 6.6 also shows that the risk of sustaining large losses can be more effectively eliminated by carefully selecting and possibly agreeing on the model. The maximum losses, whichever model turns out to be 'true', are 1924.2 for the US and 1753.9 for ROECD. Strategy E is therefore worse, for both the US and ROECD, than maintaining optimal non-cooperative policies in either the LINK or EC models. It is also worse for both countries than using cooperative policies in the MCM model. Thus both countries can eliminate risks better, while also retaining the possibility of securing some of the 'upside' gains, if they both adopt the LINK or EC models and non-cooperative policies, or if they both adopt the MCM model and cooperate.

Once again these results stress the importance of attempting to reach agreement on the choice of model and its projections. Provided models are sensibly chosen, simple rules are no substitute for a proper information exchange. That means simple rules should be used when you really have no confidence in existing models and no alternatives to suggest in their place. In all other cases, risk sensitive decision rules are preferable to either certainty equivalent or model free approximations.

Conclusions

The results in table 6.6 emphasise the importance of allowing policymakers to make a careful selection of the model (or model combination) to be used for policy design. Ideally policies and models should be jointly selected. Information exchanges sufficient to construct the relevant pay-off matrices will allow these model bargains to be identified.

Frankel and Rockett (1988) argue that the gains to one country unilaterally discovering the true model and adjusting its policies accordingly are usually much greater than the potential gains from coordination. Since they will never find the perfect model, that is not much practical help to the policymakers although it will help to set their research agenda. Our results are strikingly similar but of greater operational significance. We find that the gains (in terms of risk management) from choosing the right model, whether as a model bargain or by exchanging sufficient information to allow each country to make its own choice, are generally much greater than the gains from policy coordination itself. This result runs counter to the existing literature which has focused on the careful choice of policies and policy bargains, but not on the choice of models and model bargains.

Cooperative policies pose greater 'downside' risks as well as the possibility of larger 'upside' gains. Non-cooperative policies are more robust; the losses risked under non-cooperative policymaking are smaller but the opportunity to make policy improvements is also smaller. Consequently the arguments for policy coordination turn very much on one's attitude to risk.

Disagreement over the model exaggerates the losses risked, but less so under cooperative policymaking because of the implicit information sharing. This is the key result. An intuitive explanation is that cooperation, even if there is disagreement over the model, automatically mixes the constraints (and hence information) from different models/policymakers. If policymakers then make an active choice between models, and if the set of models spans or approximates the truth, they will be able to eliminate much of the risk of unexpected losses while retaining the expectation of making gains. Even if they fail to coordinate their policies, but recognise different models and make a systematic choice between them, they will be able to realise most of those risk reductions but without the coordination gains. Similarly if they coordinate their policies but make no effort to choose between models, they will retain the chance of coordination gains but fail to reduce any of the losses risked.

The advantage of making strategic model choices is that, in a world of multiplicative as well as additive uncertainties, it allows policymakers to go beyond certainty equivalence. It is therefore hardly surprising that the key to risk reduction is to agree on which model(s) should be used. Policy bargains, by contrast, achieve gains by making better use of a given information set (or sets, if there is disagreement). The incentives for information exchanges on the models and their conditioning information are therefore quite large.

Fixed (model free) policy rules are no substitute for using a well chosen model in either a non-cooperative or cooperative policy environment. Fixed rules are nevertheless effective for reducing downside risks although that can be done rather better by allowing agents to bargain over models.

Notes

1 See for example Kendrick (1981), or Aoki (1967) pp.103-16, for the complications which arise even in the single player context. In this case, the learning model has to be able to distinguish 'errors' made because the model is 'incorrect' from errors in the policies which have been projected for other players (possibly because we didn't know which model they would use) and from errors caused because 'incorrect' conditioning (exogenous) information has been used. And, even if that can be done with confidence, which seems most unlikely in practice (but see Ghosh and Masson, 1991), the learning model must be able to identify which of the many model parameters has caused the observed 'errors'. Note also that we focus on multiplicative (or model) uncertainties here. That appears to be the problem which concerns economists and policymakers most. The robustness of policy bargains under additive (or information) uncertainty has already been analysed in Brandsma and Hughes Hallett (1989).

2 The non-cooperative solutions, and the cooperative decisions obtained from minimising (6.5) subject to (6.6) below, are derived and analysed in Hughes Hallett (1986a).

3 The risks highlighted in this section are all evaluated with cooperative policies based on an arbitrary choice of $\alpha = \frac{1}{2}$. Would those perceived risks change with alternative bargains ? Applying the most popular bargaining model (Nash) to all ten models in the Holtham and Hughes Hallett (1987) study generated only two extra cases of cooperative gains and one extra loss. Hence, in this case, the estimated risks are extremely robust to the type of bargain struck.

4 In principle a rational expectations model like MINIMOD allows the private sector to believe a third model (different from either subscribed to by the two governments) while a fourth could turn out to be true. But in that case the expectations themselves could not be model consistent from either government's point of view, and that would violate the rational expectations assumption which each government is said to hold. So we do not consider this possibility any further.

5 This sort of argument appears in several places. Friedman (1953), for example, recommended fixed rules for counteracting uncertainty in model parameters. Fischer and Cooper (1973), Lucas (1976), and Kydland and Prescott (1977) consider fixed rules for counteracting uncertainty in the dynamics, policy responses, and the expectations. More directly, Feldstein (1988) has argued that model uncertainties may well wipe out potential gains to coordination and that fixed rules should therefore be used to eliminate that risk.

7

Is the Road to Monetary Union Paved with Recession?

John Driffill and Marcus Miller*

Introduction

Exchange-rate stability is a key feature of the European Monetary System (EMS) as most members of the Exchange Rate Mechanism are required to keep their currencies within a narrow ecu band. The initial motivation for this was to ensure stable trading conditions in the European Community, particularly for farmers. Over time, however, the EMS has evolved into a mechanism for checking inflation: the peg against the ecu has allowed other countries to use the D-Mark as a nominal anchor, a way of locking their currencies to that of Germany. The Bundesbank has been resolute in the pursuit of low inflation, so member countries without independent central banks can, in this way, benefit from the credibility already acquired by the Bundesbank. The effect this should, in principle, have on expected and actual inflation may be demonstrated using the analytical framework of Barro and Gordon (1983b). This framework has been discussed by Bean (1992) in a post-Maastricht context.

Inflation rates in Germany's partners have indeed come down; but this has taken quite some time (and has been associated with considerable economic slack). At a meeting convened by the Federal Reserve Board to discuss the EMS, Alberto Giovannini emphasised a problem that this time lag poses for the inflation convergence, namely that a country which is competitive *vis-à-vis* Germany at the time it pegs its currency will become more and more uncompetitive as long as its inflation rate exceeds that of Germany. So when its inflation rate ultimately converges, its price level will be too high: a situation which can only be corrected by a subsequent period of inflation *below* that

*We are grateful for the assistance of Francesco Giordano and Lei Zhang and for financial support from the European Commission under SPES Project No. 0016-NL, Macroeconomic Policy and Monetary Integration in Europe. This chapter draws on joint work on regime switches with Alan Sutherland and has benefited from the comments of participants at the SPES Conference on International Macro Models at Warwick in March 1992, in particular those of David Currie. Errors remain our responsibility.

in Germany. This sequence of events is illustrated in chart 7.1 where inflation differentials and relative prices are both plotted over time. The positive inflation differential disappears at T_1; but there follows a second period (T_1 to T_2) of negative inflation differentials, as required to restore competitiveness.

Chart 7.1 The problem of inflation convergence with fixed rates

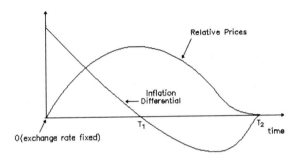

In this chapter we examine one possible cause for such a delay in achieving inflation convergence, namely the lack of credibility of the currency peg; and we spell out the possible consequences using a model of overlapping contracts.[1] Given that expectations are rational there would be no problem of inflation convergence with a fully credible currency anchor. But a lack of credibility adds an inflation premium to forward-looking wage contracts (as required to offset future expected devaluations); and this shows up as an expected inflation term in the Phillips relation between inflation and output.

Price stability requires a recession large enough to damp down the wage claims driven by these devaluation expectations. Does this mean that the 'natural rate of unemployment' will rise in countries joining the ERM? No, not if keeping exchange rates fixed reduces fears of devaluation to zero over time. If agents entertain two possibilities, either a 'high' realignment frequency (ρ_H) or zero realignment, then we show that the estimated frequency ($\hat{\rho}$) falls to zero under Bayesian learning if there are no realignments. This process of learning may ensure that long-run levels of output and employment are not affected by the regime change; but as learning takes time it gives rise to precisely the problem highlighted by Giovannini in the short term. In particular, we note that the recession caused by the overvaluation continues beyond the point when inflation rates have converged, that is, at T_1 in chart 7.1.

Superficially, it might appear that the problem can be solved by a devaluation at time T_1. But the same model of Bayesian learning outlined above also implies that agents will, in response, promptly raise their devaluation expectations; so devaluation *per se* is self-defeating. Two other ideas are briefly discussed. The first is that the perceived high realignment frequency (ρ_H) might be *state dependent*; so when inflation is brought down below the German level policymakers might benefit from a fall in ρ_H, the upper bound on the realignment frequency. The second is the proposal made in the Maastricht Treaty, which requires a two-year period without realignment as a precondition for joining the common currency bloc. This condition was designed to allow countries to correct relative prices by a last realignment two years or so before irrevocably locking parities.

Fear of devaluation, inflation and recession

The setting

Consider the case of a country with a history of persistent inflation (matched by monetary accommodation and currency depreciation), which has become embedded in overlapping wage contracts. Let the policymakers announce a change of policy, seeking instead to stabilise inflation by pegging the exchange rate against a hard (non-inflationary) currency, but without actually adopting a single currency. To keep things simple, let the policy be one of a simple peg and not an exchange-rate band. How will those setting contracts react to the pegging of the exchange rate?

Assume that they are willing to believe that the government has changed its ways, but allow also for some 'recidivism', with the initial prior attached to each of these possibilities being revised in the light of observation and experience. In the absence of capital controls (or currency bands), this recidivism is expected to take the form of random devaluations — possibly starting with the same expected depreciation as before the peg. But expected devaluation will tend to perpetuate domestic inflation despite the hard currency peg. How this affects inflation and output will be analysed in a simple model of overlapping contracts.

Overlapping contracts

To allow for the direct impact of expected future events on current wages whilst retaining some nominal inertia, we adopt the continuous-time model proposed by Calvo (1983) where we interpret forward-looking contracts as wage settlements and the price level is an exponentially weighted average of current and past wage contracts.

The model consists of the following equations

$$p(t)=\delta\int_{-\infty}^{t}x(\tau)e^{-\delta(t-\tau)}d\tau \quad \text{or} \quad \dot{p}=\delta(x-p) \tag{7.1}$$

$$x(t)=E_t\delta\int_{t}^{\infty}[p(\tau)+\beta y(\tau)]e^{-\delta(\tau-t)}d\tau \quad \text{or}$$

$$E_t(dx)=\delta(x-p-\beta y)dt \tag{7.2}$$

$$y=\eta(s-p+p^*) \tag{7.3}$$

where p = log of the price level
x = log of the current new contract
y = log of output relative to potential ($y=0$ at full employment)
s = log of the exchange rate (domestic units per unit of foreign currency)
* indicates a foreign variable
$\dot{p}$ = dp/dt denotes the (instantaneous) inflation rate
E_t = expectation operator conditional on time t information.

In equation (7.1) the current price level is expressed as an average of all outstanding contracts. The current new contract is a forward-looking integral of expected future prices and output as shown in equation (7.2), where output depends on the real exchange rate ($s-p+p^*$) as in (7.3).

We begin with the case where the exchange rate is fully credible. Let the exchange rate be fixed at c; and let p^*, the foreign price level, be constant (for convenience set $p^*=0$). As the currency peg is fully credible, then it will serve as a nominal anchor for the domestic economy. So the home price level may temporarily be too high or too low, but it will always be expected to converge to equilibrium (at c).

In these circumstances it is not surprising that new forward-looking contracts can be expressed as a weighted average of the current price level (p) and the equilibrium level (c), that is:

$$x=\theta p+(1-\theta)c \tag{7.4}$$

or equivalently,
$$x-c=\theta(p-c)$$

(Precisely how the weighting coefficient θ depends on the parameters of the model is discussed in the Appendix where it is shown that $\theta=1-\sqrt{\beta\eta}<1$).

Consequently the dynamics of price adjustment would follow from substituting (7.4) into (7.1) to obtain

$$\dot{p} = -\delta(1-\theta)(p-c) \tag{7.5}$$

which guarantees stable convergence of the price level given that $\theta < 1$.

The Phillips relation and the effect of expected devaluation

Note that, as output is proportional to p-c (see equation (7.3) above), one could alternatively express inflation as a function of current output (measured from potential). So

$$\dot{p} = \phi \ y \text{ where } \phi = \delta(1-\theta)/\eta \tag{7.6}$$

a type of 'Phillips relation' for inflation. Given that θ is chosen to be consistent with the parameters of the model, this Phillips relation will incorporate rational expectations on the part of those setting contracts, in the sense that current contracts will be the present discounted value of future nominal income (strictly $p+\beta y$) where δ is the discount factor, see equation (7.1).

The absence of any inflation expectations term in the inflation equation (7.6) above reflects the key assumptions made so far, namely that foreign prices are constant ($p^*=0$) and that the currency peg is fully credible ($s=c$). Where the peg against a hard currency lacks credibility, however, one would expect an 'inflation premium' in wage contracts to allow for expected future devaluation of the currency. Let the rate of expected devaluation be $100\hat{\mu}$ per cent points per annum over the indefinite future. How much should contracts be increased in these circumstances? Formal details are given in the Appendix, but one might have guessed that the appropriate inflation premium would be $\hat{\mu}/\delta$ since, from (7.1) one can see that steady state inflation of $\hat{\mu}$ would imply that x-$p=\hat{\mu}/\delta$. So the equation for contracts becomes

$$x=\theta p+(1-\theta)c+\hat{\mu}/\delta \tag{7.7}$$

Substituting (7.7) into (7.5), and using (7.3) as above, we find this yields a type of expectations-augmented Phillips relation:

$$\dot{p}=\phi y+\hat{\mu} \tag{7.8}$$

In short, adding an inflation premium of $\hat{\mu}/\delta$ to contracts has the result of raising the inflation rate (at any given level of output) by the expected rate of devaluation.

The size of recession (with no learning)
What does this imply for the *non-inflationary* equilibrium level of output if the authorities stick to their guns and refuse to devalue, despite widespread expectations to the contrary? One answer, found by simply setting $\dot{p}=0$ is that $y<0$, specifically

$$y=-\hat{\mu}/\phi=-\eta\hat{\mu}/(\delta(1-\theta)) \tag{7.9}$$

The effect of such a recession on the forward-looking contracts will be just sufficient to offset the inflation premium induced by devaluation expectations, so that prices will remain stable at that level of output.

This calculation seems to imply that adopting a hard currency peg must increase the natural rate of unemployment. But note that the recession we have described results from the expectation of devaluations which, given the hard currency peg, will never actually take place. Surely, in the long run, these expectations will adjust to take account of past experience so the inflation premium (and the recession associated with it) will disappear. In what follows here we give an intuitive account of the results derived in Driffill and Miller (1992), who assume that learning takes place in a Bayesian fashion in order to study the dynamics of adjustment.

The effects of learning
The anticipated inflation rate ($\hat{\mu}$) reflects an expected rate of devaluation which we can represent as $\hat{\rho}J$, where $\hat{\rho}$ is the anticipated frequency of a jump devaluation of fixed size J: specifically $\hat{\mu}=\hat{\rho}J$. We assume that $\hat{\rho}$ is a weighted average of zero and ρ_H, zero being the realignment rate of a 'committed' government, and ρ_H the high realignment rate of a 'recidivist' government. The weights reflect the probabilities that market participants attach to the two possibilities, and these possibilities depend on the observed exchange-rate outcome. On average $\hat{\rho}$ is not expected to change. However, if no realignment occurs, $\hat{\rho}$ will fall; and if a realignment occurs, which happens with a probability $\hat{\rho}dt$ in the interval of time from t to $t+dt$, then $\hat{\rho}$ jumps at once to ρ_H since a realignment reveals the government as a recidivist.

The rate at which $\hat{\rho}$ falls when no realignment occurs can be calculated from this information by noting that the unconditional expected change in $\hat{\rho}, E(d\hat{\rho})$, equals zero, that is,

$$E(d\hat{\rho}) = d\hat{\rho}\big|_N(1 - \hat{\rho}dt) + (\rho_H - \hat{\rho})\hat{\rho}dt = 0$$

where $d\hat{\rho}\big|_N$ is the change in $\hat{\rho}$ conditional on no realignment, ρ_H-$\hat{\rho}$ is the jump in $\hat{\rho}$ if a realignment occurs and $\hat{\rho}dt$ is the probability of a realignment occurring in time interval $[t,t+dt]$. Rewriting $d\hat{\rho}\big|_N$ as $d\hat{\rho}\big|_N dt$ and deleting second-order terms in dt in the limit as $dt \to 0$, we find that

$$\frac{d\hat{\rho}}{dt}\bigg|_N \equiv \dot{\hat{\rho}} = -(\rho_H - \hat{\rho})\hat{\rho} \tag{7.10}$$

Since $\rho_H > \hat{\rho}$, the latter converges to zero if there is no realignment; and so too will the 'expected inflation' terms $\hat{\mu}$, $\hat{\mu}/\delta$ as

$$\dot{\hat{\mu}} = \dot{\hat{\rho}}J$$

so

$$\dot{\hat{\mu}} = -(\rho_H - \hat{\mu}/J)\hat{\mu} \tag{7.11}$$

where $\rho_H > \hat{\mu}J$.

A diagrammatic treatment
The dynamics of inflation can be studied with the aid of chart 7.2. In the top panel the level of new contracts is charted on the vertical axis against the price level on the horizontal (both in logs, measured from the equilibrium value c). In the lower panel the rate of inflation ($\dot{p}$) is plotted against the size of recession (-y).

Take first the case where the peg is *fully credible*, so contracts lie on the schedule labelled AA which is flatter than the 45° line and passes through equilibrium E (see equation 7.4). To the right of E, new contracts will be settled below the price level, so from (7.1), prices will be falling (and *vice versa* to the left of E). It follows that prices will converge stably to equilibrium, as shown by the arrows on AA (and by equation (7.5) above). This dynamic adjustment can, of course, be viewed instead as a movement towards the origin along the schedule labelled the Phillips Relation in the lower panel. When prices are above equilibrium there will be a recession, but prices will be falling so the system will lie on the schedule at a point to the right of E, sliding towards equilibrium at the origin over time.

Chart 7.2 Speed of learning and length of recession

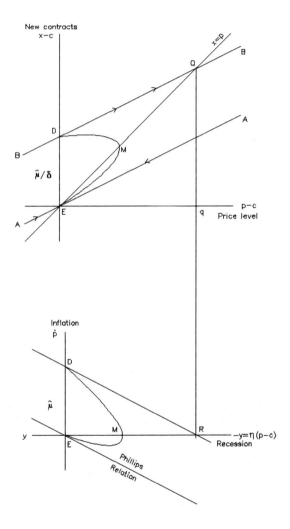

Now consider the effect of including a devaluation premium of $\hat{\mu}/\delta$ in wage contracts to reflect a lack of credibility in the currency peg. This will simply move AA vertically upwards to BB by the amount of $\hat{\mu}/\delta$, and will correspondingly shift the point of convergence from E to Q (where BB crosses the 45°line, so contracts match the price level). The effect this has on the inflation-output trade off is indicated by the vertical shift of $\hat{\mu}$ in the Phillips Relation in the lower panel (see equation (7.6) above), which moves the zero-inflation equilibrium to the point labelled R. Consequently the trajectory of contracts and the price level from D to Q in the top panel will be associated with an emerging recession shown by the movement from D to R in the lower panel.

The equilibrium just described, and the adjustment towards it, takes no account of any learning. How does incorporating Bayesian learning affect things? In the absence of any actual realignments the essential consequence of learning is to reduce $\hat{\mu}$ steadily towards zero as time proceeds. This means that there are now two forces acting on contracts and prices, both of which can be illustrated with the reference to the top panel. First, already discussed, is the movement along BB towards the quasi-equilibrium at Q as the devaluation premium lifts contracts and drives prices upward; second is the tendency for the schedule BB (and therefore Q) to subside as the intercept ($\hat{\mu}/\delta$) falls towards zero with learning. The resultant of these two forces is a trajectory like that shown as DME in the top panel. Inflation persists so long as current contracts exceed the price level (as between D and M). Then prices reach a maximum at M itself. Thereafter, with current settlements being less than the current price level, prices fall until they reach equilibrium at E.

What this implies for output and inflation is shown in the bottom panel by the trajectory DME. After time zero, output is always below potential: inflation starts at D but falls steadily first to zero, then below, before finally returning to zero. Note that the first time inflation rates converge (to zero) is associated with a recession (see point M), and this recession continues until competitiveness is gradually restored by falling prices. In short we find that lack of credibility has led to precisely the sort of scenario described by Giovannini. Inflation convergence does not signify economic convergence: it marks not the end of recession, just the bottom.

Is there any alternative to the path of recession shown in chart 7.2? The choice of two fixed realignment frequencies in the model is somewhat *ad hoc:* other possibilities might be entertained. In particular, it was suggested by David Currie that the higher realignment frequency ρ_H might be *state-dependent.* Once convergence of inflation has been achieved, for example, agents might *reduce ρ_H to a lower level*, on the grounds that by getting inflation down to that in the hard currency country, the authorities had ruled out the likelihood of a return to the high rates of devaluation implied by ρ_H. This would mean a sudden drop in contracts if the switch was not anticipated. If the state-dependent switch had been anticipated contracts would have fallen earlier. In either case the path to equilibrium would be more rapid and recession somewhat smaller. Finally, we note an argument made by David Begg and colleagues designed to allow for the correction to relative prices without triggering fears of further realignment. They argued that if entry to the common currency bloc under the Maastricht Treaty is restricted to those countries who had not realigned for at least two years, then, for a country which has signed up to join the currency bloc by a given date, an exchange-rate adjustment just two years before that could be seen as a last realignment before locking parities.

Conclusion

We have studied the effects of pegging the exchange rate to a hard currency as an anti-inflationary anchor in a model with forward-looking wage contracts and price inertia. Where the peg is fully credible, the beneficial effect this has on expectations ensures that prices promptly stabilise and output remains at a high employment level. But a lack of credibility is associated with an inflation premium in wage contracts as agents forecast future devaluations. If the peg is not in fact adjusted, then the economy tends to a low employment equilibrium where the impact of the recession on wage settlements offsets this inflation premium; so prices are stable, but at a level which is too high for full employment (given the hard currency peg).

Because it is based on the expected devaluations which never actually take place, it would be a mistake to conclude that a hard currency peg will, as a result, lead to a *permanent* recession. Allowing for devaluation expectations to be updated in Bayesian fashion implies a steady reduction of the inflation premium embedded in wage contracts as long as there is no devaluation: so, with learning, both the inflation premium and the recession associated with it will gradually disappear.

The time paths of prices and output we obtain highlight what Alberto Giovannini has dubbed the problem of inflation convergence under fixed rates: namely that the recession does *not* end when inflation has reached zero, instead, the recession must continue, as a period of falling prices is required to offset the earlier inflation and to return the economy to a competitive equilibrium. The severity of the extended recession may, however, be mitigated if defeating inflation has a direct effect on devaluation expectations. We examined a suggestion made by David Currie that getting inflation down to zero might have the virtuous result of reducing the expected frequency of devaluations faster than would result from Bayesian learning; and also the idea of a 'last realignment'.

Appendix [2]

Rational expectations restrictions on θ

Let p_0 and x_0 denote price level and contracts (in logs) measured from equilibrium at c, so $p_0 = p\text{-}c$, $x_0 = x\text{-}c$ and assume $x_0 = \theta p_0$. Then, for the fully credible peg, one can represent the dynamics of adjustment as

$$\dot{p}_0 = \delta(x_0 - p_0) \tag{7A.1}$$

$$\dot{x}_0 = \delta(\beta\eta - 1)p_0 + \delta x_0 \tag{7A.2}$$

see equations (7.1)-(7.3) in the text.

Let $x_0 = \theta p_0$, then from (7A.1)

$$\dot{p}_0 = \delta(\theta - 1)p_0 = -\delta(1 - \theta)p_0 \tag{7A.3}$$

where, for stability

$$\theta < 1 \tag{7A.4}$$

Since $\dot{x}_0 = \theta\dot{p}_0$ then from (7A.2) and (7A.3) one finds

$$\delta(\beta\eta - 1)p_0 + \delta\theta p_0 = -\theta\delta(1 - \theta)p_0$$

which implies that θ must satisfy the polynomial

$$\theta^2 - 2\theta + (1 - \beta\eta) = 0$$

hence

$$\theta = 1 \pm \sqrt{\beta\eta} \tag{7A.5}$$

Together (7A.4) and (7A.5) imply that, along the path of stable convergence to equilibrium,

$$\theta = 1 - \sqrt{\beta\eta} < 1 \tag{7A.6}$$

The effect of devaluation risk on contracts

Let

$$x_0 = \theta p_0 + k \qquad (7\text{A}.7)$$

where k is the inflation premium. To show that

$$k = \hat{\mu}/\delta$$

where $\hat{\mu} = \hat{\rho} J$.

We note that, given the risk of realignment

$$E(dx) = \delta(\beta\eta - 1)p_0 + \delta x_0 \text{ from equation (7.4) in the text,}$$

$$= dx\big|_N (1 - \hat{\rho} \ dt) + (1 - \theta)\hat{\rho} \ J dt$$

where $dx\big|_N$ is the evolution of the contracts conditional on no realignment and $(1-\theta)$ is the expected jump of the contracts on realignment, and each event is weighted by its expected probability. Denoting $dx\big|_N = \dot{x}dt$ and dropping second-order terms in dt, in the limit as $dt \to 0$ we find the evolution of contracts is

$$\dot{x} = \delta(\beta\eta - 1)p_0 + \delta x_0 + (\theta - 1)\hat{\mu} \qquad (7\text{A}.8)$$

where $\hat{\mu} = \hat{\rho} J$.

At a stationary point $\dot{x} = 0$ and $x = p = q$ so, letting q_0 denote q-c, we find from (7A.7)

$$q_0 = \frac{k}{1 - \theta} \qquad (7\text{A}.9)$$

and from (7A.8) that

$$q_0 = \frac{1 - \theta}{\beta\eta} \frac{\hat{\mu}}{\delta} = \frac{\hat{\mu}}{(1 - \theta)\delta} \qquad (7\text{A}.10)$$

since $\beta\eta = (1-\theta)^2$ from (7A.6). Together (7A.9) and (7A.10) imply that the inflation premium k is indeed $\hat{\mu}/\delta$.

The process of convergence with learning

The process of convergence discussed in the text can be described algebraically in terms of the price level and of the intercept term $\hat{\mu}$ as follows. The dynamics of inflation are

$$\dot{p}_0 = -\delta(1-\theta)p_0 + \hat{\mu}$$

as in equation (7.13) in the text, using $p_0 = p\text{-}c$ to denote the price level measured from parity c. Combining this with equation (7.11) in the text but omitting the quadratic term (since $\hat{\mu}^2 \to 0$ close to equilibrium), the dynamics of adjustment near equilibrium can be represented as a recursive linear system

$$\begin{bmatrix} \dot{p}_0 \\ \dot{\hat{\mu}} \end{bmatrix} = \begin{bmatrix} -\delta(1-\theta) & 1 \\ 0 & -\rho_H \end{bmatrix} \begin{bmatrix} p_0 \\ \hat{\mu} \end{bmatrix}$$

with stable roots displayed on the diagonal.

Notes

1 In a related paper, Miller and Sutherland (1991b) also examine the possible role of different contract structures, and of a lack of common knowledge, in delaying the adjustment of inflation.
2 For an alternative derivation of these results, see Miller and Sutherland (1991a).

8

Exchange-rate Realignments in the European Monetary System*

Andrew Britton

The exchange rate mechanism (ERM) of the European Monetary System (EMS) is neither a true fixed-rate system nor a true flexible-rate system. Exchange rates are kept within relatively narrow bands most of the time, but the possibility remains of occasional, perhaps large, realignments. The circumstances in which such realignments can take place are not at all clearly defined. Within this framework economists are attempting both to forecast exchange rates and to advise those responsible for setting them. This chapter considers whether a satisfactory analytical approach can be found to problems of both these kinds.

So far as Europe as a whole is concerned this is not a new issue. The ERM was set up in 1979, and for a number of years realignments were frequent events for all the currencies involved. What is new for those concerned with, for example, the French franc, the lira or the guilder is that realignments involving these currencies and the D-Mark have recently become much less frequent—and some are now predicting that there will never be any realignments again.

So far as Britain is concerned, of course, the issue has only arisen since the pound joined the ERM in October 1990. Indeed it was so unlikely that the pound would be realigned immediately after entry that the issue was not seriously discussed until a year after entry. The commitment of the UK to the ideal of fixed rates, ultimately embodied in an Economic and Monetary Union (EMU), is still in doubt, but interest differentials suggest that the market regards a devaluation as unlikely in the immediate future. Nevertheless the proper analysis of exchange-rate realignments remains a topic of interest to both forecasters and policymakers in this country.

*This chapter grew out of a shorter discussion of exchange-rate forecasting in the home economy chapter of the *National Institute Economic Review*, May 1991. It draws on helpful comments by members of the Institute staff, especially Ray Barrell, Peter Westaway and Garry Young. The macroeconomic programme at the Institute is financed by the ESRC.

The chapter will address these issues in an exploratory way, because there is no standard theory of realignments to which one can appeal. It begins with a description of the 'let-out clause' allowing realignments within the ERM and the way it might operate under conditions of free capital mobility. There follows a brief account of some of the relevant ideas contained in the vast literature on monetary and exchange-rate policies. The core sections of the chapter consider how policy decisions and intelligent forecasts might interact under flexible rates, fixed rates and in the ERM to determine whether, when and by how much exchange rates are realigned. Special attention is then given to some questions of obvious topical interest: ERM membership as a counter-inflation strategy, the effect of a change of government and of the prospect of transition to EMU. The conclusions at the end, as one can perhaps guess even at this stage, are in the main agnostic, but it is hoped that there is practical value in clarifying where the necessary limits to knowledge actually lie.

The nature of the realignment problem

The 'let-out clause'
The EMS was constructed to broadly the same design as the Bretton-Woods system under which international monetary relations were conducted for a generation after the Second World War. There were indeed many important differences, but it is with one common feature that we are mainly concerned here. Both systems allow realignments, that is changes in the set of parities with respect to which actual exchange rates are managed. In both systems these realignments can only be made by agreement, and the circumstances in which they can be made are not precisely defined.

The EMS currencies are free to move within a band around their central rates. To a perhaps surprising extent, the academic discussion of the EMS has concentrated on the behaviour of currencies within these bands, rather than the circumstances in which the bands themselves are moved — see for example the papers collected in Krugman and Miller (1991). Here we will go to the opposite extreme and ignore the existence of the bands altogether. In doing so we shall neglect a number of important and interesting tactical issues of exchange-rate management, such as the role of market intervention, the management of realignments when the new and the old bands overlap and the defence of currencies against speculative attack. We will treat the exchange rate as if it were an instrument under the direct control of the monetary authorities.

With capital at all free to move between currencies, a discrete change in exchange rates (or, strictly, in exchange-rate bands) must be difficult to manage. Even when capital controls were extensive and quite effective the possibility of an imminent devaluation could put great pressure on the foreign currency reserves of the central bank concerned (as Britain learnt in 1967). In today's free and very active capital market conditions it would be virtually impossible to delay a depreciation if market opinion was that a downward realignment was very likely and very imminent. Thus it is an inbuilt feature of the EMS, and of Bretton-Woods before it, that realignments must not be fully anticipated. The market must be, to some degree, surprised. Exchange-rate forecasts must be, to some degree, incorrect at the time the realignment takes place. If the authorities say anything at all to the markets in the run up to a realignment it can only be to mislead them.

Realignments will not be predictable if they come as instantaneous reactions to unexpected events. Thus the 'shock' of the oil price collapse in 1986, or the Iraqi invasion of Kuwait, or the unification of Germany, could have provoked a realignment in the EMS within days, or even conceivably within hours, so quickly that speculation had no time to build up. In practice, however, that is not the way the system works. It takes time for the authorities to assess the significance of events which are truly unanticipated. Their reactions are unlikely to be faster than those of the markets themselves. It takes time to reach agreement between governments. And the uncertainty which often surrounds an announcement of major significance may make the calculation of an appropriate new set of exchange rates quite impossible. Thus a realignment announced immediately after the Moscow coup in 1991 might have had to be put into reverse by the end of the week.

The main reason why realignments are not anticipated is that the market cannot foresee how the authorities will respond even to events which are themselves known with certainty. A typical situation in the ERM is that some currencies are regarded as being at risk of realignment upwards and others downwards. The direction for possible currency moves is clear enough, but their extent and timing is nevertheless a matter for guesswork. Relative interest rates take account of the balance of probabilities, so that the expected return from holding different currencies is the same even though some are thought more likely to rise, and others more likely to fall.

We are concerned, then, with a situation in which the behaviour of policymakers is not 'transparent'. Forecasters have to guess what policymakers' intentions may be. This is true even if they share the same knowledge or opinions about the working of the economy, and hence the likely consequences of a higher or lower exchange rate. The market participants must still guess how policymakers will evaluate different outcomes, their priorities amongst the different objectives of economic policy, what weight they attach to, say, an early reduction in inflation or to preventing unemployment from rising too high. They must also guess how much importance the authorities attach to constancy of the exchange rate as an objective in its own right, or to the future development of the ERM as a system. In other words those who try to forecast exchange-rate realignments must try to put themselves in the position of the authorities and work out what their best strategy would be — but they lack some at least of the information necessary for this calculation.

Forecasting in the ERM must therefore be a process of learning from experience. The behaviour of the authorities must be studied as a guide to the process of reasoning which is likely to govern their actions in the future. In particular information may be gleaned from the circumstances in which they do realign exchange rates, but something may be learnt from their inactivity as well.

Membership of the ERM involves some degree of commitment to a fixed exchange-rate system. The existence of the 'let-out clause' means that the commitment is not absolute. It is a promise to try reasonably hard to preserve a constant exchange rate, not a promise to sacrifice all else to that aim. Nevertheless it is a commitment, and as such it will change the character of the authorities' behaviour. We cannot hope to understand behaviour within the ERM if we treat it as if it were a flexible-rate system. Indeed it is more like a fixed-rate system, in that the authorities will seek to establish their credibility and benefit from an acquired reputation. The 'let-out clause' creates a strange hybrid, which is neither one thing nor the other. It is not easy, as we shall find, to give a logical account of how such a system works. Yet experience of the Bretton-Woods system, as well as the ERM, shows that a system of this kind can in fact endure at least as well as any of the alternatives.

Forecasting and policy analysis

Forecasting exchange rates is not often an easy or rewarding task. Under floating exchange rates a common approach nowadays is to assume that the return to holding all currencies will be the same, or differ by some constant 'risk premium'. Thus the forecast for the depreciation of sterling against the D-Mark over the next twelve months can be calculated simply as the difference between the twelve-month interest rates in the two currencies at the time when the forecast is made.

This procedure is, in fact, not so much a way of forecasting the exchange rate as a way of avoiding the need to do so. It involves accepting the 'market view' of the exchange-rate outlook as the correct one. The argument is that the market in its wisdom will have set the current level of the exchange rate such that its expected rise or fall exactly offsets the difference in interest rates.

But if the 'market view' is based on incorrect information or analysis, then the exchange rate will change as the market corrects its mistake. Someone, somewhere, must be taking a view of the 'fundamentals', the factors other than market sentiment which ultimately determine how exchange rates move — and very prominent amongst those factors in any system will be the decisions of the monetary authorities.

Under an ideal fixed exchange-rate system there would be no movements in exchange rates to forecast at all. In the ERM, however, forecasters have to take account of the possibility of realignments. It is still possible to adopt an approach based on interest-rate arbitrage, but the interpretation is a little different from that appropriate to a floating exchange-rate system.

The difference between the twelve-month interest rates for sterling and the D-Mark can be interpreted as the weighted average of a range of views as to the size of a possible realignment. A small differential may reflect the fact that the market attaches a low probability to any realignment at all, or that it attaches equal probabilities to movements in either direction. Within the ERM we cannot think of the exchange rate as the outcome of market forces in quite the same sense as it would be under a floating rate system. If we ignore the effect of actual market intervention by the authorities, however, we can say that relative interest rates have been set so as to be consistent with the exchange rate as it now is, given market expectations of future appreciation or depreciation.

Again we have to admit that this approach simply by-passes the real forecasting exercise. It is a way of reading the mind of the market, not a way of telling whether the market view is correct. If the market is to have a view at all someone has to undertake the real forecasting task of trying to read the minds of the authorities and guess in what circumstances, if any, they would change the parity — and by how much. When analysis of that kind is done at all it is usually in a rather informal way, without the benefit of much sophisticated economic reasoning.

As usual in economics, the forecasting question of what the authorities are likely to do is very closely related to the policy question of what (given their objectives) they ought to do. Economics, almost invariably, approaches the task of predicting behaviour by assuming that it will be rational. If our advice to the government were to be that realignment would be a mistake (given their objectives) in any circumstances, then we should forecast a strictly constant exchange rate unless we think the government will be misinformed or irrational in some systematic way.

In giving policy advice the costs and benefits of a higher or lower exchange rate can be set out in terms of output and inflation for a currency in the ERM as for a currency in a flexible or floating-rate system. The difference lies in the effect of one exchange-rate move on the perceived probability of another.

This is the intractable issue at the heart of policy analysis in the ERM. In discussion it is usually treated in a very informal way, and quite contradictory points of view can be expressed as if they were self-evidently true. Is the expectation of a further devaluation increased or decreased after a devaluation has occurred? Will the readiness to raise the exchange rate on one occasion be interpreted as implying an equal readiness to lower it on another?

The answers to such questions are in fact far from obvious. The existing academic literature on exchange-rate policy in the EMS does not provide ready-made answers, although it gives some guidance as to how the questions might be addressed.

Credibility and learning

The issues of credibility and learning with which we are concerned here have been discussed mainly in the context of domestic monetary policy, rather than exchange-rate systems. Blanchard and Fischer (1989) provides a very useful introduction to the field. Barro and Gordon (1983) is the starting point for most subsequent work. In that paper it is shown how policymakers who break a commitment to a money supply rule can be 'punished' by a subsequent loss of credibility. It is assumed that policy is transparent, in the sense that the preferences and intentions of the policymakers are public knowledge; that is an assumption we will be abandoning here.

The way in which actions signal intentions, and the consequent incentive in some cases to conceal information, was analysed first in the context of oligopoly, using game theory, and the ideas then transferred to macroeconomics. Vickers (1986) assumes that policymakers can be of two kinds: 'wets' and 'dries'; the public knows how either kind of policymaker will behave but can only guess which kind is in fact in power. Any government has an incentive to keep inflation low to start with so that it can build up a reputation for toughness — whether it is really tough or not. The analysis takes the form of a two-period game. In some games the 'wets' and the 'dries' can be distinguished by observation of their actions in the first period but in other games the initial move will be the same for policymakers of either sort.

Backus and Driffill (1985) similarly examine the way policies are conducted after a change of government and the incentive to 'act tough' at the start. In this case the policy choice is seen as a game played by government against a monopoly trade union, which has a strategy based on gaining a reputation for intransigence. This model of confrontation does not transfer easily to the relationship of government with the foreign exchange market which involves a multitude of independent agents.

The analysis of foreign exchange-rate policies requires an understanding of how people learn. For a brief survey of recent attempts to integrate learning into the theory of economic policy see Bullard (1991) and the references given there. Cripps (1991) anticipates some of the themes to be developed below. The context is control of the money supply rather than exchange-rate policy, but the relationships between credibility, optimal policy and learning are developed in an interesting way. Although it is always useful for actors to eventually have full understanding, it is shown that the monetary authorities can benefit from slowing down the rate at which the public learn the true value of their priorities.

Much has been written about the EMS in recent years, in particular about the behaviour of exchange rates within the bands and the effects of official intervention. The circumstances in which realignments occur and the interpretation of the 'escape clause' has not been extensively discussed. When it has been central to the analysis the issue of market learning has not often been considered. Obstfeld (1991), for example, assumes that realignments take place only in response to unforeseeable shocks. Giavazzi and Pagano (1988), by contrast, assume that realignments take place at regular predetermined intervals. Both assume that policy is transparent, so that there is no question of disclosing information about the aims of policymakers by the timing or the size of realignments.

A recent paper, Weber (1991), includes a discussion of the credibility of policy announcements within the EMS and the way in which the market learns from the observation of exchange-rate movements. Credibility is defined as 'the extent to which beliefs concerning a policy conform to official announcements about this policy' and an attempt is even made to measure it. The problems actually involved in learning from experience are simplified quite radically so that they can be addressed empirically. Weber also provides a useful summary of the history of realignments and associated policy changes since the EMS was set up.

In the sections that follow we shall try to apply ideas derived from some relatively recent developments in the theory of economic policy to the special issues identified as important to the EMS. The most convenient way of proceeding is to begin with an account of forecasting and strategy under flexible exchange rates; then to consider the alternative of a fixed exchange-rate system; and finally to turn to the ERM which has features of both.

A sketch for a formal analysis

Exchange-rate determination

Formally the determination of the exchange rate can be analysed as the consequence of interactions involving behavioural relationships of three distinct types. The first type of relationship describes the behaviour of the economy in response to actual or expected movements in the exchange rate. One could think of this as the set of relationships which are commonly embodied in an estimated macroeconomic model. The second type of relationship would specify the behaviour of the monetary authorities. This information could be set out in the form of a utility function describing their preferences together with an assumption about the procedure they adopt for maximising 'utility' measured in this way. The third type of relationship needed would describe the formation of expectations by the market in response to observations of the way the authorities behave. This third type of relationship is the most difficult to specify and the least discussed in the standard theory. The assumption of rational or consistent expectations so often used in the modern theory of economic policy has to be modified when the behaviour of the authorities is not 'transparent'.

We begin with the representation of the economy. This could be expressed by a set of equations of the form:

$$y = y(x, x^e \ ...) \tag{8.1}$$

where y represents any economic variable of interest to policymakers, for example inflation or unemployment, x represents the exchange rate and x^e represents the market expectation of exchange-rate movements in the future. A set of equations like equation (8.1) would make it possible for the authorities, and the market, to make forecasts of all future economic developments conditional on a specified path of the exchange rate and expectations about that path, which will not in general be correct. Strictly those expectations must be specified for all time periods of the future, so that at any point of time, output and inflation can be influenced by expectations of exchange-rate movements over all possible horizons.

The simplifying assumption is made that the market's views can be summarised as a single mean or representative expectation, without taking account of the dispersion of individual views or of the uncertainty attached by each individual to a central forecast.

As a further simplification, even less realistic, it could be assumed that the form and parameters of equations like equation (8.1) are known with certainty both by the authorities and by the markets. It could even be assumed that any exogenous variables which should appear in those equations can be forecast correctly. The environment is known and non-stochastic. There is no problem for example about forecasting wars and revolutions, or in interpreting their consequences for the economic variables of interests. Thus we could abstract from much of the uncertainty of real life to concentrate attention on one particular kind of learning. We shall consider later in the chapter what difference a more realistic view of the environment might make to the analysis.

Economists in fact hold a range of views as to the form of the relationships like equation (8.1), as well as the magnitudes involved. It is not necessary here to opt for a particular model of the economy. But some examples of the kind of relationship which might be involved will help the subsequent discussion.

It is very generally recognised that devaluing the exchange rate will increase inflation, unless some offsetting policy action is taken to prevent this happening. A common assumption would be that the price level will ultimately rise in proportion to the fall in the exchange rate It is also commonly believed that devaluation will raise output and reduce unemployment in the short term by stimulating the demand for exports (although account should also be taken of the fall in real incomes which will tend to reduce consumer spending). In the long term, if prices respond in proportion to the exchange rate then there will probably be no lasting effects on international trade and competitiveness, whilst the higher price level will reduce consumption for as long as it takes asset stocks to reach their new equilibrium.

The effect of exchange-rate expectations on the economy is of equal importance to the present discussion. The expectation of depreciation will almost certainly raise nominal interest rates (that is, require the authorities to raise nominal interest rates if the exchange rate is not to fall straight away). Expectation of depreciation will also increase the expectation of inflation and hence almost certainly raise inflation in fact. There is little reason to believe that expected depreciation will have much effect on output one way or the other. Thus the ultimate cost in terms of lost output of permanently reducing inflation and adjusting inflation expectations could well be greater if the exchange rate is expected to fall than it would be if the exchange rate was expected to stay constant (or to rise).

The second kind of behaviour to be described is that of the monetary authorities. Assuming that policymakers in each country can act independently of one another, only one set of preferences need be specified (although each country's effective exchange-rate index will be influenced by the decisions of all the rest). These preferences can be conveniently represented by a utility function of the form:

$$U = U(y; a) \tag{8.2}$$

where y in general includes a set of economic variables in the present and all future time periods (which could include the exchange rate, x) and a is a set of parameters which quantify their relative value to the policymakers. It may be convenient to assume that the form of $U(\ )$ is public knowledge, but that the values of the parameters a are not known. In seeking to maximise $U(\ )$ with respect to x, the authorities are subject to the constraints of equation (8.1) and also to the way in which their behaviour will influence expectations.

The third kind of behaviour to be specified defines the way in which observed exchange-rate changes influence expectations of future policy. The way in which this behaviour should be specified is itself a problem, but for the moment it could simply be written as:

$$x^e = f\{x, y\} \tag{8.3}$$

The curly brackets are used to indicate that this need not be an algebraic function at all. The variables y are included alongside x because the interpretation of a policy act must depend on the context in which it is observed. (Very different conclusions would be drawn from a devaluation when the rate of inflation is 2 or 20 per cent.) The relationship (8.3) may be understood as involving a two-step reasoning. The data on x and y for the past are used to form estimates of the parameters a in the authorities' utility function. This is a relatively simple example of an inverse optimum problem, deducing the utility function from observed behaviour. It is a case of 'rational' learning since the market is basing its expectations on reasoning about the behaviour which is in the interests of the authorities. Alternatively the process of learning may take the form of estimating a reaction function. These estimates are then used to forecast the actions of the authorities in the future. This could be called 'non-rational' learning, if it is based on statistical criteria alone, without reference to a theoretical model of the authorities' strategic decisions. Cripps (1991) shows that 'rational' and 'non-rational' learning can produce quite different behaviour. (This distinction is essentially the same as that between the strong and weak versions of the rational expectations hypothesis.)

A flexible exchange-rate system
Under a flexible exchange-rate system new data will be generated continuously, so one might imagine that estimates of the parameters of a reaction function would improve quite rapidly. The point to emphasise in the present context however is that, so long as the learning process is not complete, the authorities can be expected to take account of the effect their actions have on market expectations, that is on estimates of the parameters of their reaction function or utility function. (We can assume for the moment that the authorities know how market expectations are formed.)

A very simple example may serve to illustrate the point. By substituting equations like equation (8.1) above into a utility function like that given by equation (8.2) above, and assuming that decisions relate to one period only, the policy decision of the authorities can be restricted to the maximisation of $W(x, x^e; a)$ with respect to x. Ignoring effects on expectations, the optimum value of x would be found by solving:

$$\frac{\delta W}{\delta x}(x, x^e; a) = 0 \tag{8.4a}$$

But suppose that $\hat{a}$ is the market estimate of a, and that $\hat{a}$ depends on x. The optimum value of x is now the solution to:

$$\frac{\delta W}{\delta x}(x, x^e; a)\frac{\delta W}{\delta x^e} = \frac{dx^e}{dx} = 0 \qquad \text{(8.4b)}$$

If there is just one parameter a, then the market may in principle be able to work out its value by replicating the solution of equation (8.4b). We would then be straightaway at a consistent-expectations equilibrium.

This illustrative case, of course, vastly under-represents the complexity of a calculation of this kind in the real world. It is not to be imagined that real-world forecasters and policymakers actually approach their job in this way; they could not do so, and should not try. Expectations in general will not be consistent, but rather based on tentative hypotheses which will in general be incorrect. All that the rational expectations approach to macro policy requires is that there is no systematic bias in these hypotheses. The way the three kinds of relationships (the model of the economy, the behaviour of policymakers and expectations in the market) are involved together in the outcome will nevertheless carry over to examples more complex than this one, and to processes of reasoning that are less formal and more robust.

To illustrate the complexity of the problem two points are worth making about the process of learning. The first concerns the expectations of individual agents in the market. They will need to forecast the expectations of other agents, which will not in general be the same as their own. They may foresee a process of convergence towards a unanimous market view, but in the mean-time correct forecasting involves taking account of other people's mistakes. The second concerns the perceptions of the authorities. In deciding their optimal policy they will have to take a view of the way in which the market is learning from their behaviour. In general there is no uniquely best way for the market to form conjectures about the behaviour of the authorities – hence there is no uniquely best way for the authorities to convey to the market the information they want the market to absorb.

This section has concentrated heavily on the issue of learning, and the way it influences policy choice. Nothing has been said about commitment – the other main theme of the analysis. It is more appropriate to discuss this in the context of a fixed exchange-rate system, to which we now turn.

A fixed exchange-rate system

The advantages of pre-commitment are well known from the literature on 'time inconsistency'. In the words of a standard text, 'a policy is dynamically inconsistent when a future policy decision that forms part of an optimal plan formulated at an initial date is no longer optimal from the viewpoint of a later date, even though no relevant new information has appeared in the meantime' (Blanchard and Fischer, 1989, p.592). Rational agents will foresee that the incentive to reoptimise will exist — even if, as is emphasised in this chapter, they do not know exactly what the criteria for optimisation will be. They will therefore — to some extent at least — act in advance to nullify the benefits which might have resulted from reoptimisation viewed from the standpoint of later time periods. Thus a government which precommits itself credibly to a future plan of action may (and often could) achieve a better overall outcome than one whose discretion is unfettered, or whose commitments would not be believed.

Precommitment in the context of exchange-rate policy has no logical connection with a fixed-rate system. The authorities could precommit themselves to a rising or declining path for the exchange rate (which would have to be accompanied by appropriate interest-rate differentials). They could even, in principle, precommit themselves to respond in a prespecified way to new information as it arrives – thus overcoming a serious disadvantage of a more rigid precommitment in an uncertain world. In practice none of these options has ever been tried. The fixed-rate option is the only form of precommitment available in practice and the choice is narrowed down in effect to the way in which that commitment is specified: fixing to the US dollar, to the D-Mark, to a basket of currencies, within certain bands and so on.

In the discussion of monetary policy a commitment is deemed to be either credible or incredible. To get round the problem of time inconsistency some 'punishment mechanism' is assumed. For example, if a commitment is ever broken, no commitment thereafter will ever be believed. If a commitment is not credible then there is no point in making it. Applying this to the exchange-rate case we would conclude that the 'punishment' for breaking that commitment once would be to have to revert to a flexible rate system from then on. Given that this 'punishment' was known to be threatened, the authorities might well decide that it was never worthwhile to change the exchange rate and break this commitment. Since it would be logical for them to take that view their commitment would in fact be believed.

Reverting to the formal description of policymaking and exchange-rate forecasting set out in the previous section, relatively little needs to be changed to accommodate the case of a fixed exchange rate. The model of the economy summarised by equation (8.1) can (as a first approximation) stand — although the strict interpretation of the Lucas critique is that a change in policy regime inevitably changes behaviour, even if *mean* expectations of policy action are held constant.

It may not seem necessary to change the description of policy choice either. The underlying value judgements about such variables as output or inflation remain the same, and the aim is still to maximise 'utility' thus defined by choosing amongst all possible paths for the exchange rate. It would be reasonable for the authorities to refer to a utility function of this kind when deciding whether to accept the constraint implied by membership of a fixed rate system. They will make the implied undertaking if it pays them to do so. One might question however whether a simple utility-maximising choice is all that is involved in the decision to leave a fixed-rate system, since that involves *breaking* a commitment. As economists we do commonly analyse commitments in this way, assuming a strictly utilitarian view of decision taking. (For an example see the 'economic model' of marriage and divorce in Ermisch, 1991, chapter 4.) Many people, however, including economists no doubt, would in fact regard many commitments as morally binding, irrespective of the costs or benefits of breaking them. Considerations like this are in fact important to both behaviour and expectations in fixed exchange-rate systems. Policymakers do not as a rule wish to break commitments, especially if they are explicit and recent commitments, unless they can show that they were in some way forced to do so. It would be possible to incorporate these considerations into the design of the utility function, or the associated maximisation problem, although this seems a rather artificial procedure.

In any case the effect of a commitment must be to change the relationship (8.3) between policy acts and expectations. If reputation is an all-or-nothing matter then the relationship will be the same as it was under flexible rates with one exception. If the exchange rate has never changed since the commitment was made then it will never be expected to change in the future. If the exchange rate has changed even once since the commitment was made then it will always be expected to change in the future (except by chance when the best response under a flexible system would be precisely zero).

At any point in time the authorities can calculate the 'utility' value of keeping to their commitment. They may conclude that it should be kept for the foreseeable future, or that it should be broken straight away, reverting to a flexible system. A more complicated situation arises when they foresee that it will pay them to revert to a flexible system in the future, but not yet. If the market can read their minds then the 'punishment mechanism' of expectations comes into play straight away – quite probably resulting in an immediate move to flexible rates. However, with imperfect information the market (being ignorant of the precise way the authorities evaluate different outcomes) can at best only form a view of the likelihood that the regime will change, based on what information it has. Under a fixed-rate regime that information will be very sparse.

Under flexible rates we have suggested that the market makes deductions about the preferences of policymakers from the actions it observes. (In the simple illustrative example a single action was enough to disclose all the information required.) Under fixed rates the market has nothing to observe except inaction, unless or until the system breaks down. Inaction implies that the authorities believe a fixed-rate system will serve them best, at least for the time being. But this will be consistent with a wide range for the value of parameters or preferences. We assumed above in introducing the fixed rate system that the market gives the authorities the benefit of the doubt and never expects commitments to be broken at all.

Having looked briefly at both flexible and fixed-rate regimes we are now ready to turn to the main subject of this chapter, the ERM, which is not strictly speaking either one or the other.

The ERM: a hybrid system

Membership of the ERM does not involve an explicit commitment to a fixed exchange rate. To realign does not involve going back on one's word or breaking a promise. Utilitarian calculations are therefore not subject to the same objections as they may be in the explicit fixed exchange-rate case. The commitment is quite vague: that one will not realign lightly, or without reasonable cause, or without securing the agreement of other members. It is left obscure what reasonable grounds for realignment would be.

Under the old Bretton-Woods system exchange-rate changes were supposed to occur only in cases of 'fundamental disequilibrium', that is when exchange rates were 'misaligned' so that internal and external balance could not be restored by other means. The concept of the 'fundamental equilibrium exchange rate' (FEER) is still used today — see Williamson (1983). This is defined as the exchange rate at which reasonably full employment could be reconciled with a sustainable balance of payments position, given the price level at home and abroad. On this interpretation of the Bretton-Woods rules a case for realignment could be made if the actual exchange rate differed from the FEER by a large margin, although obviously opinions might differ as to how wide the critical margin should be. Opinions may also differ, at any time, as to where the FEER actually is. The concept itself is rather difficult to pin down — see Barrell and in't Veld (1991a). The most important limitation of this analysis is that it appears to treat prices as fixed. An orthodox view would be that *real* exchange rates (relative prices at home and abroad in terms of either currency) will come into line with the FEER sooner or later even if nominal exchange rates are unchanged. The process may be painful, with inflation in one country and unemployment in the other, but it will restore equilibrium in the end. The time horizon for such adjustment may be rather extended, and Barrell, Gurney and in't Veld (1992) suggest that it could take at least ten years for much of a real misalignment to disappear.

If we accept this view of the adjustment process, then the case for realignment rests on the argument that changing the nominal exchange rate gets the economy to equilibrium quicker or at less cost. But this is no more than a special case of the general proposition that the optimum exchange rate is not a constant. In effect the argument about FEERs simply leads us back to the point that sometimes the immediate benefit from an exchange-rate move would be substantial. The question is how large that benefit must be to outweigh the advantages of keeping the exchange rate fixed.

In a formal analysis of the ERM we can retain equations (8.1) and (8.2), describing the behaviour of the economy and policymakers' preferences, from the earlier sections of this chapter. But the relationship (8.3) describing the formation of expectations needs to be modified again. Indeed, the process of reasoning required in order to deduce policymakers' preferences rigorously from their behaviour within the ERM must be formidably complex, more so than in either a flexible or a fixed-rate system. One might even suppose that a system such as the ERM is deliberately designed in order to make forecasting difficult.

Game theorists have discussed extensively the advantages of deliberately randomising one's behaviour so as to avoid giving away useful information about one's preferences or intentions. It is not beyond the bounds of possibility that a strategy of this kind might be adopted in the setting of exchange rates, the size or timing of realignments being subject to arbitrary shifts simply to obscure their motivation, and so make prediction more difficult. However, in the ERM forecasting is likely to be so difficult even in the deterministic case that this idea will not be pursued further in this chapter.

Suppose that the exchange rate is observed to remain unchanged for a considerable period. Forecasters clearly should not conclude that it will always remain unchanged in the future, even in the absence of shocks to the system or new information about the outlook for the economy. The authorities may well be planning a realignment in the future, but intend that it should come as a surprise.

Inactivity does convey *some* information nevertheless. It indicates one set of circumstances in which the authorities do not consider a realignment is worthwhile. If exactly the same circumstances recur then the market can confidently predict that there will be no immediate realignment. Strictly speaking the circumstances must be *precisely* the same in every respect, a situation which will seldom arise, but more broadly the subjective probability must be increased that realignments will not occur if they have not happened in similar circumstances in the past. If in fact the authorities' preferences are such that they would *never* realign, then as they are observed not to realign in a variety of different circumstances eventually the market will come to treat the exchange rate as effectively fixed. Note however that the subjective probability of realignment will *not* be reduced simply by the passage of time, or by a failure to realign in circumstances which have already occurred in the past. Most information is conveyed by inactivity in new circumstances, especially where the potential gains from realignment seem to be great.

One very simple (too simple) way of summarising the circumstances of a decision to realign or not would be to compare the actual exchange rate with the FEER. If the authorities do not devalue when their currency is, say, 10 per cent overvalued, then the market will not attach much probability to a devaluation at any time when the degree of overvaluation is 10 per cent or less.

This argument could be extended to the probability of realignment when the degree of misalignment relative to the FEER is outside the range previously observed. The observation that the authorities take no action in the face of a 10 per cent overvaluation must reduce the subjective probability that they will take action when the overvaluation reaches 15 per cent — and so on. This supposes that the market forms a judgement of the probability distribution for the critical degree of overvaluation that the authorities will tolerate. Initially that threshold could lie anywhere in the range above zero; observation of inaction for small overvaluations in effect truncates the distribution, and raises its mean. The mean will always lie some way *above* the latest observation of overvaluation, so if a devaluation eventually occurs it will not be fully anticipated.

This is a rather appealing approach to exchange-rate determination in the ERM but it is subject to two important qualifications. The first is that the present degree of misalignment relative to the FEER is by no means the only consideration relevant to exchange-rate policy. In particular the authorities will base their decision on a forecast of future economic developments, not just on the current situation. If inflation is expected to be higher in their country than overseas, then overvaluation is likely to increase, whilst if inflation is lower then the problem may solve itself. The indicator which the market should really monitor is not the degree of misalignment, but the expected cost (in terms of the authorities' utility function) of keeping the exchange rate fixed from now on. Since the utility function is not public knowledge this is not an indicator which can actually be observed.

The other qualification is more fundamental. Circumstances are never the same unless market expectations are the same. The second time that the degree of overvaluation reaches 10 per cent is therefore *necessarily* different from the first time. It may not be worthwhile devaluing when the market is expecting it to happen, but still be worth devaluing at the same degree of overvaluation when the market would be caught out.

This argument suggests that forecasting the exchange rate in the ERM is simply impossible. If realignments only occur when they are unexpected, then there is no way that they can be forecast. (One is reminded of the paradox of the prisoner, who was told that he would be executed on a day when he was not expecting it. He worked out logically that no such day existed and concluded that he would never be executed. He was therefore surprised when the executioner arrived.)

Despite this argument for the impossibility of forecasting in the ERM, forecasts are in fact made, and they are influenced by the behaviour of the authorities in ways that are not wholly irrational. We have discussed the information conveyed by inactivity. What can the market learn when a realignment in fact takes place? Typically a realignment will reduce the gap between the actual exchange rate and the FEER, reducing the case for another realignment in the immediate future. If that were the whole of the story one would expect short-term interest rates to fall immediately following a devaluation, and to rise after an upward revaluation. (The effect on longer-term interest rates is less clear.) But the fact that a realignment took place will also change market perceptions of the authorities' preferences and hence expectations of realignments in the future.

The information given to the market is not just the timing and circumstances of the realignment, but also its scale. As we saw in the flexible exchange-rate case each realignment provides one data point from which the parameters of the official utility function could be estimated. It is doubtful whether such estimation is really practicable in the flexible rate case. It is considerably more difficult still in the ERM. Each observed realignment has to be interpreted as the first move in the authorities' plan. Only the first move can be observed; the rest of the plan remains a secret. Suppose one observes a small devaluation when the exchange rate is far away from the FEER. That could mean that the authorities are content to let relative inflation rates make most of the necessary adjustment. But it could also mean that another devaluation is planned in the near future.

In the flexible exchange-rate case it may be possible with sufficient observations to estimate a reaction function for the authorities. Even in that case the authorities are behaving 'strategically', so this procedure may well not be strictly valid, but it may provide a useful approximation to the authorities' behaviour in most circumstances. In the ERM the procedure would be even less reliable, and not just because of the shortage of data points. The authorities' behaviour may still result from maximising a utility function, but one could not derive a reaction function from first-order conditions of the conventional kind. The maximisation if it were ever carried out formally would involve an extremely complex grid search procedure exploring all the millions of possible combinations of different timings for planned realignments in the future. There would be non-linearities and discontinuities in the response to smooth changes in the environment, as the timing of the discrete planned realignments changed.

Despite these formal complexities it remains true that any realignment gives away more information than does inactivity. In the simplified case of the misalignment threshold discussed above, the first realignment gives away the location of the threshold. Next time it is approached the market will be confidently anticipating another realignment. This is, indeed, an argument in favour of keeping the exchange rate constant. By doing so the market is kept in ignorance, and that ignorance may be exploited to better effect on some future occasion.

It may be helpful to contrast expectation formation in the ERM with the corresponding relationships under a true fixed-rate system. We have argued that expectations under a fixed-rate system are mainly concerned with the loyalty of the authorities to the system as such, with the credibility of their commitment. Thus a single exchange-rate move, up or down, will signal that the commitment has been broken. So an upward revaluation of the currency today may encourage expectations of future devaluation. What is at stake is the attitude of the authorities to the system as such, not their attitude to inflation or unemployment. Such reasoning carries over, in attenuated form, to expectations within the ERM.

For the moment set aside the consideration that the EMS may be in the early stages of the transformation into a monetary union. It would remain true that a realignment signals something about the authorities' attitude to exchange-rate stability itself. One merit of such stability from their point of view is that it avoids the disclosure of their utility function. Information given away when the exchange rate is raised could in principle help the market to estimate the scale of a later devaluation. Moreover some observers will analyse behaviour in the ERM as if it were a fixed-rate system and apply to it the logic of precommitment, credibility and the need for punishment mechanisms. Strictly the existence of the let-out clause calls this logic into question, but it may influence expectations nevertheless.

To sum up, it is unlikely that a rigorous account could be given of optimal forecasting and policy formation in the EMS. This may explain the absence of any extensive discussion in the academic literature of the way in which the 'let-out clause' is, or should be, used. Nevertheless some useful insights may follow from a very simple approach which concentrates on the tolerable margin of misalignment. This approach could be applied either to overvaluation or to undervaluation. In the next section we shall concentrate on ERM membership as a means of curbing inflation, so that we shall be concerned mainly with situations where the exchange rate is above the FEER.

Application to the current situation

The ERM as a brake on inflation
France, Italy and several other countries have used ERM membership as part of a strategy to reduce their rates of inflation and to bring them into line with inflation in Germany. The UK is now following their example. Both forecasting and policy analysis must take account of this context. Reducing

inflation has a cost in terms of unemployment and lost output during the transition. It is argued that the cost of any given reduction in inflation will be less in the ERM than it would be outside. The case rests, of course, on the effect which the system has on expectations.

So long as the rate of inflation is higher at home than it is abroad a fixed exchange rate will become increasingly overvalued. This will raise unemployment, which in turn will slow down the rate of inflation. (If unemployment does not in fact rise as a result of losing competitiveness, fiscal policy measures may have to be taken to correct a worsening balance of payments position.) Eventually the rate of inflation will be below that abroad and the misalignment of relative prices will begin to correct itself. Meanwhile unemployment may be intolerably high. If the authorities prefer a longer, but less severe, process of adjustment they will devalue the exchange rate before the peak rate of unemployment is reached. They could indeed, by repeated devaluation, put off indefinitely the adjustment to a lower rate of inflation, but that would be to abandon the aim which led them to join the ERM in the first place.

As the earlier discussion suggested, the transition to lower inflation will be made more difficult if devaluation is expected (irrespective of whether devaluation in fact takes place). Expectations of devaluation will prolong the wage—price spiral and also necessitate a higher level of nominal interest rates. The hope is that the combination of ERM membership, a period of actual exchange-rate stability and a statement of intent to reduce inflation will transform expectations, which would otherwise have been based principally on the record of relatively high inflation in the past.

The appropriate strategy must depend on whether the problem of reducing inflation is seen as unique to the present period, or likely to recur in the future. As usual in game theory, one-off situations are quite different from 'repeated games'. It may make sense to devalue unexpectedly if one gets into difficulties, provided those difficulties are not expected to arise ever again.

Looking at this in terms of a misalignment threshold, the argument would be that the threshold should only be revealed by a realignment if it is thought unlikely that a misalignment of that scale will ever occur again. In a deterministic framework this may well be the case. When we forecast inflation, we almost invariably project it as slowing down in the medium term, as settling at a rate which we think the monetary authorities will find tolerable, somewhere quite close to zero and therefore, in the UK at least, far lower than the average rate of the past. In the absence of shocks it is indeed entirely plausible that inflation would be progressively reduced, and then held constant. If the cost of achieving that goal is a temporary spell of high unemployment, then deterministic forecasts may well on occasion show unemployment rising in the short run, but they are unlikely to show it rising repeatedly to those same levels in the long term.

We mentioned early on in this chapter the fact that the assumption of a known deterministic environment is an artificial one. It may indeed be a highly misleading one. A formal analysis in the early stages of a counter-inflation policy could well indicate that the 'optimum' strategy was to devalue on one (or perhaps a few) occasions, when the rate of inflation was still high and the rate of unemployment implied by a fixed exchange-rate regime was high as well. This seems to have been the reasoning that led France and Italy to devalue on a number of occasions in the early 1980s. These devaluations were not fully anticipated at the time, but the markets could have learnt from them roughly the degree of misalignment which the authorities in those countries were prepared to accept. Since their inflation rates are now lower, the market may not regard that information as so relevant to predicting their current behaviour. If inflation were to speed up now, or unemployment rise, in those countries the history of the early 1980s would not be forgotten.

It is easy to imagine circumstances however in which it would be back on the agenda very quickly. Moreover, it is easy to imagine some time in the future conducting a formal deterministic analysis on the lines sketched out here and then concluding that a one-off devaluation of sterling would be, on balance, worthwhile. But one message of this chapter is intended to be that such an analysis would be seriously incomplete. It is natural to hope (and even to forecast) that the rate of inflation will settle down at a tolerable rate and the need for a severe anti-inflation programme will never arise again. No-one foresaw the shocks to the world economy that resulted in repeated bursts of inflation in the 1970s. No-one even foresaw much in advance the boom in the UK at the end of the 1980s. It is possible that too relaxed an attitude to exchange-rate realignment in the short run might undermine the credibility of the ERM as an instrument of anti-inflation policy some time in the future when it is even more important to the management of the UK economy than it is now.

A change of government
The two main themes of this chapter have been commitment and learning. In developing both of them the tacit assumption has been made that the same government stays in office for ever. In fact the possibility of a change of government is always a factor in exchange-rate forecasting, especially as the time for an election approaches. The possible effect of realignment on the outcome of an election is not the least consideration in the minds of governments themselves; van der Ploeg (1989) argues that governments typically devalue the exchange rate on taking office and then allow it to appreciate gradually until the next election is out of the way.

A realignment, especially a devaluation, can easily be represented as a sign of defeat or failure. Although the ERM has a let-out clause, it is not intended that advantage should be taken of it in the normal conduct of exchange-rate policy. It is an acceptable means for solving a problem, a way of getting out of difficulties. Politicians standing for re-election do not want to present themselves as beset by problems and difficulties, even if they are not of their own making. This may be to under-estimate the sophistication of the electorate, who ought in principle to be weighing up the long-term costs and benefits of the realignment, but in fact politicians are very concerned at loss of face. The markets, knowing this, would not expect a realignment just before an election. On the other hand, the markets in the run-up to an election will naturally be influenced by the expectation of a realignment, especially (but not only) if they expect the government to lose office.

A new government might realign because its priorities as between economic objectives are different from those of the old government. If we think in terms of utility functions, then the identical situation may call for a realignment, assessed using one utility function, but not using the other. But, this will not *always* be the case. The optimal exchange rate under a flexible rate system will *always* be different for different parameters in the authorities' utility function, but under the ERM the best policy will be 'no change' for a range of parameter values.

A more interesting question concerns the effect of a change of government, if in fact the utility function does *not* change. Suppose that the new government attaches exactly the same weight to inflation as against unemployment, to the short-term future as against long-term, and so on; the very fact of a change of government will still influence the exchange rate. After a change of government the information and beliefs which the market has assembled from experience prior to the election is largely obsolete. A new government has no reputation, for good or for ill. (This is of course a simplification since the central bankers and the civil servants will be the same, and some international understandings may be inherited as well.) The market must (in most respects) begin learning afresh.

We have touched on the possibility that the best strategy in the ERM could be to build up a reputation for never realigning and then, all of a sudden, to realign when the market is not expecting it. If that is the nature of the game, then a change of government would make an immediate realignment *less* likely. It is at least as easy to imagine cases where a change of government makes realignment *more* likely (even though the utility function stays the same).

For example, the old government may have built up a reputation for resisting devaluation, and been rewarded by a reduction in nominal interest rates, thus keeping unemployment below the critical level at which devaluation would in fact be conceded. The new government, lacking reputation, may see nominal interest rates rise — and all the (true) statements it may make about its determination to halt inflation may not prevent that from happening. Higher interest rates may then push unemployment over the devaluation threshold, the expectation itself bringing about its own fulfilment.

The converse is just as possible. The old government may have realigned a few times, and hence have a reputation for resorting to the let-out clause on relatively slight provocation. In that case the new government may have *more* credibility than the old, and a realignment may be less likely.

A reputation for not devaluing can be an asset, allowing a better combination of inflation and unemployment to be achieved than would have been possible before the reputation was built up. This gives an incumbent government an advantage over a potential rival which lacks reputation. It has 'sunk costs' invested — to use terminology from a different application of game theory. A government may therefore invest in acquiring a reputation, not just because this will produce a better outcome for the economy, but specifically because it gives it an advantage over other political parties. It could achieve such an advantage in this way that its tenure of office seemed almost impossible to contest.

The transition to a fixed exchange rate

The ERM is a hybrid, an inelegant mixture of flexibility and fixity. Like the Bretton-Woods system before it, it does work, but perhaps it cannot work for ever. It may even be the case that transition to either a fixed or a flexible system is in the end inevitable. This would be the case if the ERM could work only so long as the market remained in partial ignorance of the true objectives of the authorities operating the system — and if the process of learning about those objectives converged on the truth. If the market comes to be unanimous in expecting revaluations, then revaluations must occur, either continuously or not at all. Given the inherent difficulty of learning, and given the fact that preferences change, when governments change and otherwise, the convergence on truth must be slow, and incomplete. But the system could become unmanageable — or simply not worth the effort — when the market's knowledge is still incomplete. We have also argued that, in practice, the long-term costs of using the let-out clause may always outweigh the benefits. In that case it would certainly be attractive to the monetary authorities to move to a real fixed-rate system, or a monetary union in which the question of realignment simply did not arise. That is what seems to be happening in Europe now. (The other advantages and disadvantages of a monetary union have been extensively discussed elsewhere in this volume.)

The conditions for the transition to monetary union, and the institutional arrangements to accompany it, have been settled by the treaty of Maastricht. In the meantime, realignments could slow down the process of convergence, and could even call in question whether a monetary union was feasible at all. Thus countries who are, for whatever reason, enthusiastic about EMU, and keen to play a full part in it, will be especially reluctant to realign in case they put it in jeopardy. Some flexibility has been built into the timetable. Suppose, however, that the date for the final fixing of exchange rates was decided and could not be changed. How would this affect exchange-rate forecasts and policy in the interim?

A finite-period game is a different kind of game from one with an infinite horizon. Strategy is devised by starting in the final period and working back to the beginning. In the final period of an ERM 'game' the best strategy would always be to realign. The arguments set out in this chapter for keeping the exchange rate constant have all been based on the advantage of influencing expectations, building up a reputation or even concealing one's true priorities. If the nature of the system is about to change, these considerations do not apply.

The market will know this, and be expecting a general realignment immediately before the final fixing of exchange rates takes place. It is no good therefore trying to build up a reputation for not realigning in the penultimate period. If there is no incentive to build up such a reputation then a realignment could in fact take place in the penultimate period, as well as in the ultimate period. The same reasoning can be applied to all periods, suggesting that a finite-period strategy would involve realigning in every period and that the ERM would be unstable during the transition. (A similar point is made in Froot and Rogoff, 1991.)

On the other hand, instability does not seem the inevitable result if we interpret the ERM as a device for concealing intentions. The market may know that a realignment is inevitable in the final period of the game, but it does not know how large that realignment will be (or even its direction, necessarily). It is still possible to surprise the market in the final period, so long as one does not disclose one's priorities by realigning in the interim.

Nevertheless the possibility of instability in the transition to EMU has influenced the choice of convergence criteria. One of the criteria for 'convergence', which must be fulfilled before a country is thought ready for membership of EMU, is a period in which its currency had not been devalued. The more stringent requirement has also been included that the nominal interest rates of all the countries forming the EMU should have converged before their exchange rates can be fixed. This does *not* require that realignments have not taken place, but it *does* require that no further realignments are expected by the markets, for example at the time when 'irrevocable' fixing is actually announced.

Unless the final move is made to a single currency, realignments will not in fact be technically impossible even though an 'irrevocable' commitment has been made that they will not take place. An earlier section of this chapter discussed briefly the formal analysis of a fixed-rate system. The conclusion was that it could be maintained, within a purely utilitarian framework, if a 'punish-ment mechanism' was devised to overcome the problem of time inconsistency. It was also suggested that the issue would not in fact be addressed in a purely utilitarian framework. Promises ought to be kept even if it is advantageous to break them. The implication is that the decision to join EMU cannot be addressed in a purely utilitarian framework either. Promises ought not to be made unless one means to keep them.

Conclusions

A satisfactory theory of realignments within the ERM does not exist, and is unlikely to be constructed. Two issues stand out as being particularly interesting and particularly intractible: the way the market learns from the observation of realignments and the nature of the commitment which the authorities make when they join the system. By contrast with a flexible exchange-rate system it is not possible for the market to estimate a reaction function for the authorities and much more difficult to deduce anything about their aims and objectives. By contrast with a fixed exchange-rate system there is no clear definition of the rules of the game and hence no obvious punishment mechanism to ensure that they are kept.

However the system is analysed it will never be possible to forecast realignments with confidence. It is a built-in feature of the system that exchange-rate forecasts must be incorrect, and a realignment must, to some extent, always come as a surprise. The most one could ever hope for is a rational way of assessing the subjective probability of a realignment. Even this is extremely difficult since the past behaviour of the authorities will always be open to many different interpretations, with radically different implications for what they will do next. The natural way to argue is to ask what one would do oneself in their situation, so the processes of forecasting and policy analysis are one and the same.

Ignoring the effect on expectations a realignment will always seem attractive to policymakers, often very attractive indeed. If only *foreseeable* effects on expectations are taken into account the weight attached to such strategic considerations may still be relatively small. The strongest argument against realignment is often that this is a measure which should only be used in dire emergencies, and one never knows when one might find oneself in a worse emergency than the present. A different, but related, argument is that a government which has built up a reputation for keeping the exchange rate fixed may have a better chance of being re-elected.

Applying these arguments to the present situation in Europe it would seem that the immediate incentive to realign is relatively weak for most governments including the UK, and is likely to be resisted for 'strategic' reasons of the kind outlined. The prospect of transition to a true fixed-rate system may reinforce the arguments against realignments, as they would threaten the stability of the system in its final period.

If, for such reasons, one would not recommend realignments to any (or many) of the members of the ERM in the foreseeable future (given their objectives), one would not forecast such realignments either. But here we are dealing with a balance of probabilities, and a decision to realign would not be unthinkable for any of the countries concerned. We are still in the hybrid ERM and not yet in a fixed-rate system.

The ERM has lasted for more than a decade, and the rather similar Bretton-Woods system lasted for more than two decades, yet its viability in the long term is open to question. The slow process of learning by the market progressively reduces the attraction of a system that relies on surprises. Even now the ERM has evolved some way in the direction of a fixed exchange-rate system. If it does not go the whole way, it may some day break up and Europe revert again to exchange-rate flexibility.

9

A Supply-side View on European Integration: the Case of the EMU

Anthonie Knoester and André Kolodziejak

Introduction

At the European summit in Maastricht in December, 1991, major steps forward were taken on the road towards complete European integration. The agreements signed dealt with the way in which member states should reach the ultimate goal of European integration and the establishment of European economic and monetary union (EMU). EMU is considered to be the third and final stage of European integration as advocated in the so-called Delors report of 1989.[1] The Maastricht agreements deal with the second stage, such as the economic convergence criteria that must be met by member states before they can enter EMU on 1 January, 1997 at the earliest, or on 1 January, 1999 at the latest. The first stage is the completion of the internal market on 1 January, 1993. From that date labour, goods, services and capital can move freely within the European Community.

We believe that the Maastricht agreements pay too little attention to a proper treatment of the supply-side of the economy within the continuing process of European integration. They do not contain a criterion for a maximum collective burden of member states arising from the share of taxes and social security contributions in national income. Yet such a criterion should be a cornerstone for economic policies directed towards shaping the necessary conditions for a lasting European EMU. However, under the Maastricht agreements, member states could, for instance, try to meet the officially formulated criteria through an increase in taxation in order to avoid more painful budgetary adjustments such as cuts in public spending. In the medium and long run this policy could be very counterproductive in terms of economic growth and employment.[2] Additionally, substantial differences in taxation within the European Community could induce undesired flows in labour and capital resulting in an unbalanced European income distribution and employment spread.

In this chapter we will concentrate on a treatment of supply-side economics within the context of transition to EMU. In particular, we will deal with the problems arising for member states aspiring to meet the Maastricht convergence criteria in the absence of European criteria for the collective burden. In addition, we shall formulate some policies which member states might follow in order to reach a proper starting point at which to join EMU. The plan of this chapter is as follows. In the following section we will briefly discuss the Maastricht agreements on the EMU convergence criteria. In the third section some basic supply-side elements will be discussed, followed by a quantification in the fourth section of expected policies by Germany, the Netherlands and the United Kingdom, by means of linked empirical models for these countries. The fifth section deals with so-called recovery scenarios for these member states and uses the models to analyse the effects of disturbances arising from fiscal policies in the United States. A conclusion follows in the final section.

EMU convergence criteria

The EMU convergence criteria set out at Maastricht required potential members to fulfill four criteria to be admitted to EMU. They must have an inflation rate of no more than 1.5 points above the average of the three EC countries with the lowest rates; a government deficit of less than 3 per cent of GDP; a gross government debt of less than 60 per cent of GDP; and long-term interest rates of no more than 200 base points above the average of the three EC countries with the lowest interest rates. The treaty also stipulates that the applicant's currency must have observed normal fluctuation margins for two years prior to joining the union, without devaluation or severe tension. The treaty specifies that the application tests for passage to Stage 3 will be based on these criteria. Thus failure to meet the criteria will not necessarily bar a country from joining EMU: there will be some leeway for the final political decision. The treaty therefore embodies the EC countries' genuine commitment to a shared convergence objective. No country will be disqualified on the grounds of its present economic situation. At the end of 1996, the European Council will determine, by what is called a qualified (weighted) majority, the date of the establishment of the economic and monetary union, provided at least seven member states are found to be eligible to adopt a single currency. Stage 3 of EMU could therefore begin by 1 January, 1997, at least for those seven countries. If fewer than seven countries qualify, EMU will take effect no later than 1 January, 1999, for those member states that have met the admission criteria. The basket ecu will then disappear and the ecu will become the single currency, its external parity being guaranteed by the future European central bank. The currencies of the member countries outside EMU will be defined with reference to the single currency and will fluctuate inside the present margins. These countries will be allowed to join EMU on a gradual basis according to their degree of economic convergence.

But even with some leeway for the final political decision by the end of 1996 it is clear that in order to make a successful start to EMU, at least seven countries have to meet almost all the criteria by 1 January, 1997, or it must at least be clear by then that they will be able to meet them by January, 1999, otherwise the credibility of the EMU project will be severely damaged. This suggests to us that the building of EMU must be linked with the abandonment of national Keynesian demand management and functional finance in Europe. As a consequence of growing integration government budgets of member states, like those of municipalities today, cannot and must not play an important macroeconomic role in demand management. This also explains why it was necessary (apart from German fears of giving up their strong currency) to formulate such exacting criteria in the Maastricht proposals. Although we think that these criteria are still inadequate because there is no criterion for the collective burden, it will already be difficult for most EC countries to meet the official EMU convergence criteria.

Table 9.1 shows the situation of the EC member countries with respect to the convergence criteria at the beginning of 1992. Only two countries, France and Luxembourg, meet all the criteria; Denmark and Germany meet four out of five. Four countries, namely Belgium, Ireland, the Netherlands and the United Kingdom, meet three criteria. Of these eight countries seven have to qualify for EMU entry by the end of 1996. The other four countries, Greece, Italy, Portugal and Spain, do not meet any criterion or meet only one criterion according to 1991 data. It may be clear by now that it will be very difficult for Greece, Italy and Portugal to join the EMU as full members in 1997 or in 1999. The EMU convergence criteria are not only important to the present EC member countries; they are also important for countries from the other bloc of the European Economic Space (EES): the EFTA countries. The internal market programme has led several EFTA countries to consider EC membership. Austria was the first to apply and Scandinavian countries such as Finland, Norway and Sweden seem likely to follow. It is important for EFTA countries to meet the Maastricht criteria in order that they can link themselves to the Exchange Rate Mechanism (ERM). By conforming to the EMS narrow fluctuation limits for exchange rates, Austria and Norway will have the advantage of operating more easily on EC markets within the EES (see Abrams *et al.*, 1990, pp.39-48). In this way they can borrow the credibility of monetary policies within the framework of EMS and bring down their inflation and interest rates.

A comparison with the US and Japan is also illustrative for EMU and the EES as a whole. These countries already fit perfectly in the desired fiscal pattern of the EMU. The fluctuations of the dollar and the yen *vis-à-vis* the D-Mark and the other EMS currencies meanwhile have been large during the past few years. But even this can be changed by monetary policy coordination. Only four years remain for economic policies directed towards

Table 9.1 Convergence criteria for the EMU, 1991

European economic space EC:	EMU criteria of the Treaty of Maastricht							With extra criterium	
	Govt debt < 60.0 NI (a)	Budget deficit < 3.0 NI (b)	Govt invest-ment ratio (c)	Inflation rate < 4.3% (d)	ERM perform-ance (e)	Interest rate < 11.4 (f)	EMU perform-ance	Collect-ive burden (g) < 40 NI	Overall EMU perform-ance
Belgium	129.4	6.4	1.6	3.2	+	9.3	-	44.5	-
Denmark	66.7	1.7	2.0	2.4	+	10.1	-	55.9	-
Germany	46.2	3.2	2.4	3.5	+	8.6	-	44.8	-
Greece	96.4	17.9	3.1	18.3	-	16.6	-	35.1	-
France	47.2	1.5	3.5	3.0	+	9.0	+	48.9	-
Ireland	102.8	4.1	1.9	3.0	+	9.2	-	40.4	-
Italy	101.2	9.9	3.4	6.4	-	12.9	-	43.8	-
Luxem-bourg	6.9	-1.9	6.1	3.4	+	8.2	+	53.4	-
Nether-lands	78.4	4.4	2.3	3.2	+	8.9	-	51.8	-
Portugal	64.7	5.4	2.9	11.7	-	17.1	-	39.9	-
Spain	45.6	3.9	5.2	5.8	-	12.4	-	39.5	-
UK	43.8	1.9	2.0	6.5	-	9.9	-	38.1	-
EFTA:									
Finland	18.6	3.6	3.4	4.4	-	11.4	-	39.9	-
Iceland	24.6	2.3	3.5	6.8	-	20.9	-	36.6	-
Norway	43.8	1.0	3.5	3.4	+	9.9	+	54.9	-
Austria	54.4	2.2	3.4	3.2	+	8.6	+	46.1	-
Sweden	44.8	-0.1	2.8	10.0	-	10.8	-	64.1	-
Switzer-land	10.9	-0.1	3.7	5.8	-	6.2	-	34.1	-
US	58.5	2.7	1.6	3.4	-	8.2		31.8	
Japan	63.4	-2.3	5.1	2.7	-	6.8		33.3	

Source: European Commission, OECD, IMF

Notes:

(a) Gross debt of general government. (b) General government financial balance, deficit (+) or surplus (-). (c) According to the Treaty of Maastricht when the government budget deficit is examined attention will also be paid to whether the so-called 'Golden rule' is respected. 'Golden rule' defined as not allowing general government budget deficit to exceed general government's gross capital formation as a percentage of GDP. (d) 1/3 x (2.4+3.0+3.0)+1.5=4.3, that is, calculated upper bound of growth of consumer prices. (e) Normal currency fluctuation between the narrow (2.25 per cent) ERM limits during 1989-91. (f) 1/3 x (9.2+10.1+9.0)+2.0 = 11.4, that is, calculated upper bound of long-term interest rate (government bond yield). (g) Current receipts of government as percentage of GDP.

achieving the EMU goals by 1997. For the countries closest to meeting the EMU criteria, namely Belgium, Denmark, Germany, Ireland, the Netherlands and the UK, the level of government debt and of the budget deficit are in general the most problematical criteria. Only the UK has an inflation problem. Given this situation and given the short time remaining there is a clear risk that the countries mentioned above will use tax increases to meet these criteria. There is a real danger that the European economy will be severely hit by a further increase in the collective burden. This expected interference in the supply-side of the economy requires an extra EMU criterion for the collective burden. In our opinion, a further decrease in the collective burden is necessary, to at least the average European level of 1970-80, that is, about 40 per cent of national income, or even to the average level of 1960-70, about 35 per cent, bringing Europe back into line with the other major economic blocs in the world economy.

Some basic supply-side notions

The central contention of supply-side economics is that a high level of taxation has a negative effect on economic performance. As argued in Knoester (1983, 1988, 1991a, 1991b), the so-called *inverted Haavelmo effect* can be seen as a theoretical and empirical foundation of the implementation of supply-side policies. The inverted Haavelmo-effect refers to the occurrence of a negative balanced-budget multiplier instead of a positive Keynesian one. The result of an expanding public sector, financed by extra taxes and/or social security contributions, will be a lower rate of economic growth and less employment than in the absence of such expansion. This inverted Haavelmo effect is the opposite of the Keynesian Haavelmo effect (Haavelmo, 1945). The Haavelmo effect suggests a positive balanced-budget multiplier as a result of a simultaneous increase in public spending and taxation and hence provided a perfect alibi for the postwar expansion of the public sector, which in all OECD countries was mainly financed by increasing taxes and social security contributions. Yet Haavelmo himself (1945, p.318) already toned down extreme optimism about his analysis by ending his famous paper by saying '... we only wanted to demonstrate that a 'balanced budget' has a direct multiplier effect, with a multiplier equal to one, in addition to whatever (positive or negative) effects there might be from a redistribution of income'. This effect may be associated with the phenomenon of shifting of taxation into higher wages. If higher taxes are shifted in full, each tax increase will lead to a correspondingly higher pre-tax real wage, as a result of which the ratio of profits to national income falls. Knoester and Van der Windt (1987) show that there are strong empirical indications that such shifting can be observed in the 1960s, 1970s and the early 1980s for ten major OECD countries. The shifting of taxation into higher wages can be derived from wage bargaining models, in which wages are the result of a bargaining process between employees and employers. In such wage bargaining processes claims and outcomes are based on constrained maximisation of income by both parties. Early roots of this can be found in Zeuthen (1930). A further elaboration has been given by Pen (1952), Phillips (1958) and more recently by the OECD (1978) and Knoester and Van der Windt (1987).

More taxation can change income distribution in favour of employees at the cost of employers, resulting in a lower profit ratio. This in turn will depress the investment ratio, so that economic growth will fall. Simultaneously, increased real wages will push up classical unemployment. Lower economic growth, combined with rising unemployment, will boost public spending and social security benefits, which in turn will lead to an increase in taxation and social security contributions. This rising burden of taxation will lead to a further increase in pre-tax real wages. Thus the ultimate result of this process can be a vicious circle of increasing unemployment and taxation and decreasing economic growth. These negative effects of increasing taxation can outweigh the Keynesian positive effects on economic growth and unemployment of the simultaneously increased public spending and taxation.

The question whether this will really happen and, if so, to what extent, may vary for different periods and for different countries. A clearer view of this can be obtained with the help of empirical models which contain these interactions. General models have been developed (see for example Knoester, 1983, 1988, 1991) which can be used as a suitable starting point for the empirical verification of the inverted Haavelmo effect. The details of these models will not be discussed here, only their main characteristics. An important feature of these models is that they contain a Keynesian income expenditure block and a block describing the supply-side of the economy. This is done by including equations for production capacity and excess capacity. The growth in production capacity depends on percentage changes in real wages, the investment ratio and the rate of technological progress (Knoester and Van Sinderen, 1984). In addition, these models contain a quantification of the government sector — including the social security system — and of income distribution. Of special importance is the inclusion of the wage-price block. In this block the wage equation has been derived from a wage bargaining model, implying that, in principle, an increase in direct taxes and social security contributions is shifted forward into higher real wages. the models also contain a labour market block in which employment is not only determined by effective demand — represented by excess capacity — but also by classical determinants such as real wage rate growth and the investment ratio. These models comprise a mix of Keynesian income-expenditure analysis and neoclassical growth theory. Together with an endogenous income distribution, they provide a suitable framework for analysing the effects of balanced-budget financing. The forward shifting of taxes into higher wages results in negative balanced-budget multipliers (the inverted Haavelmo effect) as a consequence of simultaneous increase in public spending and taxation. As shown in Knoester (1984), the balanced-budget multipliers are zero if the same policy measures are repeated with the exclusion of a forward shifting of taxes.

It is important to distinguish between the negative and positive effects of balanced-budget financing of public spending. The positive effects are the well-known Keynesian multiplier effects of an increase in public spending. When public-sector wages, government consumption and social security benefits go up, private consumption rises likewise as a consequence of the increase in demand. In addition, investment picks up because capacity utilisation rises. Hence these Keynesian demand effects exert an upward pressure on economic growth and national income. Yet these positive multiplier effects do not dominate the ultimate consequences of balanced-budget financing, because the forward shifting of taxes into higher real wages has direct and indirect negative effects on economic performance. The direct effects are related to the incidence of classical unemployment as explained by Malinvaud (1977) and others. When real wages go up, employment falls. This in turn leads to higher social security benefits and, consequently, to higher social security contributions or taxes, which can set in motion new rounds of forward shifting, resulting in higher real wages and lower employment. Another direct effect results from the impact of real wages on a country's competitiveness and exports. A shifting forward of taxes increases unit labour costs and thus causes competitiveness to deteriorate. As a result, exports fall, which in turn causes economic growth to decrease. The indirect negative consequences of the forward shifting of taxes follow from a change in income distribution at the expense of profits. Higher real wages depress the profit ratio, causing investment and employment to fall. This sets a negative spiral in motion, in which the negative effects of a forward shifting in taxes on the supply side of the economy plays a central role. Thus the inverted Haavelmo effect can provide an important rationale for tax cuts as advocated by supply-side economics.

In a recent survey on the effects of taxation in a set of eighteen economic models frequently used in government policy analysis in the Netherlands and the European Community, Knoester and Kolodziejak (1991) examined whether these models show a negative or a positive balanced budget multiplier. For the Netherlands fifteen models were used for the analysis of which only four models showed a positive balanced budget multiplier. For four other countries, France, Germany, the UK and the US, seven well-known empirical multicountry models were used. Of these only one on average showed a positive balanced budget multiplier. Thus one of the main conclusions of this survey is that there are strong empirical indications for the international occurrence of the inverted Haavelmo effect.

Table 9.2 Effects of a once-and-for-all 1 per cent GDP increase in direct taxes and social security contributions and a simultaneous increase in public spending, per cent

Change in levels after year	Germany		Netherlands		UK		US	
	1	5	1	5	1	5	1	5
Profit ratio*	-0.6	-1.1	-1.0	-1.2	-1.0	-1.0	-0.6	-0.5
Investment ratio*	-0.0	-0.7	-0.1	-0.8	0.0	-0.4	-0.1	-0.5
Volume of production	-0.4	-2.6	-0.7	-2.6	0.1	-1.5	0.5	-2.1
Inflation rate	0.6	1.9	1.6	2.2	0.6	4.0	0.2	1.9
Export volume	-0.1	-0.7	0.0	-0.9	-0.2	-1.3	0.1	-0.3
Utilisation rate	-0.3	-1.3	-0.6	-0.7	0.3	-0.4	-0.5	-0.4
Private employment	-0.2	-2.7	-0.2	-1.7	-0.1	-1.7	-0.4	-2.4
Unemployment rate	0.2	2.7	0.2	1.3	0.1	1.3	0.3	2.0
Public sector deficit*	0.0	0.4	-0.1	0.2	0.0	0.2	0.0	-0.2

Source: Knoester (1991b).
* per cent GDP.

Expected scenarios

As well as having to fulfill the convergence criteria agreed at Maastricht, the European countries also have to reckon with their own specific national economic conditions. In Germany, for example, the cost of reunification will remain a major topic for economic policymaking in the 1990s. In the Netherlands a reduction in the government budget deficit (that is, a lowering of the government debt ratio) is a necessary condition for joining EMU but, at the same time, Dutch policymakers have to aim at a further reduction in the unemployment rate. For all European member states such specific national conditions play a certain role in combination with the required economic policy within the framework of EMU. In this section we will discuss some plausible economic policy scenarios for Germany, the Netherlands and the United Kingdom. In addition, we will discuss a plausible policy scenario for the US since its policies can have a major effect on economic developments in Europe. The scenarios will be quantified by the empirical macroeconomic models including a well-developed supply-side (Knoester, 1983, 1988, 1991a, 1991b). A distinction is made between the effects of isolated national policy actions and simultaneous joint actions. In doing this special emphasis is given to the incorporation of the supply-side effects as discussed in the last section.

The following scenarios are considered. First, for Germany it is supposed that its reunification will result in a continuous upward pressure on public expenditure and taxation. As a result the occurrence of the inverted Haavelmo effect as discussed in the previous section forms a serious threat to German economic performance in the 1990s by including a lower rate of economic growth and a higher unemployment rate, as a result of a simultaneous increase in public spending and taxation. In addition, it appears that unification will also put upward pressure on German wages. Thus a realistic German scenario seems to be a combination of more public spending and taxation and excessive wage claims.

Dutch wage negotiations are usually significantly influenced by German wage negotiations. Hence there will be upward pressure on Dutch nominal and real wages as a consequence of upward pressure on German wages. In addition, since the beginning of the 1990s, there has been a substantial increase in Dutch nominal wages. This is, on the one hand, the result of a lower unemployment rate and, on the other, the result of a catching-up effect after the wage moderation of the 1980s. In addition, the Netherlands have to reduce both their government budget deficit and their government debt ratio in order to meet the agreed EMU convergence criterion. Upward pressure on nominal wages is expected for the UK. A specific British reason for relatively high wages in the 1990s is the fact that in the UK the inflation rate is at a substantially higher level than in, for example, the Netherlands and Germany, and this is a problem in terms of the EMU conditions. Finally, no doubt the first interest of US policymakers will be to cut the double deficit, that is, the government budget and the balance of payments deficit. Most probably the new American administration after the 1992 elections will increase taxes in order to diminish the increasingly untenable nature of the double deficit.

The results make perfectly clear that the expected scenarios for the European countries will have negative consequences on economic growth and the unemployment rate. As a consequence it becomes even more difficult for these countries to meet the EMU convergence criteria of the Treaty of Maastricht compared with the situation in 1991, as shown in table 9.1 This is also confirmed in table 9.4 which contains the same scenarios not as simulated

Table 9.3 Effects of expected national scenarios 1993-7 on production volume growth and the unemployment rate (isolated scenarios)

Expected scenarios	Volume of production %			Unemployment rate		
	1993	1995	1997	1993	1995	1997
Germany						
A	-0.28	-2.06	-5.07	0.13	1.31	3.73
B	-0.21	-2.04	-5.49	0.09	1.23	3.93
Combined	-0.49	-4.10	-10.56	0.22	2.54	7.66
Netherlands						
A	-0.21	-1.62	-2.92	0.05	0.60	1.35
C	-0.38	-0.41	0.92	0.10	0.26	-0.21
Combined	-0.59	-2.03	-2.00	0.15	0.86	1.14
United Kingdom						
A	-0.02	-0.74	-1.44	0.04	0.54	1.24
United States						
D	-0.62	-2.74	-3.30	0.39	2.93	3.57

Notes:
In all scenarios the shocks are applied each year, and hence after four years they are four times as large as in the first year.
Scenario A: 0.5 per cent wage increase.
Scenario B: positive balanced budget scenario: 0.5 per cent of GDP increase in taxes (and social security contributions) and 0.5 per cent increase of GDP in government expenditure.
Scenario C: 0.5 per cent of GDP decrease of government expenditure.
Scenario D: 0.5 per cent of GDP increase in taxes.

actions but as simultaneous actions.[3] The negative effects of expected national scenarios are even larger in an international context when they occur simultaneously. Although there are quantitative differences between the isolated scenarios and the simultaneous scenarios (table 9.4), the direction of both types of scenario is the same.

Table 9.4 Effects of the combined expected national scenarios 1993-7

	Germany			Netherlands		
Change in levels	1993	1995	1997	1993	1995	1997
Budget deficit **	0.0	0.6	1.9	-0.3	-0.6	-0.4
Government debt**	0.0	0.8	3.8	-0.3	-1.4	-2.5
Long-term interest rate	0.1	0.4	1.5	0.1	0.4	1.5
Production volume*	-0.5	-4.6	-11.5	0.8	-3.9	-6.8
Utilisation rate*	-0.4	-3.7	-8.0	0.7	-3.3	-4.9
Unemployment rate*	0.2	2.8	8.3	0.2	1.5	3.3
Profit ratio	-0.6	-2.5	-4.1	-0.3	-1.1	-1.6
Investment ratio	0.0	-0.8	-2.8	-0.1	-0.8	-1.0
Export volume*	-0.5	-4.5	-9.6	-0.1	-2.5	-6.9
Exchange rate***	0.1	0.2	0.1	0.1	0.2	0.1
Consumer prices*	0.9	3.8	5.5	0.8	1.7	1.6
Current a/c (% NI)	-0.0	0.1	0.3	0.31	-0.1	0.74
	United States			United Kingdom		
Budget deficit**	-0.3	-0.4	-0.1	0.0	0.3	0.8
Government debt**	-0.3	-1.1	-1.6	0.0	0.5	1.9
Long-term interest rate	0.1	0.3	1.0	0.1	0.6	1.7
Production volume*	-1.1	-5.6	-9.1	-0.2	-2.1	-3.9
Utilisation rate*	-1.0	-4.5	-5.4	-0.1	-1.8	-2.9
Unemployment rate*	0.7	4.7	9.0	0.1	1.3	3.0
Profit ratio	-0.3	-1.5	-1.9	-0.3	-0.8	-0.9
Investment ratio	-0.1	-0.7	-1.1	0.0	-0.53	-0.7
Export volume*	-2.3	-8.9	-12.9	-0.4	-3.6	-7.2
Exchange rate***	0.1	0.2	0.1	0.1	0.2	0.1
Consumer prices*	-0.1	0.0	-0.9	0.4	1.8	1.0
Current a/c (% NI)	-0.1	-0.1	-0.0	-0.2	-0.4	-0.3

* per cent: ** per cent GDP. In all scenarios pushes are given permanently from 1993 until 1997. See table 9.3 for the content of the scenarios.

Recovery scenarios

As noted above, the agreements signed at the 1991 European summit at Maastricht lack supply-side convergence criteria such as a maximum collective burden for member states. This is not surprising because relevant literature shows that the fiscal convergence criteria have been subject to far more discussion than monetary ones (Masson and Melitz, 1990, Bovenberg, Kremers and Masson, 1991, Buiter and Kletzer, 1991, Duwendag, 1991, Wyplosz, 1991, van der Ploeg, 1991, Langfeldt, 1992, EC Commission, 1992). As a result there is the risk that EC countries will try to meet the agreed convergence criteria by raising taxes and/or social security contributions. We have argued above that this scenario probably applies for Germany, given its need to finance the continuing cost of its reunification. In addition, a continuous upward pressure on wages in other European countries such as the Netherlands and the UK seems to be a plausible scenario for the 1990s and thus an obstacle meeting the officially agreed EMU convergence criteria for inflation and the government budget deficit. Given the drawbacks of the expected scenarios we have quantified in this section some 'recovery scenarios'. A central element in these is the need to lower, or at least to stabilise, the collective burden in EC member states and the need for wage moderation compared with the expected scenarios of the previous section. In addition, we will look at the specific starting conditions of each country as well as for a recovery scenario for the United States, given the important linkages between the European and US economies. We have quantified the recovery scenarios in standard units such as simulations by 0.5 per cent of GDP or by 0.5 per cent of the wage bill. One can, of course, multiply or divide these scenarios with a certain value in order to obtain a policy package that suits the political viabilities of each country.

Starting with the case of Germany, an obvious recovery scenario seems to be that Germany tries to avoid the simultaneous increase in public spending and taxation as a result of its reunification. The first alternative is that Germany seeks to finance the increase in public spending in the former DDR by cutting public spending in the former BRD. Such a redistribution of public spending in favour of the former DDR has the advantage that there is no longer a need for the increase in taxes and social security contributions discussed in the expected scenario for Germany. However, a far better result can be obtained if the German administration succeeds in cutting extra spending in order to achieve an overall decrease in direct taxes and/or social security contributions. Table 9.5 shows that in that case the ultimate result will be a substantial increase in economic growth and a substantial decrease in the unemployment rate. These positive effects on German economic performance are the result of the working of the supply-

Table 9.5 Effects of recovery scenarios 1993-7 on production volume growth and the unemployment rate (isolated scenarios)

Expected scenarios	Volume of production %			Unemployment rate		
	1993	1995	1997	1993	1995	1997
Germany						
E	0.28	2.06	5.07	-0.13	-1.31	-3.73
F	0.21	2.04	5.49	-0.09	-1.23	-3.93
Combined	0.49	4.10	10.56	-0.22	-2.54	-7.66
Netherlands						
E	0.21	1.62	2.92	-0.05	-0.60	-1.35
G	0.01	1.20	5.61	0.00	-0.70	-2.39
Combined	0.20	3.82	8.53	-0.05	-1.33	-3.74
United Kingdom						
H	-0.49	3.66	6.09	-0.26	-2.59	-5.45
F	0.02	1.53	2.93	-0.04	-0.89	-2.39
Combined	-0.47	5.00	9.02	-0.30	-3.48	-7.84
United States						
I	-0.39	-1.33	-0.53	0.24	1.23	1.07
J	-0.16	0.07	2.24	0.10	0.07	-1.43
Combined	-0.55	-1.27	1.71	0.34	1.30	-0.36

Notes:

In all scenarios shocks are applied permanently from 1993 until 1997, and hence are four times bigger in the fourth year than in the first.

Scenario E: 0.5 per cent wage decrease.

Scenario F: negative balanced budget scenario.

Scenario G: 2 per cent of GDP decrease in government spending and 0.5 per cent of GDP decrease in taxes.

Scenario H: 0.5 per cent of GDP decrease in wages and taxes.

Scenario I: 0.5 per cent of GDP decrease in government spending.

Scenario J: 1 per cent of GDP decrease in government spending and 0.5 per cent of GDP decrease in taxes.

supply-side mechanism as pointed out in the third section of this chapter, of which a key element is the contribution of lower taxation to wage moderation.

Apart from this, German trade unions may be persuaded to follow a policy of wage moderation even in the absence of any compensation in real earnings of employees by way of lower taxation. Table 9.5 shows that such a recovery scenario, a simultaneous cut in public spending and taxation by 0.5 per cent of GDP in each year when compared to the previous year, plus an additional wage moderation by 0.5 per cent per annum in the growth of the wage bill, will have very attractive results for the German economy in terms of economic growth and the unemployment rate. As a result of this German recovery scenario the negative consequences of the expected scenario will vanish completely.

For the Netherlands, a somewhat different recovery scenario is valid, based on specific Dutch conditions. As discussed above, the Netherlands have to cut their government budget deficit to a lower level in the years 1993-7 in order to meet the EMU convergence criteria on the government deficit and the debt ratio. At the same time an upward pressure on wages exists in the Netherlands as in other European countries. An elegant way to reach wage moderation is the policy that the Dutch government offers trade unions a decrease in direct taxes and/or social security contributions in return for wage moderation. Obviously, real net earnings of employees will not decrease as a result of such a scenario. At the same time the Dutch government cannot offer lower taxation to trade unions at the expense of an increase in the budget deficit given the need for the Netherlands to meet the EMU convergence conditions for the budget deficit. Hence for the Netherlands the only sensible way to pursue a policy of tax reduction is to finance these tax cuts with a simultaneous cut in public spending. Table 9.5 shows that the economic consequences of this policy — as was also the case in Germany — are very favourable for the Dutch economy. It should be noted that the annual additional cut in public spending is double that of the tax reduction of 0.5 per cent of GDP. This difference is due to the condition that the Netherlands should try, in order to meet the EMU convergence criteria, to reduce the government budget deficit simultaneously with the suggested tax reduction. Finally, for the Netherlands, we have also included additional wage moderation apart from that induced by lower taxes.

For the UK, unlike the case for Germany and the Netherlands, there is some room within the borders of the EMU convergence criteria to decrease taxes at the expense of an increase in the government budget deficit. Thus the combination of a tax reduction and wage moderation seems to be a plausible policy option. In this scenario — with no reduction in real net earnings for employees in spite of wage moderation — the profitability and competitiveness of the British economy can increase considerably with favourable effects on economic growth and the unemployment rate. An even better picture arises if this policy is combined with an additional reduction in taxation financed by a simultaneous cut in public spending. Here again, these favourable outcomes are the result of the supply-side mechanism pointed out in the third section. Last but not least, we have quantified a recovery scenario for the US. No doubt the American administration has to take painful decisions in the near future to diminish the US double deficit .

A plausible way to reduce adjustment costs is to lower the US government budget deficit through a cut in public spending instead of an increase in taxation, as discussed in the expected scenario for the US economy in the previous section. The results of such policy indeed show the relevance of this contention. The reason is, of course, that scenarios of spending cuts no longer have the negative supply-side effects which

Table 9.6 Effects of the combined national recovery scenarios 1993-7

	Germany			Netherlands		
Change in levels	1993	1995	1997	1993	1995	1997
Budget deficit **	0.0	-0.6	-2.1	-0.2	-1.2	-2.7
Government debt**	0.0	-0.8	-4.1	-0.2	-2.0	-6.7
Long-term interest rate	-0.2	0.6	-0.2	-0.2	0.6	-1.6
Production volume*	0.4	4.1	11.9	0.4	5.9	14.7
Utilisation rate*	0.3	3.3	48.5	0.3	4.7	9.1
Unemployment rate*	0.2	-2.5	-8.4	-0.1	-2.1	-6.3
Profit ratio	0.7	2.6	4.6	1.0	4.4	7.2
Investment ratio	0.0	0.8	3.0	0.1	1.2	5.5
Export volume*	0.2	2.6	9.0	-0.2	1.7	7.7
Exchange rate***	-0.1	-0.1	0.1	-0.1	-0.1	0.1
Consumer prices*	-1.0	-4.6	-6.8	-1.8	-5.5	-7.8
Current a/c (% NI)	0.0	-0.1	-0.7	0.1	-0.6	-0.6
	United States			United Kingdom		
Budget deficit**	-0.9	-3.1	-5.5	0.3	0.3	-0.6
Government debt**	-0.9	-6.0	-16.1	0.3	0.9	0.3
Long-term interest rate	-0.1	-0.4	1.1	-0.4	-1.6	2.5
Production volume*	-0.0	2.8	11.5	0.4	5.7	12.1
Utilisation rate*	0.1	1.8	6.3	0.3	3.8	7.4
Unemployment rate*	0.0	-2.9	-9.1	-0.3	-3.7	-9.5
Profit ratio	0.9	3.6	6.3	1.4	4.5	5.7
Investment ratio	0.2	1.6	4.4	0.0	1.1	2.4
Export volume*	1.7	4.4	6.0	0.5	5.7	14.1
Exchange rate***	-0.1	-0.1	0.1	-0.1	-0.1	0.1
Consumer prices*	-0.1	-2.1	-4.7	-1.3	-9.7	-14.9
Current a/c (% NI)	0.2	0.0	-0.4	0.1	0.0	0.3

* per cent
** per cent GDP

are apparent in the expected scenario for the US. For the US a far better economic performance is achieved if public spending cuts are increased in order to finance additional cuts in taxation. The negative consequences for the US economy then become substantially positive.

Coordinated policy action can be better than acting alone. A comparison between tables 9.5 and 9.6 shows that the direction of the isolated and simultaneous scenarios are the same, but that quantitative differences can be traced. For the combination of national scenarios the results are even more favourable. For the small open economy of the Netherlands these differences are bigger than for the relatively less open, larger countries. When we compare the favourable results of the national recovery scenarios we see that the effects on production volume are relatively large for the Netherlands and relatively small for the United States. The main reason for this is that the Dutch economy is more open than the American economy: Dutch exports and imports each amount to about 50 per cent of GDP, American exports and imports to about 10 per cent of GDP. As a consequence the Dutch economy loses national ability to act, as the American also does, although to a smaller extent. Both economies do have the ability to act at an international level (Knoester, Kolodziejak and Muujzers, 1992).

Summary and conclusions

In our opinion the Maastricht Treaty aiming at a complete European economic and monetary union in 1997 at the earliest and in 1999 at the latest, pays too little attention to the supply-side of European economies. In this chapter we have discussed this serious omission, and analysed policies for Germany, the Netherlands and the UK. Given the important links between European economies and the US economy, we have also discussed a plausible expected scenario for the United States. In addition, we have developed so-called recovery scenarios for those economies. Our main conclusions can be summarised as follows.

– For a stable and lasting EMU it is of the utmost importance that, in addition to the EMU convergence criteria of the 1991 Maastricht Treaty, extra criteria should be introduced to do justice to a proper treatment of the supply-side of the economy.
– Examples of such additional criteria are the introduction of a maximum for the collective burden, that is the share of taxes and social security contributions in national income — and the introduction of the classical rule for government budget deficits stating that deficits for current expenditure must be zero and that deficits are only allowed on the capital account, that is for government investment.

– A quantification of expected policy scenarios in the 1993-7 period shows that in Europe an upward pressure on wages in combination with an increase in the level of taxation forms a serious threat for the establishment of EMU. This destabilising development is strengthened by the possibility that the US government may decide to reduce its double deficit by an increase in taxation.

– The negative trends, as quantified in the expected scenarios, can be reversed into positive ones if Europe as well as the US pursue economic policies that will have more favourable effects on the supply-side of the economies.

– For each country such policies could be developed given the limitations of the specific starting conditions. However a central element in these policies should be to aim at a lower rate of taxation in order to promote wage moderation by trade unions, to improve economic growth and to decrease the unemployment rate.

– In an interdependent economic world national ability to act is reduced. Countries can, however, regain ability to act by coordination of recovery scenarios at an international level. This will reduce the costs of national economic adaptation processes.

Notes

1　See, for example, Committee for the Study of Economic and Monetary Union (1989), Knoester, Kolodziejak and Muijzers (1992).

2　See, for example, Knoester and Kolodziejak (1991).

3　For this purpose a conventional international linkage bloc was added to the national models (Bryant *et al.*, 1988, Kolodziejak, 1988).

10

Current account imbalances and the role of exchange rates

*Frank A.M. van Erp, Nico I.M. van Leeuwen
and Hans R. Timmer**

Introduction

In 1978 the Federal Reserve Board raised American interest rates to prevent a depreciation of the US dollar. One year later the US monetary authorities changed their policy target to reduction of the US inflation rate. The high level of US interest rates was therefore maintained. This resulted in a reduction of growth of domestic expenditure and a further appreciation of the US dollar *vis-à-vis* the currencies of the European Community. Although the interest differential did not increase continuously, the appreciation continued until 1985, probably as the result of speculative forces. The appreciation *vis-à-vis* the Japanese yen was less severe due to Japanese policy of stabilising the value of the yen in terms of the US dollar (see Feldman, 1986), so the yen appreciated *vis-à-vis* the EC currencies.

In the spring of 1985, encouraged by official statements (for example, the Plaza meeting), the US dollar depreciated in terms of both the D-Mark and the yen. As a result of volatile movements in exchange rates, the current accounts of the EC, the US and Japan showed diverging developments in the 1980s. Until the mid-1970s these regions had had an almost balanced account but after 1980 the EC and Japan showed large surpluses and the US showed a substantial deficit. Although recent figures of the US economy demonstrated a smaller deficit, the reduction of these imbalances is still on the political agenda.

Since 1979 a number of EC countries have been participating in the European Monetary System (EMS). Contrary to the United States the smaller countries of the EMS used fiscal policy to reduce their inflation rate and used their interest rates to stabilise their exchange rate *vis-à-vis* the D-Mark. In the light of the experiences with the EMS, we explore here the possible developments of the

*We would like to thank Henk Don, Geo Hana, Björn van Hamel, Wim Hulsman and Erwin Zijleman for their comments on a previous version of this chapter.

current accounts which would have occurred if the US inflation rate had been reduced by fiscal policy, and if interest rates had been used to stabilise the dollar exchange rate. Simulation results with the world model of the Dutch Central Planning Bureau over the period 1979-2002 will show that a large part of the current account imbalances would not have occurred if a more globally coordinated monetary and fiscal policy, aimed at stable exchange rates, had been implemented.[1] Although flexible exchange rates are mentioned as a potential feedback mechanism which guarantees balanced current accounts in the long run, simulation results demonstrate that the process is likely to be extensive.

In the next section we will describe the historical development of several parts of the current accounts of the three regions and summarise the main explanations mentioned in the literature for these developments. In the third section a survey of the potential feedback mechanisms will be given and this will be followed by a summary of the world model of the Dutch Central Planning Bureau. A conclusion follows our presentation of the simulation results.

Recent development of the current accounts[2]

Until the second oil crisis the current accounts of the three regions were stable and almost balanced. But during the 1980s an unprecedented surplus arose on the Japanese current account, whilst simultaneously an increasing deficit on the US current account made this country a net debtor.

These imbalances gave rise to a heated economic debate about Japanese economic and trade policies. The low level of imports of manufactured goods (as a percentage of GDP) has been frequently criticised. A most obvious explanation is the existence of tariff and non-tariff barriers to trade. However, several studies have already proven that neither import tariffs nor non-tariff barriers are higher in Japan than elsewhere. Other explanations assume home-biased preferences. Current account surpluses can be explained further by the effects of a combination of a small government deficit, by demographic structure and by a low average propensity to consume. In comparison with the EC, Japan has a relatively large section of the population between 15 and 64 years of age, and compared to the US a low average propensity to consume.[3] These features of the Japanese economy imply a high level of savings in comparison with the EC and the US. However we do not feel that this is sufficient to explain the imbalances of the previous decade. The imbalances cannot be understood without reference to oil prices and US macroeconomic policy. Here we will focus on the latter explanation.

Table 10.1 shows the average value of the components of the current account for the *United States* in four subperiods. The balances of non-factor services and current transfers did not change very much in these periods, but the deficit on the balance of goods worsened. This was mainly caused by a large fall in the balance of manufactured goods which exceeded the improvement of the energy account after the second oil crisis. This trade balance deficit led to the reduction of the surplus on factor services in the second half of the 1980s.

Table 10.1 Breakdown of the current account of the United States (per cent of GDP)

	1975-9	1980-2	1983-4	1985-87	1988-9
Goods: of which	-0.77	-0.98	-2.46	-3.32	-2.38
raw materials	0.72	0.94	0.52	0.16	0.43
energy	-1.88	-2.34	-1.49	-0.89	-0.77
manufactured goods	0.39	0.41	-1.48	-2.59	-2.04
Non-factor services	0.19	0.26	0.08	0.07	0.33
Factor services	1.10	1.26	0.97	0.42	0.19
Current transfers	-0.32	-0.30	-0.31	-0.36	-0.30
Current account (NA basis)	0.21	0.24	-1.72	-3.19	-2.17

Source: See note 2 at the end of the chapter.

The aggregated current account balance of the *European Community* can be broken down in a similar way. The surplus of the non-factor service account and the deficit on (current) transfers has not changed very much since 1975. Major changes took place in the balance of goods, which deteriorated after the second oil price shock in 1979, but recovered strongly after 1982.

In 1983 and 1984 the improvement in the current account was mainly caused by the energy account and the growing surplus on the account of manufactured products. After some delay and partly becaused of the developments in the trade balance in previous years, the balance of factor services worsened in this period. After the depreciation of the US dollar and the sharp fall in oil prices, the improvement of the energy account continued, but the EC lost part of its surplus on manufactured goods.

The causes of the change in the *Japanese* current account position are almost identical to those for the EC. The reduction of the import costs of raw materials and energy was mainly responsible for the emerging surplus on the balance of goods (see table 10.3). This decline, in terms of GDP, exceeded the reductions

Table 10.2 Breakdown of the European Community current account (per cent of GDP)

	1975-9	1980-2	1983-4	1985-87	1988-9
Goods: of which	-0.37	-0.94	0.01	0.76	0.25
raw materials	-1.73	-1.06	-1.03	-0.79	-0.77
energy	-2.49	-3.64	-3.22	-1.90	-1.06
manufactured goods	3.85	3.76	4.27	3.44	2.08
Non-factor services	0.71	0.59	0.84	0.92	0.58
Factor services	0.12	-0.10	-0.27	-0.30	-0.32
Current transfers	-0.48	-0.44	-0.41	-0.46	-0.51
Current account (NA basis)	-0.02	-0.89	0.17	0.92	0.00

Source: See table 10.1.

Table 10.3 Breakdown of the Japanese current account (per cent of GDP)

	1975-9	1980-2	1983-4	1985-87	1988-9
Goods: of which	1.46	1.02	2.95	4.19	2.98
raw materials	-3.11	-2.78	-2.43	-1.75	-1.82
energy	-3.84	-5.86	-4.68	-2.42	-1.32
manufactured goods	8.42	9.67	10.06	8.37	6.13
Non-factor services	-0.80	-0.80	-0.68	-0.66	-1.12
Factor services	-0.02	-0.07	0.14	0.44	0.68
Current transfers	-0.06	-0.10	-0.08	-0.08	-0.09
Current account (NA basis)	0.59	0.05	2.33	3.89	2.45

Source: See table 10.1.

in the EC and the US due to the higher Japanese dependency in this field. Until 1984 the surplus on the balance of manufactured products grew and compensated the deficit on other components of the trade balance. After the fall of the US dollar the surplus of manufactured goods diminished, but by less than the reduction of the deficit on the other accounts. Contrary to the EC and the US, Japan featured a constant deficit in non-factor services and current transfers. A large improvement has taken place in the balance of factor services, due to a period of current account surpluses. The surplus on the factor services account has been growing by almost 0.75 per cent of GDP since 1983.

Just looking at the trends in the value of the current accounts we may conclude that all three regions had an improvement in their energy account. The diverging development of the current accounts centres mainly on the balance of manufactured goods. Reduced US export performance and increased US imports coincide with the appreciation of the US dollar since 1980 and US fiscal policy in 1982/3. A few years later the surplus on factor services diminished due to the earlier trade deficits. The balance of manufactured goods and the current accounts have shown some convergence since the depreciation of the dollar in 1985, particularly in the last three years of the 1980s. However, major imbalances still exist.

Current account imbalances and traditional feedback mechanisms

International capital mobility has increased significantly during the 1980s and facilitated the financing of the American deficit. However, because international capital mobility was not perfect, the financing of the deficit was accomplished by means of monetary incentives. During the first half of the 1980s, the inflow of capital was encouraged by high interest rates in the United States, giving foreign portfolio investors a relatively high yield. In the second half of the decade the depreciation of the dollar gave rise to a further inflow as a result of revaluation of stocks.

The existence of a current account deficit only becomes a problem when other countries are no longer willing to finance it. Preventing a perpetual accumulation of foreign debt, accelerated by deficits on the factor services account, could be another reason to reduce deficits. Without adjustment, debt accumulation will lead to destabilising monetary tensions or a continuous impoverishment of the debtor country. Here we assume the necessity of a reduction in current account imbalances and, in that case, an increase in interest rate differentials and currency depreciation in the deficit country are traditional feedback mechanisms in an economy with flexible and fixed exchange rates. Because the factor service account results mainly from former current account balances, the elimination of current account imbalances requires a change in the trade balance. A lasting improvement of that balance requires a structural change in the propensity to consume or the propensity to invest or changes in the government account. The accounting identity underlying this statement can be written:

$$(X - M)/Y = (1 - C/Y) - I/Y + (T - G)/Y.$$

where X and M represent the value of exports and imports respectively, C and I are the values of consumption and investment, whilst T and G represent total government revenues and expenditure, and Y is the value of GDP. All are in current prices.

We first discuss the current situation of *flexible exchange rates*. A depreciation of the US dollar would improve American competitiveness and the value of US exports. On the other hand import prices expressed in dollars will increase and the volume of imports will therefore diminish. Assuming the J-curve effect, the value of imports may still increase and the current account may even deteriorate further in the short run. After this first effect we may assume that the Marshall-Lerner condition will hold and that the current account improves. In the short run, the price setting behaviour of enterprises determines the influence on consumer and export prices. If American firms accept a loss of their profit margins or foreign firms increase their margins, the impact on prices will be reduced, but still we may expect an improvement in the current account position.

The ultimate effect of the depreciation depends on the flexibility of wages and prices in the long run. If the wage-price system in the domestic economies is homogeneous of degree one,[4] the change in relative prices will disappear in the longer run. In that case a depreciation of the US dollar will lead to inflation in the US and deflation in other countries, leaving relative prices unchanged. The neutralisation of changes in the exchange rate may arise because costs are institutionally passed on to prices and prices are institutionally passed on to wages. The neutralisation can also arise as a result of tensions on the supply side of an economy. For instance, a depreciation of the dollar will lead to an increase in US output, a reduction of unemployment and an increase in capacity utilisation. The resulting tensions on the supply side may lead to wage and price increases offsetting the initial depreciation effect. In other words, exchange rate adjustments, that is, changes in relative prices, are likely to be neutralised in the long run if domestic prices and wages are flexible (see also Dornbush, 1980).

If wages and prices are not flexible, changes in the exchange rate could be effective. In that case a depreciation of the dollar would lead to an increase in output and a reduction in unemployment. However, it is uncertain whether the current account would improve. That depends on the influence of the exchange rate on the propensity to consume and to invest. A reduction of unemployment may increase government savings, but these may be offset by an increase in capital formation. Besides growth of output, the real interest rate is also a factor determining savings and investments. Although US nominal interest rates will rise due to a depreciation of the dollar, it is not certain whether the real interest rate will rise too.

We conclude, therefore, that the long-run effectiveness of the use of flexible exchange rates to reduce current account imbalances is doubtful and that therefore the recent movements of the US dollar were an unnecessary destabilisation of the current account in the short run. This conclusion implies that the loss of the exchange rate as a traditional shock absorber, by opting for a system of fixed or managed floating exchange rates, is a small loss.

In the case of *fixed nominal exchange rates* and given imperfect international capital mobility, the financing of the US current account deficit will require a larger interest rate differential between the US and the rest of the world. Because the interest rate differential is the only available instrument, the increase will be larger than in the case of flexible exchange rates.

Assuming that only the US interest rate is rising, US consumption and US capital formation will decline and hence national savings will increase. The reduction of domestic expenditure will diminish US imports, lower the capacity utilisation rate and raise unemployment. It depends on price setting behaviour whether the combined total effect on prices of the rise of capital costs and the utilisation effect is positive or negative, but probably prices will decline and the competitiveness of the US will increase and therefore exports will grow. If the decline in prices cannot prevent an increase in unemployment, the total effect on the current account will be partly mitigated by a larger government deficit caused by fewer receipts and more outlays.

We may conclude that in the case of fixed exchange rates adjustment of the domestic savings rate is more likely than in the case of flexible exchange rates. Nevertheless, if with fixed exchange rates a larger interest rate differential does not occur or is not effective enough, only one instrument is left to influence directly the saving rates and thereby the balance on current account – fiscal policy.

Outline of the world model of the Central Planning Bureau

Purpose of the world model: the highlights
In order to get a better understanding of foreign developments relevant tor the Dutch economy a quarterly world economic model has been constructed. This model, simply called World Model (WM), should provide a framework for making a consistent set of forecasts and simulations for the foreign determinants which are exogenous in the economic model of the domestic economy.

Empirical macroeconomic models, and especially large models dealing with the international economy, tend to become, after using them for several years, more and more like a black box. Continuous changes in separate parts of the model, because of empirical evidence, can alter the working of the complete system in an unintended and undesirable way. Consequently, simulations, which are one of the main purposes of such a model, may give counterintuitive results. Only models which are developed in a very tight theoretical framework can resist such an erosion. At this stage we think that WM has become too much of a black box, therefore at this moment a critical analysis and rebuilding of the model is taking place. Nevertheless, using an adapted version of the model, we will still be able to illustrate some of the relevant mechanisms mentioned in the previous section. We will, therefore, pay less attention to numerical values and instead stress the importance and direction of these mechanisms.

Aggregration in the world model

In WM three national economies are modelled (West Germany, United States, Japan) and three regions: Major European Community countries – MEC: Italy, France, United Kingdom; Small European Community countries – SEC: other EC countries; and the remaining OECD economies. For each of these the model contains a real and a monetary sector. In the real sector the supply side, demand side and prices are distinguished. The monetary sector of Germany and the United States is based on a portfolio model. The monetary sector of other regions is limited to interest- and exchange-rate equations. A block for the 'rest of the world' is used to close the external trade balances and no attempt was made to model the domestic economies within this region.

A closer view on the real side of WM

The real growth of *consumption* depends on the real growth of disposable income and the (first difference of the) real interest rate. An adjustment mechanism ensures a long-run income elasticity of unity and the level of the long-run average propensity to consume depends on the (long-run) growth of disposable income and the level of the real interest rate.

Three types of *capital formation* are distinguished in WM: inventories, residential investments, non-residential investments. The main determinants of non-residential capital formation are the accelerator mechanism, the capacity utilisation rate and profitability relative to the real interest rate. Investment in inventories is related to demand, and investment in dwellings is explained by disposable income, interest rates and the unemployment ratio. The *capital stock* is determined by net capital formation in equipment. Scrapping of fixed capital is a function of technology and profits. Capacity is determined in an aggregated vintage model. *Labour demand* follows from this and actual output. *Labour supply* is determined by the population and partly endogenous to the discouraged worker effect. *Wages* are influenced by price indexation and changes in labour productivity. In all economies the growth of wages reflects entirely the changes in labour productivity. The model has a downward sloping non-linear long-run Phillips curve. The *price of consumption* is one of the key prices in the model. The change of this price is specified as a linear homogeneous function of the change in unit labour costs, the change in the average import price and the change in capacity utilisation. The institutional elements in the wage-price system denote that an increase in the import prices will result in a 30 per cent increase in export prices and labour productivity is neutral. Near homogeneity of degree one and the strong Phillips effect combined with the historically determined investment ratio guarantee long-run homogeneity in the wage-price system.

In the submodels of West Germany and the United States the *government sector* is disaggregated. Different taxes and expenditure including unemployment benefits are distinguished. In the other parts of the model a more aggregated description is chosen. In all cases the specification of taxes ensures a constant tax ratio in the long run. The growth of government outlays is related to the growth (volume and price) of GNP. These specifications denote a constant government surplus (percentages of GNP).

Imports of raw materials (SITC 0,1,2,), energy (SITC 3), manufacturing (SITC 5-9) and non-factor services are modelled separately. For all categories total sales and the price differential between the domestic price (GNP price) and the relevant import price are explanatory variables. Because bilateral trade of raw materials and industrial products is explicitly modelled, the relevant import prices are a weighted average of the export prices of foreign supplier countries. The *export volume of raw materials and manufactured goods* follows from the total imports of these regions and relevant market shares. Changes in relative export prices alter the market shares. Besides the explanatory variables of the consumer price, *export prices* of raw materials and manufacturing are also determined by competitor prices. The export price of manufactured goods is the second key price in the model of an economy.

Energy exports from the OECD-region are given by an extrapolation of the past and energy exports from the rest of the world are determined as the difference between total imports and exports of the OECD-region (quantity adjustment). Just one global energy price is assumed. The growth of the volume of *exports of non-factor services* is equal to the growth of the exports of goods. The *export price of non-factor services* is a weighted average of the consumer price and a competitor price. These weights are fixed. The balance of *factor services* is defined by the interest rate, previous current account balances and the exchange rate.

A closer view of the monetary side of WM
In the complete version of WM the US and German *interest rates* and the D-Mark/dollar *exchange rate* are endogenously determined by supply and demand. Demand and supply of various assets are derived from a portfolio model and the

monetary policies of the US and Germany are explicitly modelled. Exchange rates *of other economies vis-à-vis* the US dollar are based on the D-Mark/dollar rate and modified by differences in current account position and inflation relative to Germany. A similar approach is used for the determination of the short-term and long-term interest rates in other regions.

In some of the simulations in this chapter we have used a smaller version of the monetary block of WM. In the next section the main features of these monetary blocks will be discussed in relation to the simulations.

Simulations

In this section the results of five simulations are presented. All simulations start in the first quarter of 1978 and end in the fourth quarter of 2002. After a survey of the baseline, the impact of the flexible exchange-rate system on the current account imbalances is shown. The third simulation describes the transition from flexible towards nominal fixed exchange rates. During a transition period of fifteen years, starting in the first quarter of 1980, the nominal and real exchange rates converge towards constant rates. As a byproduct of stable exchange rates a change in the structural inflation rates is assumed after 1990.

Although a fixed exchange-rate regime will result in a stable economic development the ultimate effect on the current account positions is limited. Therefore we add in our fourth simulation a more restrictive US fiscal policy. The results of this simulation show a substantial reduction in the US current account deficit. Just to stress the advantages of international policy coordination we also present in a fifth simulation the results of a globally coordinated policy consisting of the transition from real fixed to nominal fixed exchange rates, expansive fiscal policy in Germany and Japan and a restrictive fiscal policy in the US in 1980.

The baseline
Up to the end of 1989 the results of the baseline are identical to the historical data. For the period 1990, up to and including 2002, the baseline is based on the technical assumption that real interest rates and real exchange rates are fixed.[5] Therefore changes in nominal interest rates are only an adjustment for inflation and alterations of nominal exchange rates reflect differences in inflation between countries.

$$\dot{e}_i = a_t (\dot{p}_i - \dot{p}_u)$$

$$r_i = \begin{bmatrix} r_{i-1} + \Delta \dot{p}_i \text{ for Germany} \\ \alpha_t (r_{i-1} + \Delta \dot{p}_i) + (1 - \alpha_t)(r_g - \dot{e}_g) \text{ for the United States} \\ \alpha_t (r_{i-1} + \Delta \dot{p}_i) + (1 - \alpha_t)(r_g - \dot{e}_g + \dot{e}_i) \text{ for other regions} \end{bmatrix} \quad (10.1)$$

in which $\dot{p}_i$ is inflation in country i, r_i is the nominal interest rate in country i, e_i the exchange rate of the US dollar (local currency country i /\$), subscript g indicates West Germany, subscript U the United States and in the baseline α_t is 1.

After 1994 the baseline may be characterised as a stable economic development. The growth rates of exports, imports and GNP (all volumes) become almost constant towards the end of the simulation period. Looking at the current account the EC and Japan have a constant surplus (as a per cent of GNP) while the deficit of the US is constant as a ratio of GNP. The government balances of all economies stabilise as a ratio of GNP. The US dollar shows a continuous nominal depreciation.

Flexible exchange rates
In this simulation we used the interest- and exchange-rate equations of the original monetary block for the Major European Community region, Smaller European Community region, Japan and the Remaining OECD block. These equations imply that the exchange rates and nominal interest rates may change in response to inflation rate differentials and current account imbalances. The numerical specification indicates that real interest rates will decline in response to inflation. The monetary blocks for Germany and the United States are replaced by simple reduced form interest- and exchange-rate equations. The US real short-term and long-term interest rates remain fixed in this monetary block. The specification of the German short-term interest rate depends on the US nominal short-term interest rate and German inflation. The change in the German long-term interest rate is equal to the change in short-term interest rates. A simple reduced form consisting of the interest rate differentials, differences in the inflation rate and differences in current account balance between the US and Germany, determines the D-Mark/US dollar exchange rate. The actual development in the 1980s is reproduced by this version of the model.

Table 10.4 contains the results in deviation of the baseline after 1989. Volumes are expressed as cumulative differences (differences in levels) while figures of prices (including exchange and interest rates) are absolute differences between price changes in the simulation and in the baseline. These figures, therefore, show the difference in inflation rates. Ratios are also expressed as absolute differences.

Table 10.4 Flexible exchange rates

Description		1990	1992	1994	1997	1999
		Deviations from baseline (%)				
Balance on current account (% GNP)	D					
European Community		0.3	-0.0	-0.1	-0.2	-0.6
United States		-0.3	0.1	0.2	0.3	0.5
Japan		0.1	-0.3	-0.6	-0.8	-0.8
Government surplus (% GNP)	D					
European Community		-0.1	-1.8	-2.0	-2.8	-3.8
United States		0.0	0.3	0.4	0.5	0.7
Japan		0.1	0.2	0.4	0.6	0.9
Domestic expenditure (volume)	%					
European Community		-1.4	-3.1	-2.8	-3.3	-3.4
United States		0.1	0.4	0.3	0.4	0.6
Japan		-0.1	-1.2	-2.2	-4.0	-6.8
Gross national product (volume)	%					
European Community		-1.3	-3.3	-3.1	-3.9	-4.9
United States		0.2	0.7	0.8	0.9	1.3
Japan		-0.3	-2.0	-3.5	-5.7	-8.7
Exports of goods and services (volume)	%					
European Community		-1.4	-4.3	-3.9	-5.0	-6.4
United States		0.2	1.9	3.0	3.2	5.0
Japan		-1.3	-5.5	-9.3	-13.1	-16.8
Imports of goods and services (volume)	%					
European Community		-1.6	-3.9	-3.3	-3.7	-3.4
United States		-0.4	-1.9	-1.8	-1.6	-0.7
Japan		0.0	-0.2	0.4	-0.3	-2.1

Notes: Simulation minus baseline; per cent = cumulative relative differe ce (in percentages); D = absolute difference (in percentages).

Table 10.4 continued

Description		1990	1992	1994	1997	1999
		Deviations from baseline (%)				
Domestic expenditure (price)	D					
European Community		-0.5	-0.3	-0.7	-0.5	-0.6
United States		0.2	0.1	0.3	0.2	0.2
Japan		-0.5	-0.6	-1.5	-2.0	-2.6
Exports of goods and services (price)	D					
European Community		-1.0	-0.3	-1.1	-1.0	-1.2
United States		0.3	-0.2	0.4	0.2	0.2
Japan		-1.6	-1.2	-2.7	-2.8	-3.2
Imports of goods and services (price)	D					
European Community		-1.9	-0.4	-1.3	-1.4	-1.5
United States		3.6	-0.7	0.4	0.1	-0.3
Japan		-5.1	-2.9	-4.0	-4.1	-3.8
Exchange rates	D					
D-mark/US dollar		-5.7	0.7	-1.7	-1.7	-1.6
Yen/US dollar		-7.1	-2.1	-4.3	-4.2	-3.8
Long-term interest rates (%)	D					
European Community		2.9	3.5	4.1	4.5	4.9
United States		-0.5	-0.1	0.0	-0.1	-0.0
Japan		2.5	1.8	2.6	2.9	3.2
Unemployment rate (% labour force)	D					
European Community		0.1	1.0	1.0	1.4	1.8
United States		-0.0	-0.3	-0.5	-0.5	-0.7
Japan		0.0	0.1	0.3	0.5	0.9
Wage rates	D					
European Community		-0.1	-1.6	0.0	-0.6	-0.5
United States		0.0	0.4	0.2	0.2	0.3
Japan		0.0	-1.0	-1.5	-2.3	-2.8

Relative to the baseline, the US current account causes a depreciation of the US dollar in 1990. Import prices outside the US, expressed in local currencies, fall and induce a process of deflation in these economies. In the first year the current accounts show the J-curve effect in all the economies.

After a few years the US starts to benefit from its improved competitiveness. However, nominal wages grow less rapidly in the EC and Japan. In addition to lower import prices and partly automatic price compensation this reduction follows from a worsening export performance, which leads to a fall in the capacity utilisation rate and a rise in unemployment. The flexibility in wages and prices results in a decline of European and Japanese export prices expressed in local currencies which thereby offsets part of the loss of competitiveness. In the US an opposite adjustment process occurs. Apart from the impact on prices, the worsened export performance to the EC and Japan also leads to a reduction of domestic expenditure and therefore to a reduction in the volume of imports. Except for the cutback in income, the increase in European and Japanese real interest rates are part of the explanation for the fall in domestic expenditure. Improved US competitiveness is then partly mitigated by a fall in export prices and the import volume of the EC and Japan.

After a few years the economies have reached a new stable path and the US current account balance has improved, but this requires a continuous depreciation of the US dollar. This implies that a once and for all depreciation of the dollar will not guarantee balanced accounts in the long run. This result agrees with our economic theory and seems also confirmed by dollar shock simulations of world models involved in the Brookings and SPES project (Bryant *et al.*, 1988, vol. 2, table F and Whitley, 1992, table A7).[6]

Towards fixed nominal exchange rates

In this simulation we assume a different exchange-rate policy. The new policy is introduced in the first quarter of 1980 and describes the transition process from fixed real exchange and real interest rates to nominal fixed exchange rates and a common global nominal interest rate determined by the monetary policy of Germany. In accordance with the EMS experiences we assume this process will take fifteen years. Therefore the parameter α_t, mentioned in equation (10.1) above, is:

$$\alpha_t = \begin{bmatrix} 1 & \text{1978.1 until and including 1980.1} \\ \alpha_{t-1} - \dfrac{1}{60} & \text{1980.2 until and including 1994.4} \\ 0 & \text{1995.1 until and including 2002.4} \end{bmatrix}$$

Starting in the first quarter of 1990 the Phillips curves are adjusted to obtain changes in structural inflation rates due to the new exchange-rate policy.

In deviation from the baseline, this simulation means a depreciation of the US dollar in the first half of the last decade and an appreciation in the second half. In the period 1981 up to and including 1985 the relative depreciation improves US export performance and therefore domestic activity increases, employment increases, domestic expenditure rises and the government deficit declines. Although strong first year effects, current account imbalances would still have existed in 1985, due mainly to the increased import value. Apart from the rise in import prices, the negative price effect is compensated by a positive income effect due to an increase in total expenditure (domestic as well as exports). Hence we may conclude that flexible exchange rates are not the main cause of the current account deficit. The main cause lies somewhere else.

In the second half of the last decade the opposite development appears. The dollar appreciation relative to the baseline causes a worsening of the export performance and therefore a reduction in GNP growth and employment, but once again current account imbalances would have existed at the end of the 1980s. In the second half of the last decade the fall in US import prices limits the effect on the US current account.

According to our world model, the strong appreciation and subsequent depreciation of the US dollar had hardly any effect on the existence of the current account imbalances in 1985 and 1989. In both periods the change in the value of US exports was more or less compensated by a change in the value of US imports. However, this does not mean that the US economy is insensitive to movements of the dollar exchange rate. It is, therefore, quite plausible that the increase in unemployment in the beginning of the 1980s as a consequence of increased interest rates and the appreciation of the dollar, and the priorities of the Reagan administration (tax reduction, national defence) led to an expansionary fiscal policy (see Boskin, 1987). Because an increase in the government deficit without compensating domestic savings almost by definition means a deterioration in the current account, this could have been the driving force of the imbalances we have seen in the 1980s. In the next simulation we will further investigate the plausibility of this presumption.

In the long run nominal fixed exchange rates and a common global nominal interest rate result in a stable growth path. All regions have an annual real growth of GNP of about 2 per cent, the volume growth of exports is about 6 per cent and import growth is higher only in Japan. Apart from Japan the level of the inflation rate is almost zero. However, the nominal fixed exchange-rate system does not lead to balanced current accounts in the long run, so another policy instrument is necessary.

Table 10.5 Towards nominal fixed exchange rates

Description		1980	1985	1989	1990/4	1995/9
		Deviations from baseline (%)				
Balance on current account (% GNP)	D					
European Community		0.4	-1.0	0.6	1.0	1.3
United States		-0.8	0.6	-0.6	-0.7	-0.3
Japan		0.3	-0.8	2.1	1.4	-0.2
Government surplus (% GNP)	D					
European Community		0.0	2.0	2.8	2.7	2.4
United States		-0.2	4.1	1.0	0.7	0.5
Japan		0.4	0.8	0.7	0.9	1.0
Domestic expenditure (volume)	%					
European Community		0.8	1.1	3.1	1.1	0.1
United States		0.1	6.1	-0.5	-1.4	-2.4
Japan		1.0	2.0	2.2	3.6	4.4
Gross national product (volume)	%					
European Community		1.4	-1.3	2.9	1.6	0.9
United States		-0.6	9.0	-1.8	-2.5	-2.8
Japan		-0.2	0.4	3.9	4.6	3.2
Exports of goods and services (volume)	%					
European Community		2.8	-6.1	5.3	6.4	5.6
United States		-4.1	35.8	-7.7	-6.6	-3.4
Japan		-5.9	4.2	26.6	22.3	11.0
Imports of goods and services (volume)	%					
European Community		0.9	3.2	6.8	6.0	4.8
United States		1.2	-1.7	9.0	6.3	0.2
Japan		2.4	12.6	1.9	7.8	13.9

Notes: Simulation minus baseline; per cent = cumulative relative difference (in percentages); D = absolute difference (in percentages).

Table 10.5 continued

Description		1980	1985	1989	1990/4	1995/9
		Deviations from baseline (%)				
Domestic expenditure (price)	D					
European Community		1.2	-1.9	-0.9	0.3	0.4
United States		-0.5	2.7	0.0	-1.5	-2.6
Japan		-3.2	-0.1	0.9	1.8	2.4
Exports of goods and services (price)	D					
European Community		2.5	-2.0	-3.0	0.2	0.5
United States		-0.9	3.2	1.0	-1.3	-2.5
Japan		-12.0	-1.5	-1.2	0.4	-1.2
Imports of goods and services (price)	D					
European Community		2.8	-0.4	-3.4	0.3	0.6
United States		-2.0	4.2	3.2	-0.7	-1.8
Japan		-15.4	2.9	-6.9	-0.2	-0.1
Exchange rates	D					
D-mark/US dollar		4.3	-5.6	-6.9	1.3	2.8
Yen/US dollar		-10.4	-2.8	-8.2	0.6	2.1
Long-term interest rates (%)	D					
European Community		1.4	-4.8	-2.5	0.1	1.1
United States		-1.6	-2.8	-1.9	-2.1	-2.8
Japan		-3.6	-2.4	1.7	2.9	2.9
Unemployment rate (% labour force)	D					
European Community		-0.2	-0.1	-0.7	-0.7	-0.3
United States		0.3	-4.2	0.2	1.0	1.3
Japan		0.0	-0.1	-0.3	-0.5	-0.5
Wage rates	D					
European Community		1.1	-2.4	1.3	0.3	0.4
United States		-0.6	2.6	-1.1	-1.8	-2.8
Japan		0.5	0.3	1.9	2.5	2.7

Table 10.6 Towards nominal fixed exchange rates including US fiscal policy

Description		1980	1985	1989	1990/4	1995/9
		Deviations from previous simulation (%)				
Balance on current account (% GNP)	D					
European Commun ty		-0.1	-0.3	-0.5	-0.7	-1.2
United States		0.3	0.5	0.7	0.9	1.2
Japan		-0.1	-0.3	-0.4	-0.4	0.2
Government surplus (% GNP)	D					
European Community		0.0	-0.3	-0.5	-0.8	-1.3
United States		0.6	0.4	0.2	0.3	0.7
Japan		0.0	-0.1	-0.1	-0.1	-0.1
Domestic expenditu e (volume)	%					
European Community		-0.0	-0.2	-0.3	-0.5	-0.6
United States		-2.2	-4.0	-4.3	-4.1	-3.4
Japan		-0.0	-0.7	-1.5	-2.3	-3.5
Gross national product (volume)	%					
European Commun ty		-0.1	-0.6	-0.9	-1.4	-2.1
United States		-1.9	-3.4	-3.3	-2.7	-1.8
Japan		-0.2	-1.3	-2.1	-3.0	-3.4
Exports of goods and services (volume)	%					
European Community		-0.5	-1.8	-2.6	-4.0	-5.6
United States		-0.3	-2.1	-1.7	-1.3	-1.1
Japan		-1.4	-4.5	-5.8	-6.8	-5.6
Imports of goods and services (volume)	%					
European Community		-0.2	-0.5	-0.7	-1.3	-1.9
United States		-3.3	-6.6	-8.1	-8.6	-7.9
Japan		-0.2	-1.6	-2.8	-4.4	-7.3

Notes: Simulation minus baseline; per cent = cumulative relative difference (in percentages); D = absolute difference (in per cent).

Table 10.6 continued

Description		1980	1985	1989	1990/4	1995/9
		Deviations from previous simulation (%)				
Domestic expenditure (price)	D					
European Community		-0.0	-0.2	-0.2	-0.3	-0.4
United States		0.1	-0.6	-1.2	-1.0	-0.6
Japan		-0.0	-0.3	-0.6	-0.9	-1.4
Exports of goods and services (price)	D					
European Community		-0.1	-0.3	-0.3	-0.4	-0.5
United States		0.0	-0.6	-1.3	-0.9	-0.6
Japan		-0.0	-0.3	-0.6	-0.8	-1.0
Imports of goods and services (price)	D					
European Community		-0.2	-0.4	-0.3	-0.4	-0.5
United States		-0.2	-0.6	-0.7	-0.7	-0.7
Japan		-0.4	-0.5	-0.6	-0.7	-0.6
Exchange rates	D					
D-mark/US dollar		-0.1	0.3	0.4	0.2	0.0
Yen/US dollar		-0.1	0.2	0.3	0.1	0.0
Long-term interest rates (%)	D					
European Community		-0.0	-0.2	-0.2	-0.3	-0.4
United States		0.2	-0.5	-0.3	-0.4	-0.4
Japan		0.0	-0.2	-0.3	-0.4	-0.4
Unemployment rate (% labour force)	D					
European Community		0.0	0.2	0.3	0.5	0.8
United States		0.3	2.0	2.2	1.9	1.5
Japan		0.0	0.1	0.2	0.3	0.4
Wage rates	D					
European Community		0.0	0.0	-0.1	-0.3	-0.4
United States		-0.1	-1.0	-1.2	-0.9	-0.5
Japan		0.0	-0.3	-0.7	-1.2	-1.6

Table 10.7 Towards nominal fixed exchange rates and globally coordinated fiscal policy

Description		1980	1985	1989	1990/4	1995/9
		Deviations from baseline (%)				
Balance on current account (% GNP)	D					
European Community		0.3	-1.2	0.3	0.6	0.9
United States		-0.4	1.3	0.4	0.8	2.0
Japan		0.0	-2.0	0.4	-1.0	-3.4
Government surplus (% GNP)	D					
European Community		-0.2	1.6	2.4	2.1	1.7
United States		0.4	4.6	1.4	1.6	2.4
Japan		-0.8	-1.0	-1.5	-1.4	-1.7
Domestic expenditure (volume)	%					
European Community		1.2	1.8	3.8	1.8	1.1
United States		-2.0	2.0	-4.7	-5.1	-4.9
Japan		2.5	6.6	8.2	10.4	12.4
Gross national product (volume)	%					
European Community		1.7	-0.9	3.2	1.6	1.3
United States		-2.4	5.6	-4.5	-4.2	-1.9
Japan		0.9	3.5	7.8	8.1	6.1
Exports of goods and services (volume)	%					
European Community		2.8	-6.7	4.5	5.0	5.1
United States		-3.9	36.1	-5.8	-2.3	7.3
Japan		-6.9	1.8	21.7	14.9	1.9
Imports of goods and services (volume)	%					
European Community		1.3	3.7	7.3	6.2	5.6
United States		-2.1	-8.0	0.5	-2.5	-7.1
Japan		4.1	18.6	9.9	19.2	34.5

Notes: Simulation minus baseline; per cent = cumulative relative difference (in percentages); D = absolute difference (in per cent).

Table 10.7 continued

Description		1980	1985	1989	1990/4	1995/9
		Deviations from baseline (%)				
Domestic expenditure (price)	D					
European Community		1.2	-1.9	-1.0	0.2	0.5
United States		-0.4	2.2	-1.0	-2.2	-2.7
Japan		-3.3	0.5	1.9	3.0	3.9
Exports of goods and services (price)	D					
European Community		2.5	-2.0	-3.0	0.1	0.6
United States		-0.7	2.6	-0.0	-2.0	-2.7
Japan		-12.0	-1.0	-0.6	1.0	2.0
Imports of goods and services (price)	D					
European Community		2.7	-0.5	-3.5	0.2	0.7
United States		-2.1	3.8	2.7	-0.9	-1.6
Japan		-15.6	3.1	-6.7	-0.2	-0.0
Exchange rates	D					
D-mark/US dollar		4.3	-5.3	-6.4	1.5	2.8
Yen/US dollar		-10.5	-2.0	-7.3	1.1	2.1
Long-term interest rates (%)	D					
European Community		1.4	-4.7	-2.5	0.1	1.3
United States		-1.4	-3.1	-2.2	-2.2	-2.6
Japan		-3.7	-1.8	2.3	3.2	3.0
Unemployment rate (% labour force)	D					
European Community		-0.2	-0.2	-0.8	-0.7	-0.4
United States		0.6	-2.4	2.1	2.5	1.6
Japan		-0.0	-0.3	-0.7	-0.8	-0.8
Wage rates	D					
European Community		1.1	-2.3	1.3	0.2	0.5
United States		-0.7	1.8	-2.2	-2.5	-2.9
Japan		0.6	1.1	3.2	3.9	4.4

Towards fixed iominal exchange rates including additional US fiscal policy
In addition to the previous simulations a 2 per cent GNP reduction in US government outlay is assumed in 1980. The shock is distributed equally over the four quarters and the size is smaller than the opposite fiscal impulse of the Reagan administration in 1982/3. In table 10.6 the results of this simulation are presented as deviation from the previous simulation. Because the model is almost linear, the sum of the deviations presented in tables 10.5 and 10.6 gives an indication (˙ the total effect.

In the *short un* the change in US fiscal policy mainly affects the domestic economy. All elements of domestic expenditure and imports decline. As the interest rate hardly changes the reduction of consumption is caused by a cutback in disposable income and the drop in sales is mainly the current account and the export performance of the EC and especially Japan. The reduction in domestic expenditure without compensating exports lessens US employment and capacity utilisation. The dampening effect of the capacity utilisation rate on inflation is fully comper iated by an increase in unit labour costs due to a decline in labour productivity w ich is not yet translated into lower wages. The rise in domestic prices causes ¿ small increase in US interest rates and a small depreciation of the US dollar.

In the *medium term*, five to ten years, the negative effect on the US reaches its maximum. In contrast to the initial effect, lower unit labour costs cause a fall in US prices and therefore the US interest rate declines and an appreciation of the dollar takes place. The changes in the latter two variables are smaller than the changes in prices, due to the far advanced stage of the transition process to fixed nominal xchange rates and therefore the global common interest rate. The reduction (f the US current account deficit continues and after ten years the deficit is almos. ¾ per cent of GNP below the level in the previous simulation.

In the *long run*, fifteen to twenty years after the policy change,the world economy reaches a new stable path. The ultimate effect on US gross national product, consumption and capital formation is limited. US imports are reduced and the US current account improved by more than 1 per cent of GNP. The fall in US inflation during the transition period causes a nominal dollar appreciation and somewhat 'ower US interest rates. In contrast to the EC, Japan adjusts its imports in resp nse to reduced exports to the US and therefore keeps its surplus on the current account, while the external balance of the EC deteriorates. However the EC maintains a surplus in comparison with the baseline.

Towards fixed nominal exchange rates including global fiscal policy
With regard to exchange-rate policy and US fiscal policy this simulation is identical to the previous one. The main difference is the addition of a 2 per cent (of GNP) expansionary fiscal policy in Germany and Japan in 1980.[7] Because the mechanism which determine the ultimate impact on the world economy are

identical to those in the previous simulation, although the effect is mitigated, we will only describe the outcomes. These results are presented in table 10.7and expressed in deviation of the baseline (table 10.4).

In the *short run* the impact on the US economy is equal to the previous simulation. Major but opposite changes take place in the EC and Japan. The growth of government expenditure increases consumption, capital formation and imports in these economies.

In the *medium term* the globally coordinated policy alternative has a smaller negative impact on the world economy than the unilateral restrictive US policy. In spite of a reduction of exports, Japan enlarges its imports and hence reduces its current account surplus. The reduction of US government outlays and the increase of government outlays in the EC and Japan improves the US current account more than in the previous simulation. Because of the expansive fiscal policy measures in the EC and Japan unemployment hardly changes in the EC, decreases in Japan, while the rise in US unemployment is smaller than in the case of unilateral reduction in government outlays. The relative strength of the US economy is improved and it is reflected in a higher value of the US dollar than in the previous simulation.

In the *long run* all three regions will benefit relative to the baseline. The initial fall in the US economy is almost completely compensated for by more growth in the EC and Japan. Although the annual growth of US real consumption and real capital formation is almost the same as in the baseline, the level of these aggregates is lower, reflecting increased private savings. Also government savings rise due to the initial reduction in outlays and increase in taxes caused by little additional economic growth.

Notes

1 Technically we implement such coordinated policy by assuming an EMS-like policy in the US, given an independent monetary policy in Germany which stabilises German inflation and given one world capital market.
2 To collect a complete set of international trade data concerning the bilateral export and import of several types of goods (SITC-categories, volume and value), non-factor services, factor services and so on, various statistics (custom, national accounts, balance of payments) have to be used. Unfortunately in most cases these statistics are mutually inconsistent, sometimes even internally. For example exports of goods on a custom basis do not correspond to exports of goods on the balance of payments and a discrepancy exists between world exports and world imports for each category of goods. In our view the discrepancies among several sources can frustrate the simulation analysis. We have therefore developed a procedure to adjust basic statistics to obtain a mutually consistent set of

data, leaving National Accounts data unchanged. The figures ₁ resented in the tables in this section are derived from this adapted dataset, but a more or less similar picture can be obtained from figures derived from customs and balance of payments statistics.

3 OECD, Historical Statistics, table 2.1 and table 6.1

4 A condition imposed in most empirical macroeconomic models.

5 This assumption and the disregard of the developments in 1990 and 1991 give the base not only a technical character, but it also does no correspond with the official forecasts of the CPB.

6 Probably not all adjustments have taken place after six years (see Whitley, 1992). This is probably also the case in the Brookings project in which the dollar shock was smoothly implemented in a three-year period and the simulation period was also six years.

7 The sum of these changes in government outlays of these three areas is negative.

11

German Reunification
and European Monetary Policy

Jean-Pierre Chauffour, Hélène Harasty and Jean Le Dem*

Introduction

German reunification took place during the debate over the progress towards European Economic and Monetary Union (EMU). This timely coincidence served to highlight the constraints linked to the workings of the European Monetary System (EMS). As an asymmetrical shock in Europe, reunification caused an overheating of the West German economy accompanied by inflationary pressures. Just when its European partners were faced with a major slowdown in growth, Germany adopted a restrictive monetary policy that spread immediately to other EMS countries, which found it extremely costly and cyclically ill-timed. The management of such asymmetrical shocks in the EMS framework appeared to be more unsatisfactory than ever, emphasising the need for a switch to a different system. EMU is the alternative adopted by the European Community (EC) in Maastricht. EC countries wanted to abandon a fixed exchange-rate system in which monetary decisions are taken by one dominant country.

German reunification provides a case study in the management of an asymmetrical macroeconomic shock in Europe under different exchange-rate systems. The MIMOSA model allows us to simulate its short and medium-term effects in Europe. This chapter comprises two sections. First, we describe the impact of reunification and the prospects based on the model, under the present exchange-rate system (EMS). We begin by outlining the scenario adopted for the East German economy in the medium term. We then simulate the effects of its integration with western Germany under the present EMS mechanism. A retrospective simulation of 1990-91 and a forward simulation to 2000 enable us to determine the impact of the different elements of

*The authors wish to thank Jonathan Mandelbaum for translating this chapter into English.

reunification on Germany, on other European countries, and on the rest of the world: first, the initial shock of higher demand (migration flow, opening of the East German market, and massive public transfer payments). We then analyse the effects of the adoption of a fiscal financing policy in Europe (higher interest rates and concomitant appreciation of European currencies). We can then answer the fundamental question: on balance, has German unity stimulated or hindered growth among Germany's European partners? Did the depressive effects of higher interest rates and the D-Mark's climb wipe out or even reverse the positive effects of the demand stimulus?

But whatever the bias of the ultimate effect of German reunification on European growth, the fact remains that the rise in European interest rates was particularly unwelcome in the current sharp cyclical downturn. The responsibility for steeper rates lies indisputably with the EMS. The system induces a full repercussion of German monetary policy—in this case, its tightening due to reunification—on other member countries. This leads to another question: would such a macroeconomic shock have been better managed under another exchange-rate system —either flexible exchange rates in which the D-Mark alone would have been revalued; or, on the contrary, a single-currency system (an already operating EMU) in which Europe would have framed a common monetary policy?

The short-term impact of German reunification

Prologue: A scenario for medium-term trends in the East German economy
To simulate the macroeconomic effects of German reunification in the short and medium term, we need to define a scenario of the economic development of the East German economy to the year 2000. Using a small model of the East German economy whose principles we have described elsewhere (Harasty and Le Dem, 1990), we evaluated a median scenario based on the most likely trends in the key variables of East German economic development: the speed of convergence of East German wages towards West German wages, the scrapping rate for old capital, and the rate of accumulation of new capital.

In the scenario which is reported in table 11.1, private investment (including housing), which represented 25 per cent of GDP in 1991, grows to 35 per cent of GDP by 1996, then gradually decreases to 29 per cent in 2000. By then, 20.8 per cent of German private investment takes place in the eastern Länder, still a distinctly higher percentage than the proportion of jobs there (16.2 per cent) because the convergence towards the West German model would still be far from complete. Admittedly, the capital stock per head would have reached 87 per cent of the western level, but only half of the installed capital would consist of investment meeting western standards. On these assumptions, labour productivity would reach 71 per cent of the West German level. Productive capacity growth would grow at 6.5 per cent a year over the decade, but there would not be enough new jobs to ensure the convergence of the eastern and western labour markets. The unemployment rate would exceed 25 per cent until 1995 and fall rapidly thereafter, but in 2000 it would still be at 14 per cent despite a net migration of 1.8 million East Germans to the western part during the decade and a downward alignment of participation rates — in particular that of women — towards those of western Germany.

Table 11.1 Long-term scenarios for East Germany

	1991	1995	2000
Real wages (a)	52	81	91
Investment rate (b)	24	34	29
Cumulated depreciation rate (c)	33	60	69
Potential labour productivity (a)	35	56	71
Unemployment rate (d)	27	26	14
West public transfers (e)	6.0	4.6	3.6
East to West migratory balance (f)	330	140	65
Contribution to the global current account (g)	5.0	5.7	4.9
Contribution of the German trade (h)	4.6	4.9	5.1

Source: MIMOSA CEPII-OFCE.
(a) As a percentage of the West level.
(b) Per cent of West German GDP.
(c) Per cent of the 1990 production capacity.
(d) Unemployed persons plus part-time unemployment and collective utility jobs, in per cent of the potential workforce.
(e) Primary deficit of social security regime, of Länders and of West German communes, in per cent of West German GDP.
(f) Thousands.
(g) East German net imports, including those from West Germany, in per cent of West German GDP, 1990 prices.
(h) East German net imports of West German origin only, in per cent of West German GDP, 1990 prices.

Real short-term effects: direct effects and fiscal policy
Despite the seeming inevitability of a slowdown after two years' robust growth, West Germany saw a sharp acceleration of its GDP growth in 1990 to its highest rate since 1976. Conversely, Germany's European partners have been caught in a sharp cyclical downturn since 1990. Yet the standard transmission mechanisms via external trade did function, since West German imports surged.

It is possible that the hard-line monetary policy adopted in Frankfurt, the impact of reunification in the financial sphere – namely, higher interest rates and the appreciation of European currencies against the dollar – completely offset or even reversed the direct expansionary effect of reunification on Germany's European partners. However, it could be argued that reunification has had a broadly positive effect, but that this was masked by the adverse factors affecting the global economy in the past two years – the Gulf crisis, the recession in the English speaking countries, and the end of the investment boom.

Direct effects of German reunification on western Germany
The direct effects of German reunification on western Germany can be summarily subdivided into three components: heavy immigration from eastern Germany, the opening of new markets for West German exports, and massive public transfer payments to the new eastern Länder. Immigration from eastern Germany was not perceptibly halted by the signing of the unification treaty. The main effects of the immigration on the West German economy have been an increase in consumption and housing demand, and an additional supply of labour. The immediate rise in household consumption has been coupled with higher public spending, mainly for integrating and training the newcomers. East German immigration provided a timely easing of pressures in the West German labour market, curtailing the sharp wage pressures that appeared there in 1990. However, it is hard to imagine that the newcomers, poorly trained and lacking labour union support, will have an immediate impact on the pay talks in the same way as the 'local' West German unemployed. In our simulation, therefore, we have kept an effect of immigration on West German wage formation via the Phillips curve, but reduced it by half.

The penetration of West German products in East German markets has exceeded all forecasts. Consumer preferences switched instantly and almost completely from East German products to West German ones. Indeed, the output shift from east to west reached such proportions that in 1991 East Germans imported as much as they produced. Commercially speaking western Germany was the clear winner in the collapse of the East German economy. More than 80 per cent of east Länder 'imports' are now West German. Sales to those Länder contributed 5.5 per cent and 8.5 per cent to West German export growth in 1990 and 1991 respectively, representing contribu tions to GDP growth of 1.8 and 2.8 points. But western Germany also financed that expansion via massive central government transfers of approximately DM98 billion in 1990 and DM150 billion in 1991, or 4 and 5.5 points of GDP respectively. In this sense, reunification may be likened in the short run to a Keynesian stimulus.

Our model suggests that, together, the demand and supply effects allow a non-inflationary recovery in the short run. The results are reported in table 11.2. Price pressures engendered by the extra demand are entirely offset by growth induced productivity gains and the labour market easing. The impact on growth is very strong in the first two years, peaking at 4.1 per cent in 1991 – at the price, however, of a deterioration of more than five points in the current account balance as a ratio of West German GDP, and a 5.4 point increase in the budget deficit the same year.

Table 11.2 Impacts of reunification on West Germany with exogenous interest rates and exchange rates

	Direct impacts			Restrictive fiscal policy			Total		
	1990	1991	1992	1990	1991	1992	1990	1991	1992
GDP growth (a)	2.1	4.1	0.6	-	-0.9	-0.6	2.1	3.2	0
Inflation (a)	-0.1	0.2	0.7	-	1.4	1.6	-0.1	1.6	2.3
Current a/c (b)	-3.5	-5.4	-5.8	-	0.6	1.2	-3.5	-4.8	-4.6
Gov't a/c (b)	-3.8	-5.4	-5.0	-	1.7	2.0	-3.8	-3.7	-3.0

Source: MIMOSA CEPII-OFCE.
(a) Per cent deviation from baseline.
(b) Absolute deviation from baseline as a percentage of GDP.

The fiscal financing of reunification

As early as 1990, reunification costs were seen to have been grossly underestimated. In 1991, Germany acted to curb its budget deficit. The government did not want to go back on the third stage of the tax reform begun in 1990, which cut personal income taxes by DM20 billion. It therefore decided to institute a once-for-all levy of about DM11 billion on household income, to be collected in the second half of 1991 and the first half of 1992. The rest of the package, being designed to cause less pain, was therefore more inflationary: it included a rise in unemployment insurance contributions and a deferral of the business tax reform from 1991 to 1992. Spending cuts were also planned, including reductions in subsidies to west Berlin and to corporations, as well as a sizeable slowdown in public spending increases – particularly for the existing Länder and municipalities, which have been asked to make solidarity contributions to the new Länder. We estimate the fiscal financing measures, including tax increases and spending cuts, at an overall DM45 billion in 1991.

The simulation of these economic policy measures, reported in table 11.2, shows a negative impact of 0.9 points on West German growth in 1991. The rise in indirect taxes has a sharp inflationary effect, adding 1.4 points to inflation. The deficit reduction impact represents 1.7 points of GDP. It is worth noting that, according to MIMOSA, the inflationary impact of reunification in 1991 is due far more to the policy of raising indirect taxes than to the reunification shock itself. The model attributes greater weight to supply shocks and labour market tensions than to goods market pressures in explaining inflation. In the short run, buoyant demand brings productivity gains to domestic firms and boosts sales by foreign suppliers but does not incite domestic firms to raise their prices. This finding is corroborated by the observed moderation of producer price growth compared to consumer price growth — respectively 1.9 per cent and 3.9 per cent in the third quarter of 1991 over the same quarter of 1990.

In our forecast for 1992, the direct effects of reunification on the West German economy are likely to fall off sharply, once western firms have acquired eastern market share and production in the eastern Länder picks up. We project extra growth of only 0.6 points in this year for western Germany. This weak, but nevertheless still positive, effect should be entirely offset by the negative impact of the budget increases. The real effects of reunification on West German growth are thus likely to cease. By contrast, the rise in indirect taxes will continue to exert an inflationary effect, adding a further 2.3 points to the price increase.

Indirect effects via the financial sphere
The impact effects of reunification appear to be easy to identify. Assessing the shock's impact on interest rates and exchange rates is more complex. The approach adopted here consists in endogenising these variables by incorporating, if needed, the impact of long-run expectations on the financial markets.

Monetary policy
The German money market rate, which is determined by Bundesbank policy, has risen continuously from the start of 1988 to year-end 1990, in both real and nominal terms. This trend was not reproduced in all OECD countries. EMS countries, of course, have followed the German rates. The Bank of Japan also gradually lifted its rates in 1989 and 1990. But US rates edged down steadily from 9.4 points at the beginning of 1988 to 4.75 points at year-end 1991. What share of the rise in German short-term rates is attributable to reunification?

Inflationary pressures existed in Germany well before unity. The quickening of inflation and the rise of short-term rates in 1989 cannot be ascribed to reunification, which did not take place until the following year. We can assume that, even without reunification, inflationary pressures would have persisted in 1990. In that year, high wage demands would have undermined price stability, while the enactment of the third stage of tax reform would have boosted growth significantly. The most delicate task, therefore, is to measure the Bundesbank reaction to the reunification shock alone.

A reaction function estimated on quarterly data gives a fairly coherent account of Bundesbank behaviour (see appendix). From 1988 to early 1991, it explains the gradual hardening of monetary policy by the rising pressures on productive capacity and the steady increase in inflation, despite the decline in US short-term rates. The Bundesbank's confrontation with the government over the financing of reunification and the inflationary consequences of Bonn's choices explain the 1991 interest rate rises, which are less well reproduced by the equation. But, overall, the equation's behaviour justifies introducing it in its present form in the simulation.

According to our simulations with endogenous interest rates, reunification does not seem responsible for more than a very small share of the 1990 increase in short-term rates, since its inflationary effect was still weak. (Our conclusion may of course depend upon the dynamic structure of our equation.) Admittedly, the productive capacity utilisation rate, used here as a leading indicator of inflationary pressures, moves up 1.2 points, causing a slight rise in short-term rates. In 1991, by contrast, the simulation shows a bigger rise of 1.6 points.

Long-term rate movements

The movement of real long-term rates in West Germany deserves fuller discussion. Bond yields followed a fairly downward slope until the second quarter of 1989, but then turned around sharply. From mid-1989 to early 1990, long-term rates climbed more than 2 points. Such a pattern is not charted by our simple equations linking long and short-term rates, but this trend is easy to interpret. Expectations on short-term rates prior to the fall of the Berlin Wall are correctly reflected in a simple average of earlier inflation. By contrast, reunification – which by year-end 1989 appeared inevitable – radically altered market expectations on long-term inflation. Traders now expected higher budget spending over the next several years, and made assumptions about how it would be financed. Inflationary expectations, the uncertainty over the future course of monetary policy, and the consequent increase in risk combined to propel long-term rates beyond 9 per cent at year-end 1990. The subsequent fallback has been modest, because the government's financing choices raise the prospect of a stern response from the Bundesbank.

Another interpretation has sometimes been put forward, based on the supply and demand mechanisms of the German long-term capital market (Raedalli *et al.*, 1991; Augory *et al.*, 1991). The rise in long-term rates, it is argued, is due to the increased requirements for private and public long-term capital due to reunification. The authors effectively demonstrate a slight effect of long-dated government issues on long-term rates, but it is too weak to explain the current increase .

To sum up, we feel we can use our reaction function for short-term simulation rates, but not the one that determines long-term rates. We shall subsequently assume that the simulation error for the long-term rate equation is entirely due to the reunification effect. Long-term rates would therefore have risen 2.1 points in 1990 and 2.5 points in 1991 (see appendix). From 1992 to 2000, the positive impact of reunification on long-term rates diminishes owing to the inflation slowdown and the gradual return of short-term rates to their baseline level.

Exchange rate

By the fourth quarter of 1989, the D-Mark had risen sharply against the dollar, which moved down from DM1.95 in September 1989 to DM1.70 in January 1990. After a relative stabilisation in the first half of 1990, the dollar's slide persisted through the second half of the year. In the following year, the dollar experienced wide swings, ending at DM1.60. On an annual average, the D-Mark gained 14 per cent against the dollar in 1990 and lost 4.5 per cent in 1991. These changes are not, of course, entirely attributable to the impact of German reunification. After all, it is highly improbable that exchange rates would have remained perfectly stable if reunification had not taken place. Other shocks influenced the currency markets. The Gulf crisis and events in the ex-USSR exerted upward pressure on the dollar, while the easing of US short-term rates fuelled the downward pressure.

Unlike interest rate estimation, the estimation of an exchange rate equation would be difficult and of little help in interpreting these movements. We have therefore adopted a rule suggested by Fischer *et al.* (1990), based on the rationality of currency market participants. The rule assumes that the markets expect the foreseeable portion of future economic change. When an unexpected shock occurs, the exchange rate jumps to a new level high enough to ensure that, in each subsequent year, the expected returns on investment in different currencies are made to match, allowing for a risk factor for countries with current account deficits. This method obliges us to take into account the effects of German reunification over the long term, our cutoff date being 2000. We describe the effects in greater detail in the next section. Currency market expectations are obviously not observable but, in keeping with rational expectations theory, we will assume they are identical to our model's scenario.

Table 11.3 Total impact on West Germany with endogenous interest rates and exchange rates

	Impact of interest rates			Impact of exchange rate			Total impact of reunification		
	1990	1991	1992	1990	1991	1992	1990	1991	1992
GDP growth (a)	-0.8	-0.8	-0.3	-0.9	-0.4	0.0	0.5	2.1	-0.3
Inflation (a)	0.0	0.0	0.0	-0.7	-0.6	-0.5	-0.8	1.1	1.8
Current a/c (b)	0.6	1.0	1.0	0.3	-0.1	-0.2	-2.8	-4.1	-3.9
Gov't a/c (b)	-0.4	-0.8	-1.1	-0.3	-0.7	-0.8	-4.5	-5.2	-4.2
Short-term interest rate (c)	0.1	1.6	1.9	-	-	-	0.1	1.6	1.9
Long-term interest rate (c)	2.1	2.5	1.9	-	-	-	2.1	2.5	1.9
Exchange rate appreciation (a)	-	-	-	10.6	10.7	9.5	10.6	10.7	4.5

Source: MIMOSA CEPII-OFCE.

(a) Percentage deviation from baseline.

(b) Absolute deviation from baseline as a percentage of GDP.

(c) Absolute deviation from baseline in percentage points.

Quantified with the aid of that long-range scenario, the D-Mark would have risen by 10.6 per cent in 1990 and 10.7 per cent in 1991 against the dollar. Because of the rise in German short-term rates induced by reunification, the cumulative German–US cumulative interest rate differential between 1990 and 2000 would have been 14 points. Pressures on German productive capacity, followed by the inflationary impact of reunification starting in 1992, would then send short-term rates up 1.6 points in 1991 and 1.9 points in 1992. Then, as pressures on productive capacity eased and the inflationary impact stabilised, the effect on short-term rates would subside, virtually disappearing by 2000. The D-Mark's appreciation is also dampened by the risk premium linked to the sharp drop in Germany's current account surplus. The surplus contraction represents 2.8 points of GDP in 1990, 4.1 points in 1991. Thereafter, as the growth differential between Germany and its partners narrowed, the German current account surplus would tend to rise again. The negative effect on the exchange rate of the cumulative reduction in German net external assets to 2000 is estimated at 3.4 per cent in 1990 and 3.2 per cent in 1991.

Overall, the interest rate rises and the D-Mark's appreciation would have a negative impact of 1.2 points on German growth in 1990 and 1991, and the total effect of reunification would be only 0.5 points and 2.1 points respectively, compared with 2.1 points and 3.2 points in the simulation using exogenous interest and exchange rates (table 11.3); inflation is reduced by the parity appreciation, and the current account balance improves. Thus, in the simulation with endogenous interest and exchange rates, reunification has a disinflationary impact of 0.8 points in 1990 and an inflationary impact of 1.1 points in 1991. Germany's current account surplus is cut by 2.8 points and 4.1 points of GDP respectively, while the general government deficit increases by 4.1 and 4.6 points respectively. Monetary policy is effective in restraining inflation, but at the price of slower growth.

In 1992, interest rate rises are projected to continue weighing on German growth, dragging it down by 0.3 points. As a result, the overall impact of reunification – with zero real effects – should become slightly negative. Despite the fact that the D-Mark would begin losing ground against the dollar, the disinflationary effects of its sharp climb would persist, but the additional inflation linked to the reunification shock would reach 1.8 points owing to higher taxes.

Effects of reunification on Germany's partners

Table 11.4 gives our model-based estimates of the impact of unification. The direct impact of reunification on growth in Germany's European partners is 0.4 points a year in 1990 and 0.8 points in 1991, with a weak inflationary impact. Reunification also improves the partners' current-account balances by an average 0.7 points of GDP in 1991, and public deficits by 0.4 points. In 1992, by contrast, the impact on growth, inflation, and the current account balance would become nill.

We simulated the impact of higher interest and exchange rates assuming a perfectly efficient functioning of the EMS. The rises in German interest rates and the D-Mark's appreciation are therefore fully transmitted to all EC countries. This hypothesis no doubt heightens the impact on interest rates in certain countries. Reunification narrowed some countries' inflation gaps with Germany; it enhanced the credibility of parities inside the EMS, and thus promoted a faster convergence of interest rates. For the other European countries, the increase in interest and exchange rates translates into a significant slowdown in growth (of the order of 0.5 points in 1990 and 1991), a widening of current account and public deficits, but also a lowering of inflation of the order of 0.7 points in 1990 and 1991. This exercise, therefore, clearly shows that the 'direct' effects of reunification, which were very strong in 1990 and 1991, were considerably diminished by the German financing policy as well as by interest and exchange rate movements.

When those effects are taken into account, our model suggests that the benefits of reunification for Germany's European partners are sharply reduced, but they are not transformed into a negative impact. In 1991, the partners obtained half a point of extra growth. At the same time they enjoyed a disinflationary effect, an improvement in their current account balances equivalent to 0.3 points of GDP, and a slight improvement in their public sector deficits.

Table 11.4 Total impact of reunification on EC countries (excluding Germany). Endogenous interest rates and exchange rates.

	GDP growth (a)			Inflation (a)		
	1990	1991	1992	1990	1991	1992
Direct effects	0.4	1.2	0.2	0.1	0.3	0.4
Restrictive fiscal policy	-	-0.1	-0.1	-	0.0	0.1
Interest rate rise	-0.2	-0.3	-0.1	0.0	0.1	0.0
Exchange rate appreciation	-0.2	-0.3	0.0	-0.8	-0.6	-0.4
Total	*0.0*	*0.5*	*0.0*	*-0.6*	*-0.2*	*0.1*

	Current a/c balance (b)			Gov't a/c (b)		
	1990	1991	1992	1990	1991	1992
Direct effects	0.2	0.7	0.8	0.1	0.4	0.5
Restrictive fiscal policy	-	-0.1	-0.2	-	0.0	-0.1
Interest rate rise	-0.1	-0.1	-0.1	-0.1	-0.1	-0.1
Exchange rate appreciation	0.1	-0.3	-0.4	-0.1	-0.2	-0.1
Total	*0.3*	*0.3*	*0.1*	*0.0*	*0.1*	*0.3*

Source: MIMOSA CEPII-OFCE.
(a) Percentage deviation from baseline. (b) Absolute deviation from baseline as a percentage of GDP.

Managing German reunification in Europe under alternative exchange-rate systems

Exchange-rate systems: EMS and its alternatives
The analysis of the macroeconomic effects of reunification underscores the constraints linked to the transitional stage between the asymmetrical EMS in

its current form and the projected monetary union approved in Maastricht. A fixed exchange rate system with one dominant country works well when the countries find themselves in the same economic situation and in pursuit of the same goals. By tying their monetary policies to that of Germany, EMS members were able to minimise the cost of coping with asymmetrical shocks in Europe. The EMS also functions efficiently in certain asymmetrical situations by curbing the use of nominal parity swings. It has thus enabled some members, notably France and Italy, to change their economic strategy. These countries abandoned their practice of accommodating inflationary behaviour through chronic devaluations. They switched to competitive disinflation, a more arduous path in the short run, but sounder in the medium term. Many countries have come to perceive the EMS as the source of successful disinflation, even though at present that strategy may seem to carry a heavy cost in unemployment and in lost growth.

Conversely, in the EMS, the European countries most committed to the search for fixed parities lose their basic means of macroeconomic regulation. European monetary policy is constrained by EMS mechanisms. Fiscal policy ceases to be an effective regulatory instrument, since any significant deviation intended as a short-term stimulus impairs the credibility of a country's economic policy and generates expectations prejudicial to its exchange rate stability. In such a system, sovereignty in economic policy is the privilege of the dominant country. The Bundesbank's high interest rates are inappropriate to the situations in other EC countries.

Flexible exchange rates

In a flexible exchange rate system, domestic economic policies are sovereign. Whether the shock is transitory or structural, whether it affects all the economies or only selected ones, it can be accommodated in the short run by each country independently. But this type of adjustment quickly reached its limits for macroeconomic regulation in Europe. It does not incite countries to fight inflation; that inflation, soon incorporated in pay demands and interest rates, ceases to sustain growth; exchange rates, turned over to market forces, are unstable, and the lack of economic policy coordination leads to collectively inefficient strategies.

To analyse what the impact of German reunification would have been in a flexible exchange rate system, we made several assumptions. We postulated a German fiscal policy identical to what it is under the EMS. The Bundesbank's response obeys the same determinants as in the EMS: the money market rate rises with inflation and with pressures on domestic productive capacity. The rise in long-term rates partly reflects an identical risk premium linked to future inflation expectations. This causes a unilateral rise of the D-Mark against all other currencies. The effects of reunification are concentrated in Germany and are too weak to modify the macroeconomic aggregates of its European partners. Imported inflation and the transfer of demand by Germany's main partners are not significant enough to trigger a hardening of monetary policy in European countries other than Germany. There is also no special risk premium affecting the foreign exchange market since the fiscal and current account balances of Germany's partners are not significantly modified.

EMU

In the diametrically opposite scenario where the single currency replaces the European currencies, the European monetary authority sovereignly defines its interest rate and exchange rate policy *vis-à-vis* the rest of the world according to the movements of macroeconomic aggregates defined on a European scale. To evaluate the consequences of reunification in such a system, we need to define beforehand the fiscal and monetary policy rules characterising EMU – which we assume will comprise today's twelve EC members. We take the rules defined in Maastricht.

Under the terms of the Maastricht accord, the EC states have pledged continuous compliance with criteria for 'sound management' of their public finances. The public debt is not to exceed 60 per cent of GDP, the public deficit 3 per cent of GDP. However, on the Commission's recommendation, the Council will be authorised to grant exemptions from these rules. Germany would no doubt have obtained such an exemption in view of the singularity of reunification. We will therefore assume in the EMU scenario that no additional budget constraint weighs on Germany. The Community also agreed in Maastricht to set up a European Central Bank System (ECBS) with identical targets and policy instruments as the Bundesbank today.

We incorporate these elements to simulate the course of reunification if EMU had already been implemented. European short-term interest rates are determined by an ECBS reaction equivalent to that of the Bundesbank but based on EC inflation and productive capacity utilisation rates. Similarly, the inflation risk premium linked to the shock influences the formation of European long-term rates. The premium is proportional to the one estimated in the EMS scenario, taking into account Germany's relative weight in the Community. In the same manner, the rule for determining the ecu's parity against the dollar and yen is the European-scale equivalent of the rule adopted for the D-Mark under the EMS — enlarged to adopt European indicators as determinants. There is one difference, however. While EMU would tolerate a rise in the German budget deficit, the financing of that deficit would have to be modified to comply with EMU fiscal harmonisation rules. Part of the public transfer payments entailed by reunification were financed by an increase in indirect taxes — a procedure that would be disallowed in the harmonised framework of the single European market. In order to take this fact into account, we have made two different simulations under EMU rules. The first simulation assumes the same fiscal policy as in the EMS and flexible exchange rate scenarios. This simulation therefore allows a direct comparison between the alternative exchange rate systems, without incorporating different inflationary effects of fiscal policy. The second simulation assumes the extra revenues required to meet the cost of reunification would have been levied exclusively through a direct income tax on households. That hypothesis does not distort relative prices in Europe.

Table 11.5 offers a comparison of the impact of reunification prior to a monetary policy reaction in two alternative scenarios: a tax rise partially affecting direct taxes (as was actually the case) or an increase in personal income tax alone. In the second scenario, we made the arguably questionable assumption that wage earners would accept this direct tax rise without demanding compensatory pay rises. In these conditions, the simulation shows a particularly strong inflationary effect of indirect taxation. Inflation would climb an average 1.1 per cent annually during the eleven years under review versus 0.3 per cent if only direct taxes are increased. However, the tax rise is less harmful to growth, and therefore causes a slightly wider external deficit. But the results clearly show that the inflation cost of the tax rise is enormous compared to its benefits.

How financial variables react to the reunification shock under alternative exchange rate systems
We can now compare the consequences of the shock under the three possible exchange rate systems.

Interest rates

It is in the EMS that reunification has the sharpest impact on short-term rates. The German money market rate increases 1.5 points in 1991 and a further 0.5 in 1992, leading to tighter monetary policies all over Europe (chart 11.4). In the mid-term, the German authorities ease their policy and short-term rates fall back by just over a quarter point each year from the present to the year 2000. By contrast, EMU significantly dampens the rise of European, hence German, short-term interest rates. The extra increase is a single point in the first year and practically zero in the second. In the medium term, European interest rates would have been about one point lower under EMU than in the EMS.

On the other hand, flexible exchange rates would lead to a smaller rise in the German short-term rate than the EMS. That is because the D-Mark's effective appreciation is steeper in a flexible exchange rate system than in the EMS, since the D-Mark is the only currency to be revalued. As a result, it also rises against the other European currencies, dampening the shock's inflationary impact and thus moderating the Bundesbank reaction. The EMS is therefore responsible for some of the vigour of the German interest rate rise. By

Table 11.5 Direct impact of restrictive fiscal policy: impact on West Germany

		EMS or EMU1 or flexible exchange rates	EMU2
GDP (level in points	1990	2.0	2.0
	1991	5.1	5.0
	1992	5.0	4.7
	1995	4.1	3.9
	2000	1.9	2.3
Consumption deflator	1990	-0.1	-0.1
(level in points)	1991	1.6	0.8
	1992	3.9	1.8
	1995	8.8	1.8
	2000	12.3	3.8
Current account balance	1990	-3.5	-3.5
(% of GDP)	1991	-4.8	-4.7
	1992	-4.6	-4.3
	1995	-2.7	-2.3
	2000	-1.9	-1.4
Government account	1990	-3.7	-3.7
(% of GDP)	1991	-3.6	-3.8
	1992	-2.9	-3.1
	1995	-2.3	-2.5
	2000	-2.8	-2.7

Source: MIMOSA CEPII-OFCE.
Deviations from baseline.

contrast, flexible parities have the virtue of preserving the sovereignty of other EC members, so that reunification triggers no interest rate rise there.

Finally, European long-term interest rates move up less in EMU than in the EMS, because medium-term inflationary expectations are lower for EMU than for Germany alone. In Germany, long-term rates react identically under the EMS or flexible exchange rates. EMU, for its part, would have enabled Germany to protect itself against an excessive increase in long-term rates.

Exchange rates

In both the flexible exchange rate system and the EMS, the impact of German reunification on the German exchange rate might depend on the cumulative German-US short-term interest rate spreads until 2000 and on the relative variations in the two countries' current account balances. The short-term appreciation of the D-Mark against the dollar is identical at about 10 per cent in both systems. While short-term rates climb more steeply in the short run in the EMS, they are higher in the mid-term under a flexible exchange rate system. In the short run, the shock's inflationary impact is thus stronger under the EMS than with flexible exchange rates because of the lesser rise in the effective exchange rate. The opposite occurs in the medium term, when the D-Mark's effective depreciation becomes sharper under a flexible exchange rate system than in EMU. Consequently the cumulative interest rate spread with the US is identical in both exchange rate systems. In the medium term, the exchange rate returns to its baseline level under both systems as the cumulative interest rate spread narrows. EMU, however, curtails the ecu's immediate appreciation against the dollar.

While there is hardly any difference in the D-Mark's nominal rise against the dollar in the EMS or with flexible exchange rates, the D-Mark's effective exchange rates move in radically different ways under the two systems. With flexible exchange rates, the nominal and effective appreciations are obviously identical since the D-Mark is revalued unilaterally. By contrast, the EMS generates a common appreciation of all its currencies, reducing the D-Mark's effective rise to just 4 per cent as against 10 per cent with flexible parities. In EMU, German reunification causes an effective revaluation of the German currency – now the ecu – of only 2 per cent, since the ecu's nominal rise against the dollar is smaller and parities between European countries are fixed.

Impact on growth and inflation

In Germany

In western Germany, EMU is the most favourable exchange rate system over the short run, as far as growth is concerned, since it maximises the extra growth induced by reunification. Output expands 1.5 per cent in the first year, peaking at 4.3 per cent above baseline in the second year (table 11.6). Interest rate rises are smaller and therefore less growth inhibiting than under other exchange rate systems. Meanwhile, the slacker rise in the D-Mark/dollar parity and in the D-Mark's effective exchange rate has a less adverse effect on competitiveness. Up to 1997, EMU is the system that maximises German growth, which dips slightly thereafter. The smaller appreciation of the effective exchange rate under EMU is balanced in the alternative simulation by a weaker

Table 11.6 Total impact of German reunification on West Germany in the three scenarios

		EMS	Flexible exchange rates	EMU1	EMU2
GDP (level in points	1990	0.5	-0.1	1.4	1.5
	1991	2.6	1.8	4.3	4.3
	1992	2.3	1.5	4.1	4.0
	1995	2.9	2.9	3.7	3.6
	2000	1.9	2.7	1.9	2.3
Consumption deflator	1990	-0.8	-1.1	-0.5	-0.5
(level in points)	1991	0.4	-0.4	0.8	0.2
	1992	2.2	1.0	3.0	1.1
	1995	6.5	4.3	7.8	3.0
	2000	11.3	9.8	11.9	4.5
Current account balance	1990	-2.8	-2.5	-3.4	-3.4
(% of GDP)	1991	-4.1	-4.1	-5.0	-4.9
	1992	-3.9	-3.9	-4.8	-4.6
	1995	-2.9	-2.9	-3.1	-2.7
	2000	-2.4	-2.2	-2.3	-1.7
Government account	1990	-4.1	-4.3	-3.8	-3.9
(% of GDP)	1991	-4.6	-5.0	-3.9	-3.9
	1992	-4.2	-4.6	-3.3	-3.4
	1995	-3.2	-3.4	-2.6	-2.8
	2000	-3.2	-2.8	-3.0	-2.8
Short-term interest rate	1990	0.1	-0.1	0.1	0.2
(level in points)	1991	1.6	1.1	1.0	1.0
	1992	1.9	1.4	1.1	1.1
	1995	1.5	1.5	0.6	0.5
	2000	0.6	1.0	0.4	0.3
Long-term interest rate	1990	2.1	2.0	0.6	0.6
(level in points)	1991	2.5	2.4	0.7	0.7
	1992	1.9	1.8	0.5	0.5
	1995	0.8	0.8	0.2	0.2
	2000	0.2	0.3	0.1	0.1
Exchange rate DM/$	1990	10.6	10.3	6.9	6.2
(appreciation in points)	1991	10.7	10.7	6.8	6.1
	1992	9.5	10.0	6.0	5.2
	1995	5.3	6.9	3.4	2.9
	2000	0.3	0.8	0.4	0.3

Source: MIMOSA CEPII-OFCE.
Deviations from baseline.

disinflationary impact (the alternative assumes the same fiscal policy as in EMS and flexible exchange rate scenarios. The flexible exchange rate system yields a slightly better figure owing to the D-Mark's weaker effective revaluation, which entails smaller competitiveness losses. More significantly, this reduced deterioration in trade performance persists throughout the period. The dynamics of the reunification shock, therefore, do not exhibit the same profile in the flexible exchange rate scenario. Excluding 1992, marked by a slowdown unrelated to the exchange rate system, robust growth is sustained for a full seven years with flexible parities. Conversely, with EMU, growth is concentrated in the first two years and then quickly loses steam. Over the long run, German growth is relatively independent of the exchange rate mechanism in force. But over the short run each exchange rate system accommodates the shock in a distinctive manner. German fluctuations are weakest in the EMS. EMU concentrates the impact in the initial years, whereas the flexible exchange rate system spreads it over several years.

As regards inflation, the most significant comparative advantages emerge in the medium-to-long term. The flexible exchange rate system, in which the D-Mark is the only appreciating currency, appears to be less inflationary than EMS, despite the smaller rise in interest rates. A Nash equilibrium is the most efficient system to combat inflationary pressures in Germany in the medium term, but the main explanation for that is the choice of the financing procedure. Consequently, on the inflation score, the EMS seems more virtuous than EMU1 but not more virtuous than EMU2. By 1992, the virtues of flexible exchange rates, and therefore of imported disinflation for Germany, are superseded by EMU2. The general level of German prices stabilises rapidly when a European monetary policy is introduced and when the government decides to raise direct taxes. In the alternative scenarios, inflation runs higher throughout the period.

Overall, we find the EMS to be the most unfavourable exchange rate system for Germany since it produces slacker growth and higher inflation than the other systems.

The effects on the rest of the EC

Growth is higher under flexible rates in the rest of the EC, whilst a German-dominated EMS in the short run significantly reduces the expansionary effect of unification (see chart 11.1). The EMU results are in between. Under flexible rates unification causes more inflation, but under EMU and EMS the effects of demand are more than offset by the appreciation of the ecu. The appreciation is less under EMU than in the EMS (see chart 11.2).

Chart 11.1 Impact on GDP

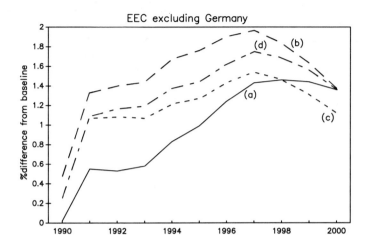

Notes: (a) EMS: (b) Flexible exchange rates: (c) EMU2: (d) EMU 1.

Chart 11.2 Impact on consumption deflator

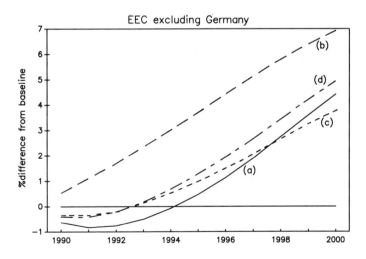

Notes: As for chart 11.1.

In the United States

Our model suggests that the rest of the world, particularly the US, also benefited from extra growth in Germany (chart 11.3). In the short run, the EMS is the alternative that provides the highest growth transfer to the US, since it gives the US sizeable competitiveness gains relative to EMS countries as a group. The simulation shows US growth rising by an additional 0.3 points in the first year, 0.7 points in the second. Paradoxically, German reunification under the EMS provides a bigger boost to US growth than to growth in Germany's European partners, because of the rise of interest rates in Europe and the appreciation of European currencies against the dollar. Under flexible exchange rates and EMU, by contrast, it is the European countries that gain the most from the demand transfer, owing to their closer trade links with Germany. In the medium term, flexible exchange rates provide steady additional growth to the US until 1997. The EMS and EMU exhibit different dynamics. Most of the effect is concentrated at the start of the period, when European currencies climb sharply against the dollar. Also, US inflation is significantly higher when US growth itself is more buoyant — in this particular case, when Europe adopts the EMS mechanisms (chart 11.4), since the US pays for its competitiveness gains with a dose of imported inflation.

Chart 11.3 Impact on GDP

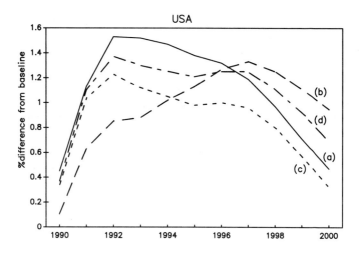

Notes: As for chart 11.1.

Chart 11.4 Impact on consumption deflator

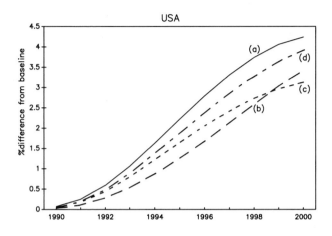

Notes: As for chart 11.1.

Conclusion

There are three points worth making about the management of the German reunification shock by European economic policy as actually practised in 1990 and 1991. First, it would seem that the fiscal policy adopted by Germany to finance reunification had exactly the inflationary effects that its monetary policy was seeking to avoid. German policy – based on the principle of strict autonomy between monetary and fiscal authorities – did not produce the best compromise in the admittedly exceptional circumstances of reunification. If a cut in the public deficit was needed to reassure the financial markets and the Bundesbank, the German government would have done better to apply a sharper increase in direct taxes on households.

Secondly, the German experience shows the limit of the EMS and the desirability of moving towards Economic and Monetary Union. In the absence of the current European exchange rate mechanism, the D-Mark would have appreciated alone, the Germans would have imported disinflation – which would have curbed the rise in their interest rates – and Germany's partners would have benefited from a welcome transfer of demand, although they would have paid for it with slightly higher inflation. In the EMS, such a readjustment would have been impossible, for it would have undermined the credibility of member countries' exchange-rate policies and the convergence towards German interest rates. Fixed exchange rates, as applied under the EMS, are therefore particularly costly when the dominated countries and the dominant country find themselves in contrasting phases of the economic cycle. By contrast, in EMU, the extra German inflation would have had less impact on the European interest rate since monetary policy management would have been based on average EC inflation. Moreover, European harmonisation constraints would have made it harder for Germany to raise its indirect taxes. The financial markets would not have feared such an abrupt reaction by the monetary authorities, so their expectations would not have sent interest rates and the exchange rate as high as they actually went.

However, we do not intend to join those who are casting stones at the German authorities. The scale of western Germany's transfer payments clearly shows that the country has done its utmost to integrate the eastern Länder. Indeed, Germany's conduct is a model for action by the European Community in favour of all its eastern and southern neighbours.

Appendix

Interest-rate and exchange-rate equations used in the simulation

Interest rate and exchange rate in the EMS
To endogenise European interest and exchange rates, we estimated an equation for the German short-term rate and an equation for the German long-term rate; we also wrote a rule for the change in the DM/dollar exchange rate compatible with rational behaviour by currency traders. Next, we assumed that German rate movements were fully passed on into other EMS countries' interest rates, and that EMS countries' exchange rates were fixed against the D-Mark. All estimates reported here are based on quarterly data for 1979I to 1991I.

Equation for the German short-term rate: The German monetary authorities set the short-term interest rate on the basis of the US interest rate, the inflation rate, and the productive capacity utilisation rate, which they regard as a leading indicator of inflation. Hence:
$$MMR = 0.78MMR_{-1} + 0.37QCP + 0.11PCU + 0.19USB - 10.0$$
$$\quad\quad (19.0) \quad\quad (2.7) \quad\quad (6.5) \quad\quad (5.8) \quad\quad (-6.3)$$
SEE: 0.45; DW:2.18.
MMR: German money market rate.
USB: US Treasury bond yield.
QCP: Quarterly growth rate of German consumer prices.
PCU: Productive capacity utilisation rate in West German industry.

Equation for the German long-term rate: This is a term-structure equation in which the German long-term rate depends on the short-term rate and a smoothed inflation rate that proxies expected inflation. Also included is the US long-term rate.

$$GBY = 0.40GBY\text{-}1 + 0.48[MMR\text{-}MMR_{\text{-}1}] - 0.18[GBY_{\text{-}1}\text{-}MMR_{\text{-}1}]$$
$$(3.9) \qquad (7.0) \qquad\qquad (\text{-}3.3)$$

$$+ 0.22USM + 0.03GCP + 0.014GCP_{\text{-}1} + 0.021GCP_{\text{-}2}$$
$$(4.5) \qquad (2.1) \qquad (2.8) \qquad\quad (2.0)$$

$$+ 0.026GCP_{\text{-}3} + 0.027GCP_{\text{-}4} + 0.025GCP_{\text{-}5}$$
$$(3.1) \qquad\quad (2.9) \qquad\quad (2.5)$$

$$+ 0.020GCP_{\text{-}6} + 0.012GCP_{\text{-}7} + 1.95$$
$$(2.3) \qquad\quad (2.1) \qquad\quad (4.0)$$

SEE: 0.28; DW: 1.66.
Method: Almon for inflation
GBY: German Treasury bond yield.
GCP: German consumer price increase, quarter q over quarter q-4.
USM: US medium-dated paper yields (7-10 years).

German exchange-rate equation: The equation assumes currency market speculators are fully rational and fully informed. Their expectations of long-term economic change (here, up to 2000) are identical to our scenario. In response to an unforeseen shock, the exchange rate jumps to a new level high enough to ensure that its later movement makes up for the interest rate differential adjusted by a risk premium, assumed to be proportional to the current account balance. The exchange rate rise is therefore equal to the cumulative total from now to 2000 of the interest rate differential minus the accumulated current account balance deterioration multiplied by a special coefficient, whose size is proportional to the risk premium. Following Fisher *et al.* (1990), we adopt a coefficient of 0.1. This equation is further analysed in the chapter by Whitley in this volume. We do not attempt to solve our model in consistent expectations mode, and our results would be significantly altered if we did so.

$$\dot{DM_t} = \sum_{i=t}^{2000}(USB - MMR)_i + 0.1 = \sum_{i=t}^{2000}100(\frac{USCA}{GDPU} - \frac{GCA}{GDPG})_i$$

DM: DM/$ exchange rate.
GCA: German current account balance.
USCA: US current account balance.
GDPG: German nominal GDP.
GDPU: US nominal GDP.
All EMS currencies are assumed to move in line with the D-Mark.

Interest rates and exchange rates under flexible exchange rates
In a flexible exchange rate system, only the German interest rates respond to the reunification shock. We use the same equations as in the EMS model. Similarly, the D-Mark is revalued against all other currencies according to the rule used for the EMS.

Interest rates and exchange rates under EMU
In EMU, there is only one short-term European rate, one long-term European rate, and a single currency. Short-term rate movements are determined by the European central bank. The latter has the same reaction function as the Bundesbank since its status of independence from EC governments and its main target of monetary stability, as defined in Maastricht, are identical to those of the German central bank. The only difference lies in the variables used to determine European monetary policy, which are EC inflation, the EC productive capacity utilisation rate, and the US short-term rate. Similarly, the European long-term rate reacts in the same manner as the German long-term rate today, the determinants being EC variables rather than German variables. We accordingly assume that the reunification shock on the German long-term rate in the EMS would have affected the European long-term rate under EMU. The shock's intensity would have been proportional to Germany's weight in the EC.

Lastly, the European exchange rate rises against the dollar according to the cumulative spread from now to 2000 between European and US interest rates, while the risk premium is estimated on the basis of the relative changes in European and US current account balances.

References

Abrams, R.K., Cornelius, P.K., Hedfors, P.L. and Tersman, G. (1990), *The Impact of the European Community's Internal Market on the EFTA*, IMF Occasional Paper no. 74, Washington DC, IMF, December.

Alesina, A. and Grilli, V. (1992), 'The European Central Bank: reshaping monetary politics in Europe' in Canzoneri, Grilli and Masson, (Eds) *op. cit.*

Alogoskoufis, G. and Portes, R. (1992), 'European monetary union and international currencies in a tripolar world' in Canzoneri, Grilli and Masson (Eds), *op. cit.*

Anderton, R. and Barrell, R. (1992), 'The ERM and European Labour Markets', paper presented at RES conference, April.

Anderton, R., Barrell, R. and McHugh, J. (1992), 'Nominal convergence in European wage behaviour: achievements and explanations' in Barrell (Ed), *op.cit.*

Aoki, M. (1967), *Optimisation of Stochastic Systems*, London and New York, Academic Press.

Aoki, M. (1976), *Optimal Control and System Theory in Dynamic Economic Analysis*, Amsterdam, North-Holland.

Artis, M. (1988), 'How accurate is the world economic outlook? A post-mortem on short-term forecasting at the IMF', *IMF Staff Studies.*

Artis, M. and Nachane, D. (1990), 'Wages and prices in Europe, a test of the German leadership hypothesis', *Weltwirtschaftliches Archiv*, no. 126.

Artis, M. and Ormerod, P. (1991), 'Is there an 'EMS effect' in European labour markets?', Manchester University, mimeo.

Artis, M. and Taylor, M. (1988), 'Exchange rate, interest rates, capital controls and the European Monetary System: assessing the track record' in Giavazzi, F., Micossi, S. and Miller, M. (Eds), *The European Monetary System*, Cambridge, Cambridge University Press.

Augory, C., Avouyi-Dovi, S. and Bauer, A. (1991), 'Les effets de la réunification sur les taux d'intérêt allemands', Working paper no. 1991-16T, Paris, Caisse des dépôts et consignations, September.

Backus, D. and Driffill, L. (1985), 'Rational expectations and policy credibility following a change of regime', *Review of Economic Studies.*

Baer, G.D. (1991), 'Der Delors-bericht: ausgangspunkt für die weitere diskussion' in Weber, M. (Ed), *Europa auf dem Weg zur Währungsunion*, Darmstadt.

Barrell, R. (1990a), 'European currency union and the EMS', National Institute Economic Review, no. 132, May.

Barrell, R. (1990b), 'Has the EMS changed wage and price behaviour in Europe?' *National Institute Economic Review*, no. 134, November.

Barrell, R. (1992a), 'The prospects for monetary union in Europe', in Barrell (Ed), *op. cit.*

Barrell, R. (Ed) (1992b), *Economic Convergence and Monetary Union in Europe*, London, Sage Publications.

Barrell, R., Darby, J. and Donaldson, C. (1990), 'Strructural stability in European wage and price systems', National Institute Discussion Paper no. 188.

Barrell, R. and Gurney, A. (1990), 'Fiscal and monetary policy simulations with forward-looking exchange rates using the National Institute Global Econometric Model (GEM)', National Institute of Economic and Social Research Discussion Paper no. 200.

Barrell, R. and Gurney, A. (1991), 'Fiscal and monetary policy simulations with forward looking exchange rates', National Institute Discussion Paper no. 200.

Barrell, R., Gurney, A. and in't Veld, J.W. (1992), 'The real exchange rate, fiscal policy and the role of wealth: an analysis of equilibrium in a monetary union', *Journal of Forecasting*, May.

Barrell, R. and in't Veld, J. (1991), 'FEERs and the path to EMU', *National Institute Economic Review*, no. 137, August.

Barrell, R. and in't Veld, J.W. (1992), 'Wealth effects and fiscal policy in the National Institute Global Econometric Model', *National Institute Economic Review*, no. 140, May.

Barro, R. and Gordon, R. (1983a), 'Rules, discretion and regulation in a model of monetary policy', *Journal of Monetary Economics*, July.

Barro, R. and Gordon, D. (1983b), 'A positive theory of monetary policy in a natural rate model', *Journal of Political Economy*, August, no. 91.

Bartolini, L. and Bodnar, G. (1992), 'Target zones and forward rates in a model with repeated realignments', mimeo, IMF.

Bean, C.R. (1992), 'Europe 1992: a macroeconomic perspective', mimeo London School of Economics, February, forthcoming in *The Journal of Economic Perspectives*.

Becker, R.G., Dwolatsky, B., Karakitsos, E. and Rustem, B. (1986), 'Simultaneous use of rival models in policy optimisation', *Economic Journal*, vol. 77.

Begg, D. *et al.* (1991), 'The making of monetary union', *CEPR Annual Report of Monitoring European Integration*, no. 2, London School of Economics, CEPR.

Blanchard, O. and Diamond, P. (1990), 'Unemployment and wages: what have we learned from the European experience?', London, Employment Institute.

Blanchard, O. and Fischer, S. (1989), *Lectures on Macroeconomics*, Cambridge, Mass., MIT Press.

Boskin, M.J. (1987), *Reagan and the Economy: the Successes, Failures and Unfinished Agenda*, San Francisco, ICS Press.

Bovenberg, L., Kremers, J. and Masson, P. (1991), 'Economic and monetary union in Europe and constraints on national budgetary policies', *IMF Staff Papers*, no. 38, Washington, IMF.

Brandsma, A.S. and Hughes-Hallet, A.J. (1989), 'Macroeconomic policy design with incomplete information', *Economic Modelling*, vol. 6.

Bryant, R., Henderson, D., Holtham, G., Hooper, P. and Symansky, S. (1988), *Empirical Macroeconomics for Interdependent Economies*, Washington, Brookings Institution, two volumes.

Bryant, R., Hooper, P., Mann, C. and Tryon, R. (1992), *Evaluating Policy Regimes: New Research in Empirical Macroeconomics*, Washington, The Brookings Institution.

Buiter, W. and Kletzer, K. (1991), 'Reflections on the fiscal implications of a common currency' in Giovannini, A. and Mayer, C., *European Financial Integration*, Cambridge University Press.

Bullard, J.B. (1991), 'Learning, rational expectations and policy', *Federal Reserve Bulletin of St Louis*, January/February.

Calvo, G.A. (1983), 'Staggered contracts and exchange rate policy' in Frenkel, J. (Ed.), *Exchange Rates and International Macroeconomics*, Chicago, University of Chicago Press.

Canzoneri, M. and Edison, H. (1988), 'A new interpretation of the coordination problem and its empirical significance', Board of Governors of the Federal Reserve, Washington, DC, Working Paper, May.

Canzoneri, M., Grilli, V. and Masson, P.R. (Eds) (1992), *Establishing a Central Bank: Issues in Europe and Lessons from the US*, Cambridge, Cambridge University Press.

Canzoneri, M. and Minford, P. (1988), 'When international policy coordination matters: an empirical analysis', *Applied Economics*, vol. 20, no. 9, September.

Canzoneri, M. and Minford, P. (1989), 'Policy interdependence: does strategic behaviour pay?' in Hodgman, D.R. and Wood, G.E. (Eds), *Macroeconomic Policy and Economic Interdependence*, Macmillan.

Chadha, B., Masson, P.R. and Meredith, G. (1992), 'Models of inflation and the costs of disinflation', IMF Working Paper no. WP/91/97, October, forthcoming in *IMF Staff Papers*.

Chow, G.C. (1981), *Econometric Analysis by Control Methods*, New York, J. Wiley & Sons.

Collins, S.M. (1987), 'PPP and the peso problem: exchange rates in the EMS' in Claassen, E.M. (Ed), *Proceedings of Workshop on International Monetary Arrangements,* held at European University Institute, Florence, forthcoming, Praeger.

Committee for the Study of Economic and Monetary Union (1989), 'Report on economic and monetary union in the European Community (Delors Report)', Luxembourg, Office for Official Publications of the European Communities.

Cripps, M. (1991), 'Learning rational expectations in a policy game', *Journal of Economics Dynamics and Control*, vol. 15.

Currie, D. (1992a), 'Hard ERM, hard ecu and European Monetary Union' in Canzoneri, Grilli and Masson (Eds), *op. cit.*

Currie, D. (1992b), 'European Monetary Union: institutional structure and performance', *Economic Journal*, 102.

Currie, D.A. and Wren-Lewis, S. (1990), 'Evaluating the extended target zone proposal for G3', *Economic Journal*, 100.

Delors, J. (1989), 'Report on economic and monetary union in the European Community', European Commission, 'The Delors Report', Luxembourg, Office for Official Publications of the EC.

DIW (1991), 'Die lage der weltwirtschafts und der deutschen wirtschaft im herbst 1991' (*Rapport commun des cinq instituts allemands*), *DIW Wochenbericht* 42-43/91, 24 October.

Dornbusch, R. (1980), *Open Economy Macroeconomics*, New York, Harper International edition, Basic Books.

Dornbusch, R. (1991), 'Problem of European monetary integration', in Giovannini, A. and Mayer, C. (Eds), *European Financial Integration*, Cambridge, Cambridge University Press.

Driffill, J. and Beber, M. (Eds) (1991), *A Currency for Europe*, London, Lothian Foundation Press.

Driffill, J. and Miller, M. (1992), 'Learning about a shift in exchange rate regime', mimeo, Department of Economics, University of Warwick, Department of Economics, QMC, University of London, forthcoming in *Economic Journal*.

Dubois, E. and Kenigswald, L. (1991), 'L'écart de croissance franco-allemand entre 1990 et 1992', Economie et Statistique, no. 246-247, September-October.

Duwendag, D. (1991), 'Zur frage eines tragfähigen policy mix; sind adequate regeln für die fiskalpolitik unentbehrlich? in Weber, M. (Ed), *Europa auf dem Weg zur Wahrungsunion*, Darmstadt.

EC Commission (1990), 'One market, one money', *European Economy*, no. 44, October.

EC Commission (1992), 'The economics of community public finances', *European Economy*, special issue, te verschijnen.

Edison, H.J., Miller, M.H. and Williamson, J. (1987), 'On evaluating and extending the target zone proposal', *Journal of Policy Modeling*, vol. 9, Spring.

Eichengreen, B. (1990), 'One money for Europe? Lessons from the US currency union', *Economic Policy*, April.

Emerson, M. and Italianer, A. (1990), 'Comments on 'The price of EMU" in *Britain and EMU*, London School of Economics, CEPR.

Ermisch, J. (1991), *Lone Parenthood, an Economic Analysis*, Cambridge University Press.

Feldman, R.A. (1986), *Japanese Financial Markets: Deficits, Dilemmas and Deregulation*, Cambridge, Mass., MIT Press.

Feldstein, M. (1988), 'Thinking about international economic coordination', *Journal of Economic Perspectives*, no. 2.

Fischer, S. and Cooper, J.P. (1973), 'Stabilisation policy and lags', *Journal of Political Economy*, no. 81.

Fisher, P. and Salmon, M. (1986), 'On evaluating the importance of non-linearity in large macroeconomic models', *International Economic Review*, October.

Fisher, P.G., Tanna, S.K., Turner, D.S., Wallis, K.F. and Whitley, J.D. (1990), 'Econometric evaluation of the exchange rate in models of the UK economy', *Economic Journal,* 100.

Flood, R.P., Rose, A.K. and Mathieson, D.J. (1990), 'An empirical exploration of exchange rate target zones', NBER Working Paper no. 3543, New York, December.

Frankel, J. and Rockett, K.E. (1988), 'International macroeconomic policy coordination when policy makers do not agree on the true model', *American Economic Review*, no. 78.

Fratianni, M. and von Hagen, J. (1990), 'The European Monetary System ten years after', North-Holland, Carnegie-Rochester Conference Series on Public Policy, vol. 32, Spring.

Frenkel, J.A., Goldstein, M. and Masson, P.R. (1989), 'Simulating the effects of some simple coordinated versus uncoordinated policy rules' in Bryant, R. *et al.* (Eds), *Macroeconomic Policies in an Interdependent World*, Washington, IMF.

Friedman, M. (1953), *Essays in Positive Economics*, Chicago, University of Chicago Press.

Froot, K.A. and Rogoff, K. (1991), 'The EMS, the EMU, and the transition to a common currency', New York, NBER Working Paper no. 3684.

Ghosh, A.R. and Masson, P. (1988), 'International policy coordination in a world with model uncertainty', *IMF Staff Papers*, no. 35.

Ghosh, A.R. and Masson, P. (1991), 'Model uncertainty, learning and the gains from coordination', *American Economic Review*, no. 81.

Giavazzi, F. and Giovannini, A. (1989), *The European Monetary System – Limiting Exchange Rate Flexibility*, Cambridge, Mass, MIT Press.

Giavazzi, F. and Pagano, M. (1988), 'The advantage of tying one's hands: EMS discipline and Central Bank credibility', *European Economic Review*, vol. 32, no. 5, June.

Giavazzi, F. and Spaventa, L. (1990), 'The 'new' EMS', CEPR Discussion Paper no. 369, London School of Economics, CEPR.

Godfrey, L.G. (1988), *Misspecification Tests in Econometrics*, Cambridge, Cambridge University Press.

Grauwe, P. de (1987), 'Fiscal policies in the EMS: a strategic analysis' in Claassen, E.M. (Ed), *Proceedings of Workshop on International Monetary Arrangements, held at European University Institute, Florence*, forthcoming, Praeger.

Grauwe, P. de (1988), 'Exchange rate variability and the slowdown in growth of international trade', *IMF Staff Papers*, vol. 35.

Grauwe, P. de (1989), 'The cost of disinflation and the European Monetary System', CEPR Discussion Paper no. 326, London School of Economics, CEPR.

Haas, R.D. and Masson, P.R. (1986), 'MINIMOD: specification and simulation results', *IMF Staff Papers*, vol. 33.

Haavelmo, T. (1945), 'Multiplier effects of a balanced budget', *Econometrica*, no. 13.

Harasty, H. and Le Dem, J. (1990), 'Les conséquences macroéconomiques de la réunification allemande', *Economie Prospective Internationale*, no. 43, 3éme trimestre.

Holtham, G. and Hughes Hallett, A.J. (1987), 'International policy coordination and model uncertainty' in Bryant, R. and Portes, R. (Eds), *Global Macroeconomics: Policy Conflict and Cooperation*, London, Macmillan.

Holtham, G. and Hughes Hallett, A.J. (1992), 'Policy cooperation under uncertainty: the case for some disagreement', *American Economic Review*, no. 82.

Howrey, E.P. and Kelejian, H. (1971), 'Simulation versus analytical solutions: the case of econometric models' in Naylor, T.H. (Ed), *Computer Simulation Experiments with Models of Economic Systems*, New York, John Wiley.

Hughes Hallett, A. (1979), 'On methods for avoiding the *a priori* numerical specification of preferences in policy selection', *Economic Letters*, no. 3.

Hughes Hallett, A. (1986a), 'Autonomy and the choice of policy in asymmetrically dependent economies', *Oxford Economic Papers*, vol. 36.

Hughes Hallett, A. (1986b), 'International policy design and the substainability of policy bargains', *Journal of Economic Dynamics and Control,* no. 10.

Hughes Hallett, A. (1987), 'How robust are the gains to policy coordination to variations in the model and objectives?' *Ricerche Economiche*, vol. 41 (special issue on game theory and coordination).

Hughes Hallett, A., Holtham, G. and Hutson, G.J. (1989), 'Exchange rate targeting as surrogate international cooperation' in Miller, M., Eichengreen, B. and Portes, R. (Eds), *Blueprints for Exchange Rate Management*, London and New York, Academic Press.

Hughes Hallett, A. and Minford, P. (1989), 'Exchange rate agreements as a policy regime, their performance and design characteristics' in Christodoulakis, N. (Ed), *Dynamic Modelling and Control of National Economies*, Oxford and New York, Pergamon Press.

Hughes Hallett, A. and Minford, P. (1990), 'Target zones and exchange rate management regimes: a stability analysis of the European Monetary System', *Open Economies Review*, vol. 1.

Hughes Hallett, A., Minford, P. and Rastogi, A. (1991a), 'The European Monetary System: achievements and survival', CEPR Discussion Paper no. 502, London School of Economics, CEPR, January.

Hughes Hallett, A., Minford, P. and Rastogi, A. (1991b), 'The European Monetary System – problems and evolution' in Driffill and Beber (Eds), *op. cit.*

Hughes Hallett, A., Minford, P. and Rastogi, A. (1992), 'The European Monetary System: achievements and survival', revised version in Bryant *et al, op. cit.*

Hughes Hallett, A. and Rees, H.J.B. (1983), *Quantitative Economic Policies and Interactive Planning*, Cambridge and New York, Cambridge University Press.

Hughes Hallett, A. and Vines, D. (1991), 'Adjustment difficulties within a European Monetary Union: can they be reduced?' in Driffill and Beber (Eds), *op. cit.*

in't Veld, J.W. (1992), 'The diverse experience of the Netherlands, Belgium and Denmark in the ERM' in Barrell (Ed)(1992b) *op.cit.*

Ireland, J. and Westaway, P. (1990), 'Stochastic simulation and forecast uncertainty in a forward looking model', Working Paper, London, National Institute of Economic and Social Research.

Ishii, N., McKibbin, W. and Sachs, J. (1985), 'The economic policy mix, policy cooperation and protectionism: some aspects of macroeconomic interdependence among the United States, Japan, and other OECD countries', *Journal of Policy Modelling*, vol. 7.

Kendrick, D.A. (1981), *Stochastic Control for Economic Models*, New York, McGraw-Hill.

Knoester, A. (1983), 'Stagnation and the inverted Haavelmo effect: some international evidence', *De Economist*, vol. 131, no. 4.

Knoester, A. (1988), 'Supply-side policies in four OECD countries' in Motamen, H. (Ed), *Economic Modelling in the OECD Countries*, London and New York, Chapman and Hall.

Knoester, A. (1991a), 'Supply-side economics and the inverted Haavelmo effect' in Phelps, E.S. (Ed), *Recent Developments in Macroeconomics*, The International Library of Critical Writings in Economics 13, Hants/Vermont, Edward Elgar Publishing Company.

Knoester, A. (1991b), 'The inverted Haavelmo effect and the economic consequences of fiscal policies in the 1970s and 1980s', paper presented at the 1991 Conference of the Confederation of European Economic Associations (CEEA), Amsterdam, June 12-14, forthcoming in Knoester, A. (Ed), *Taxation and Economic Policy in Europe and the United States*, London, Macmillan.

Knoester, A. and Kolodziejak, A. (1991), 'Effects of taxation in economic models; a survey', Research Memorandum 9102, Nijmegen, forthcoming in *Economic Modelling*.

Knoester, A., Kolodziejak, A.M.M. and Muijzers, A.P.M. (1992), 'Economic policy and European integration', paper presented at the 1990 conference of the Confederation of European Economic Associations 'Exchange Rate Regimes and Currency Unions', Deutsche Bundesbank, Frankfurt/Main 22-24 February 1990, in Baltensperger, E. and Sinn, H.W. (Eds) (1992), *Exchange-Rate Regimes and Currency Unions*, London, Macmillan.

Knoester, A. and Van Sinderen, J. (1984), 'A simple way of determining the supply side in macroeconomic models', *Economic Letters*, 16, nos. 1-2.

Knoester, A. and Van der Windt (1987), 'Real wages and taxation in ten OECD countries', *Oxford Bulletin of Economics and Statistics*, vol. 49, no. 1.

Kolodziejak, A. (1988), 'Multicountry models with respect to the European Community', Catholic University Nijmegen (in Dutch).

Kolodziejak, A.M.M. and Muijzers, A.P.M. (1992), 'Het rapport van het comité-Delors (The report of the Delors committee)', *Economische Statistische Berichten*.

Krugman, P. and Miller, M.H. (Eds) (1991), *Exchange Rate Targets and Currency Bands*, Cambridge, Cambridge University Press.

Kydland, F.E. and Prescott, E.C. (1977), 'Rules rather than discretion: the inconsistency of optimal plans', *Journal of Political Economy*, no. 85.

Langfeldt, E. (1992), 'European monetary union: design and implementation' in Barrell, R. (Ed), *Economic Convergence and Monetary Union in Europe*, London, Sage Publications.

Lawrence, R.Z. (1991), 'Efficient or exclusionist? The import behavior of Japanese corporate groups', *Brookings Papers on Economic Activity*, no. 1.

Layard, R. and Nickell, S. (1985), 'The causes of British unemployment', *National Institute Economic Review*, no. 111, February.

Layard, R., Nickell, S. and Jackman, R. (1991), *Unemployment: Macroeconomic Performance and the Labour Market*, Oxford, Oxford University Press.

Lipschitz, L. and McDonald, D. (1990), 'German unification, economic issues', IMF Occasional Paper no. 75, December.

Lucas, R.E. Jr. (1976), 'Econometric policy evaluation: a critique' in Brunner, K. and Meltzer, A.H. (Eds), *The Phillips Curve and Labor Markets,* Carnegie-Rochester Conference Series on Public Policy, no. 1.

Malinvaud, E. (1977), *The Theory of Unemployment Reconsidered*, Oxford University Press.

Marquez, J. and Ericsson, N. (1990), 'Evaluating the predictive performance of trade account models', paper presented at Conference on the Empirical Evaluation of Alternative Policy Rules, Washington.

Masson, P. and Melitz, J. (1990), 'Fiscal policy coordination in a European Monetary Union', IMF Working Paper 90/24, Washington, IMF.

Masson, P.R. and Melitz, J. (1991), 'Fiscal policy independence in a European Monetary Union', *Open Economies Review*, vol. 2.

Masson, P. Symanski, S., Haas, R. and Dooley, M. (1988), 'Multimod: a multi-region econometric model', Working Paper 88/23, Washington DC, IMF.

Masson, P.R., Symansky, S. and Meredith, G. (1990), *MULTIMOD Mark II: A Revised and Extended Model*, IMF Occasional Paper no. 71, Washington, IMF, July.

Masson, P.R. and Symansky, S. (1992), 'Evaluating policy regimes under imperfect credibility', in Bryant *et al., op. cit.*

Meese, R.A. and Rogoff, K. (1983), 'Empirical exchange rate models of the seventies: do they fit out of sample?' *Journal of International Economics*, vol. 14.

Melitz, J. (1985), 'The welfare case for the European Monetary System', *Journal of International Money and Finance*, vol. 4, no. 4, December.

Miller, M. and Sutherland, A. (1991a), 'The 'Walters Critique' of the EMS: a case of inconsistent expectations?', *The Manchester School*, no. 49 (Supplement), June.

Miller, M. and Sutherland, A. (1991b), 'Contracts, credibility and common knowledge: their influence on inflation convergence', mimeo, Economics Department, University of Warwick, forthcoming in Torres, F. and Giavazzi, F. (Eds), *The Transition to Economic and Monetary Union in Europe*, Cambridge University Press.

Miller, M. and Weller, P. (1989), 'Target zones, currency options and the dollar' in Miller, M., Eichengreen, B. and Portes, R. (Eds), *Blueprints for Exchange Rate Management*, Cambridge University Press.

Minford, P. (1989a), 'Do floating exchange rates insulate?' in MacDonald, R. and Taylor, M. (Eds), *Exchange Rates and Open Economy Macroeconomics*, Oxford, Basil Blackwell.

Minford, P. (1989b), 'Ulysses and the Sirens: a political model of credibility in an open economy', *Greek Economic Review*, vol. 11.

Minford, P. (1989c), 'Exchange rate regimes and policy coordination' in Miller, M., Eichengreen, B. and Portes, R. (Eds), *Blueprints for Exchange Rate Management*, Cambridge University Press.

Minford, A.P.L., Agenor, P. and Nowell, E. (1986), 'A new classical econometric model of the world economy', *Economic Modelling*, vol. 3, no. 3.

Minford, P., Matthews, K. and Rastogi, A. (1990), 'A quarterly version of the Liverpool model of the UK', Working paper 90/60, Liverpool Research Group in Macroeconomics.

Minford, P. and Rastogi, A. (1990a), 'Testing the stability of nominal rules by stochastic simulations', Working paper 90/05, Liverpool Research Group in Macroeconomics.

Minford, P. and Rastogi, A. (1990b), 'The price of EMU' in Dornbusch, R. and Layard, R. (Eds), *Britain and EMU*, London, Centre for Economic Performance in association with Financial Markets Group, London School of Economics.

Minford, P., Rastogi, A. and Hughes Hallett, A. (1991), 'The price of EMU revisited', unpublished, University of Liverpool.

Minford, A.P.L., Spraque, A., Matthews, K.G.P. and Marwaha, S. (1984), 'The Liverpool macroeconomic model of the United Kingdom', *Economic Modelling*, January.

Nagar, A.L. (1969), 'Stochastic simulations of the Brookings Econometric Model' in Duesenberry, J.S., Fromm, G., Klein, L.R. and Kuh, E. (Eds), *The Brookings Model: Some Further Results*, Amsterdam, North-Holland.

Nickell, S.J. (1984), 'The modelling of wages and employment' in Hendry, D.F. and Wallis, K.F. (Eds), *Econometrics and Quantitative Economics,* Oxford, Basil Blackwell.

OECD (1978), *Public Expenditure Trends*, Paris, OECD.

OECD (1989), *OECD Economic Survey of France*, Paris, OECD.

Obstfeld, M. (1991), 'Destabilizing effects of exchange rate escape clauses', CEPR Discussion Paper no. 518, London School of Economics, CEPR.

Oudiz, G. and Sachs, J. (1984), 'Macroeconomic policy coordination among the industrial economies', *Brookings Papers on Economic Activity*, no. 1.

Pagan, A. (1984), 'Econometric issues in the analysis of regressions with generated regressors', *International Economic Review*, vol. 25, no. 1.

Pen, J. (1952), 'A general theory of bargaining', *American Economic Review,* vol. 4, no. 1, March.

Philips, A.W. (1958), 'The relation between unemployment and the rate of change of money wage rates in the United Kingdom, 1861-1957', *Economica*, 25.

Ploeg, F. van der (1989), 'The political economy of over-valuation', *Economic Journal*, September.

Ploeg, F. van der (1991), 'Macroeconomic policy coordination during the various phases of economic and monetary integration in Europe' in EC Commission, 'The economics of EMU', *European Economy*, special issue.

Radaelli, G., Edwards, J. and Holtham, G. (1991), 'German unification: implications for interest rates and debt', Shearson Lehman Brothers, November.

Sachs, J. and Wyplosz, C. (1986), 'France under Mitterand', *Economic Policy*, vol. 2.

Svensson, L.E.O. (1991), 'Assessing target zone credibility: mean reversion and devaluation expectations in the EMS', IMF Working Paper WP/91/96, Washington, IMF, October.

Taylor, J. (1979), 'Staggered wage setting in a macroeconomic model with rational expectations', *American Economic Review*, Papers and Proceedings, vol. 69.

Taylor, J. (1988), 'The treatment of expectations in large multicountry econometric models - appendix' in Bryant *et al., Empirical Macroeconomics for Interdependent Economies, op. cit.*

Ungerer, H., Evans, O., Mayer, T. and Young, P. (1986), 'The European Monetary System: recent developments', IMF, Occasional Papers, 48.

Vaubel, R. (1989), 'Comments on Manfred Wegner' in Vosgerau, H.J. (Ed), *Studies in International Economics and Institutions*, Berlin and Heidelberg, Springer-Verlag.

Vickers, J. (1986), 'Signalling in a model of monetary policy with incomplete information', *Oxford Economic Papers.*

Walters, A.A. (1990), *Sterling in Danger: the Economic Consequences of Pegged Exchange Rates*, London, Collins (Fontana) with the Institute of Economic Affairs.

Weber, A. (1991), 'Reputation and credibility in the European monetary system', *Economic Policy*, no. 12, April.

Whitley, J.D. (1992), 'Comparative simulation analysis of the European multicountry models', *Journal of Forecasting*, May.

Williamson, J. (1983), *The Exchange Rate System*, Washington, Institute for International Economics, revised edition 1985.

Williamson, J. (1991), 'FEERs and the ERM', *National Institfute Economic Review*, no. 137, August.

Wyplosz, C. (1991), 'Monetary union and fiscal discipline' in EC Commission, 'The economics of EMU', *European Economy*, special issue.

Zeuthen, F. (1930), *Problems of Monopoly and Economic Warfare*, London.